THE ADVENTURES OF
FAT RICE

THE ADVENTURES OF

FAT RICE

RECIPES FROM THE CHICAGO RESTAURANT INSPIRED BY MACAU

ABRAHAM CONLON
ADRIENNE LO
HUGH AMANO

photography by Dan Goldberg
illustrations by Sarah Becan

TEN SPEED PRESS
Berkeley

CONTENTS

INTRODUCTION

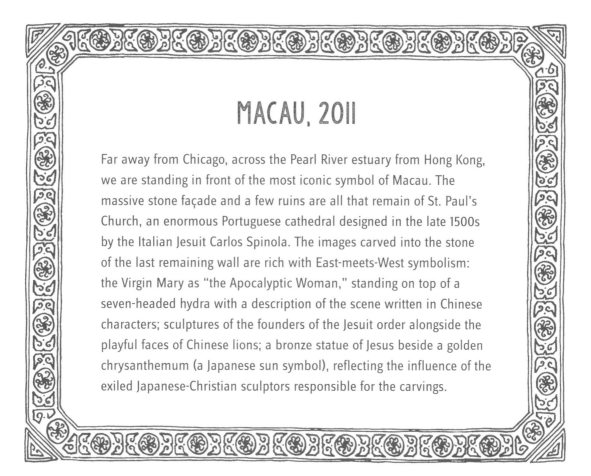

MACAU, 2011

Far away from Chicago, across the Pearl River estuary from Hong Kong, we are standing in front of the most iconic symbol of Macau. The massive stone façade and a few ruins are all that remain of St. Paul's Church, an enormous Portuguese cathedral designed in the late 1500s by the Italian Jesuit Carlos Spinola. The images carved into the stone of the last remaining wall are rich with East-meets-West symbolism: the Virgin Mary as "the Apocalyptic Woman," standing on top of a seven-headed hydra with a description of the scene written in Chinese characters; sculptures of the founders of the Jesuit order alongside the playful faces of Chinese lions; a bronze statue of Jesus beside a golden chrysanthemum (a Japanese sun symbol), reflecting the influence of the exiled Japanese-Christian sculptors responsible for the carvings.

After exploring the ruins, we make a quick jaunt to another place that reinforces the feeling of Macau's historic position as a crossroads between East and West (and makes mainland Chinese tourists feel like they're in faraway Europe): the Fortalaza do Monte, built in 1624 as protection against Dutch invaders. The fortress's massive lower stone walls are scattered with a few windswept, withered buds and blossoms of a papaya tree. Known as *fula papaia*, these male flower buds used to be a staple in Macanese cooking, essential to dishes like crab with papaya flower (*caranguelo fula-papaia*) and stir-fried greens with shrimp paste and papaya flower (*bredo raba-raba*, see page 110). But today, nearly all of the papaya trees that bear these beautiful, slightly bitter buds are gone, along with the people who once cooked these traditional Macanese dishes. This is why we are here: to learn about and try to understand a cuisine that may soon be forgotten.

This was our first visit to Macau, but we had only allotted thirty-six hours for our culinary excursion. We had eaten the famous Portuguese egg tarts (*pastéis de nata*), pork chop buns (*zhu pa bao*), grilled sardines, garlicky suckling pig (*leitao*), and curried *everything*, from chicken to oxtail to crabs, that Macau is known for. We'd caught a very brief glimpse of Macau's rich culinary history–but our trip was too short and we wanted more. Even after just thirty-six hours, we were hooked on the island's intermingling of Chinese, Portuguese, Indian, Malay, and African influences.

Macau was actually the last stop of a much longer journey for us. The week before, we had been in metropolitan Hong Kong, feasting on live seafood and simple Cantonese cuisine; before that, we had learned the techniques of the numbing and fiery (*ma-la*) dishes of Sichuan province at the Sichuan Institute of Higher Cuisine. We had embarked on this trip to learn more about the regional cuisines of China and to get inspiration for the series of underground dinners we were hosting back in Chicago. Since we were in the neighborhood, we knew we had to stop in Macau, but nothing could have prepared us for its eerie, fantastical mélange of cultures: towering, shiny casinos alongside drab, aging colonial architecture; fair-skinned Asians speaking Portuguese while eating brothy noodles with chopsticks, as well as mainland Chinese tourists eating baked spaghetti dishes with forks; olive oil-rich *bacalhau* (Portuguese salt cod) on the same menu as steamed fish with ginger and scallion; the scent of curry and soy sauce mingling with that of freshly baked bread and strong coffee.

This is Macau today: a gambling mecca larger than Las Vegas, but formerly one of the world's most thriving trading ports, with a history of cultural confluence dating back to the mid-1500s. In 2011, twelve years after Portugal handed it back over to China, Macau was still in a state of transition. Most Portuguese-speaking Macanese people, along with their multicultured, trilingual (English-Portuguese-Cantonese) offspring, had moved away–to Portugal, Canada, the United States, Brazil–to be with their families or start new ones of their own.

We were due back in Hong Kong that evening and only had a few hours before we had to catch the ferry. So, with nothing but a *Lonely Planet* guide tattered map in hand (this was well before phones were as smart as they are today), we embarked on our last culinary adventure of the trip: a stop that would change our trajectory forever.

"Okay, let's get outta here. It's already 1 p.m., and I think this place closes at 3. Let's go right up here on to Rua de Dom Belchior Carneiro."

We were looking for a specific restaurant that was located near the reservoir. The cobblestone streets, pastel buildings, and shops with Portuguese names like *Fatima* made us feel like we were a world apart from central China, despite the fact that Hong Kong is a mere hour's ferry ride away.

"After the Rotundo do Almirante Costa Cabral, this street will turn into Rua de Tomas Vieira. What's up with these street names? They're all named after Portuguese guys. You think we're on the right track?"

The duality of the city–partly a product of the "One Country, Two Systems" principle of China's dealing with both socialism and capitalism–is apparent, for even though the names of streets and storefronts are written in Portuguese, Chinese characters are not direct translations and often mean something completely different. Bus and taxi drivers don't recognize the streets by their Portuguese names; you have to know their Chinese names to get around. Don't get into a cab and expect that you can speak Portuguese because your Cantonese is rusty; take it from us, that *doesn't* work.

"Didn't you say this was supposed to turn into Rua de Tomas something-or-other?"

"Yeah, isn't this it?"

"No, this is Rua do Almirante Costa Cabral! The same dude that roundabout was named after back there! Ugh. Let's double back."

The vibrant colonial architecture framed in skeletal bamboo scaffolding is another of Macau's dichotomies, and the narrow, winding, one-way roads are clearly a product of a rapidly growing society that outpaced any urban planning.

"I think we can turn right up here, onto Rua de Jorge Álvares, then left."

"You know that dude?"

"I think I've heard of him before; sounds familiar."

Jorge Álvares was the first European to reach China, sailing out from Burma under the Portuguese flag and landing on Nei Lingding Island in 1513. This established highly sought-after trading opportunities with China, solidifying the Age of Exploration and all of the ensuing commerce. Macau became a hub of all of this new, multinational trade.

"Where are we now? We should be back on Costa Cabral."

"What's that sign say? Estrada de Cemitario? What the . . . ? Let's turn back and get to that intersection by Electronicos Yek Wo or whatever."

"Really?!"

"Yeah, we need to go back by the cemetery."

Cemiterio Sao Miguel Arcanjo is the largest Catholic cemetery in Macau. On the gravestones and tombs one sees more of that Christian imagery with Chinese characters that symbolizes the blended cultures of the city's past. Many of the people buried in this cemetery cooked wonderful dishes with those withered, drying *fula papaia* of the past.

"I think it's this way–let's go up Rua de Tap Siac."

"Okay . . . yeah, here's the Macau Central Library, so it shouldn't be too far now. I'm getting hungry."

We continued though the cultural mash-up that is Macau, passing storefronts with signs in Chinese and relics of Portuguese history, and it reminded each of us of our own backgrounds: Abe of Portuguese descent, Adrienne of Chinese. Over the years, we had dabbled with Macanese cooking. We'd never actually been to Macau, but had heard of and studied the legends–dishes with unexpected combinations, like soy sauce with olive oil; or that simultaneously did and didn't make sense, like salt cod fried rice, coconut-scented curries with olives, or the strangely named "African chicken." We started cooking our own renditions of these dishes at our illegally operated, disguised-as-an-antique-store speakeasy restaurant, where we'd feed forty diners a night. But we knew we just had to get to Macau one day, to taste these dishes in their birthplace.

"We've made it! Thank God they aren't closed!"

Beyond our worries about finding the restaurant, we were worried about its very existence. The caption in our guide book didn't say much. It merely said, "This unpretentious eatery near the reservoir is one of the best kept secrets among the local Macanese community. Choices are sparse, but its homemade Macanese dishes, like *feijoada* (pork with kidney beans) and *minchi*, as well as its flan, deserve a thumbs-up."

Looking back, we're not entirely sure what drove us there, but upon arrival, it all made sense.

We found a very humble-looking, semisubterranean, cafeteria-style restaurant with white tile walls awash with images of old Macau. The owner, chef, and *grande dame* of Macanese cooking, Dona Aida de Jesus, was in the corner, perfectly composed, silently reading a newspaper with one eye and monitoring the food coming out of the kitchen with the other. Hungry out of our minds from the journey there, and not knowing what anything was, we got a bit of everything available. To our surprise, Dona Aida offered many new things that we didn't see on the touristy food streets of Taipa (one of the three islands that make up the Macau municipality). We ate *galinha bafassa*, a smothered, braised chicken with turmeric and potatoes, and spicy curried oxtail with peas and carrots. A Macau-style *feijoada* of pork knuckle with cabbage, kidney beans, pig ears, frankfurters, and tomato included a chouriço reminiscent of Portuguese linguiça found in Abe's home state of Massachusetts, but seemed crossed with *lap cheong* (the fragrant Chinese sausage scented with rose wine and soy). This was humble, soul-satisfying cuisine, *not* a soft-shelled turtle or some exotic sea creature braised in a mouth-numbing sauce like we experienced on the mainland. This was hearty and subtle, nourishing and natural. The food brought Abe back to a story in *Saveur* ("Original Fusion" by Margaret Sheridan) that he read as young chef, a story that had ultimately brought him to Macau. Eating through these dishes with so much history, so much adaptation, development, and soul, he started to realize that Dona Aida was *the* lady he had read about in the magazine twelve years prior, who along with her daughter, Sonia Palmer, was billed as one of the very few people preserving this forgotten fusion. Noting we weren't from around these parts, Dona Aida came over to our table, and we clumsily tried to string together some Portuguese to speak with her. But we quickly learned that her English is strong and graceful, and at the age of ninety-six she spoke with a deep voice that made Abe think of his Madeiran grandmother Bea's famous Pavarotti impression. From afar, Dona Aida looked quite Chinese, but as

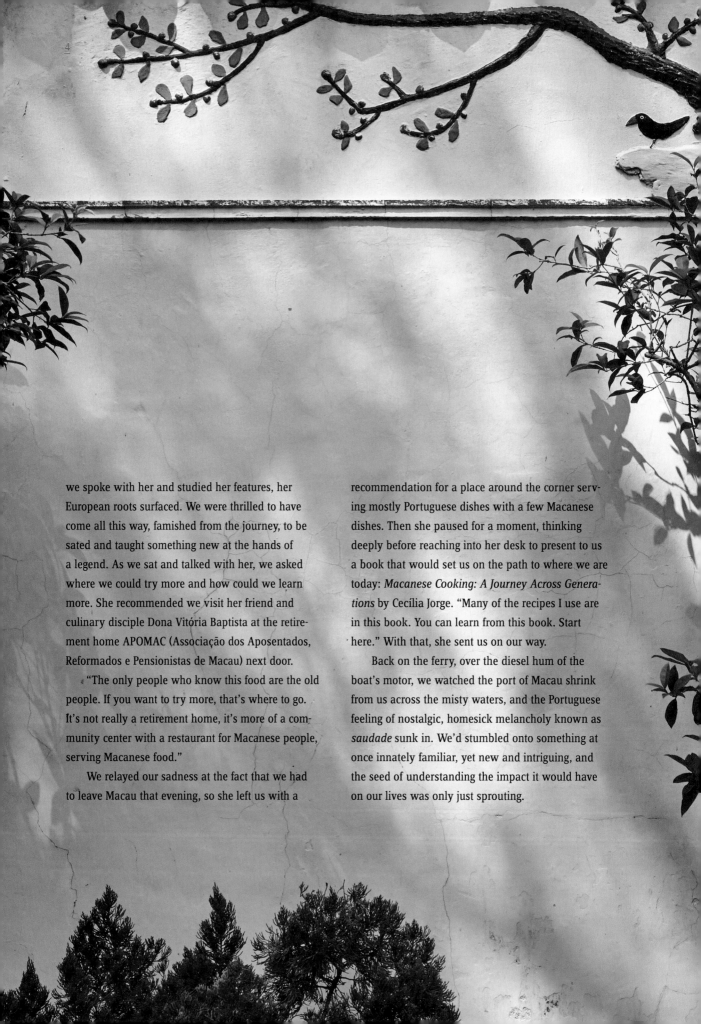

we spoke with her and studied her features, her European roots surfaced. We were thrilled to have come all this way, famished from the journey, to be sated and taught something new at the hands of a legend. As we sat and talked with her, we asked where we could try more and how could we learn more. She recommended we visit her friend and culinary disciple Dona Vitória Baptista at the retirement home APOMAC (Associação dos Aposentados, Reformados e Pensionistas de Macau) next door.

"The only people who know this food are the old people. If you want to try more, that's where to go. It's not really a retirement home, it's more of a community center with a restaurant for Macanese people, serving Macanese food."

We relayed our sadness at the fact that we had to leave Macau that evening, so she left us with a recommendation for a place around the corner serving mostly Portuguese dishes with a few Macanese dishes. Then she paused for a moment, thinking deeply before reaching into her desk to present to us a book that would set us on the path to where we are today: *Macanese Cooking: A Journey Across Generations* by Cecília Jorge. "Many of the recipes I use are in this book. You can learn from this book. Start here." With that, she sent us on our way.

Back on the ferry, over the diesel hum of the boat's motor, we watched the port of Macau shrink from us across the misty waters, and the Portuguese feeling of nostalgic, homesick melancholy known as *saudade* sunk in. We'd stumbled onto something at once innately familiar, yet new and intriguing, and the seed of understanding the impact it would have on our lives was only just sprouting.

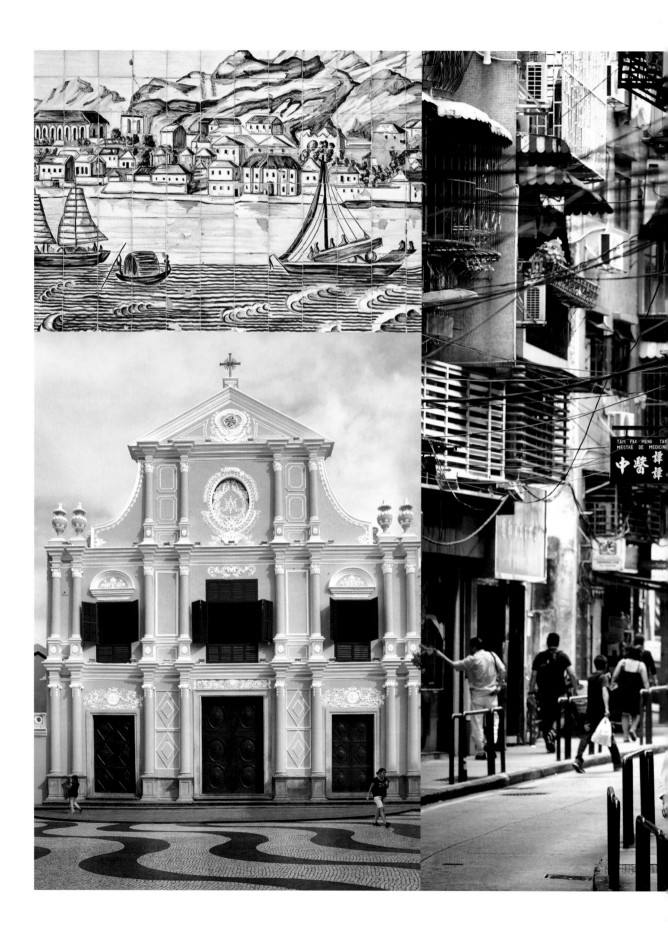

CHICAGO, 2012

"What the f&!% do you want to name this restaurant and what the f&!% are we going to cook!?!?"

Hugh was freaking out. Thirteen months after starting the process of building our restaurant, the floors were laid, the walls were up, the basements were dug, and the concrete was poured. The hood fan was up and running, and the walls had just been painted. We were getting close. We *had* to open soon. Abe was bringing in wok burners and the wood-fired grill and digging through old barns for vintage cast-iron pans and trivets. Adrienne was trying to rein in the obscene spending required just to get a new restaurant off the ground, and we had yet to really nail down the concept of the restaurant—or pick a name, for that matter. What were we thinking?

For the previous five years, Abe and Adrienne had run the underground (*technically* illegal) dining club X-marx, where, more or less, the menu changed nightly. Being underground gave us the flexibility to rotate themes and experiment in directions that traditional restaurant work would have never allowed. We'd explored a lot of flavors and a lot of history, investigating the crazy-plentiful foodways and cultures Chicago has to offer: Vietnamese groceries on Argyle Street, Indian and Pakistani shops and spice houses on Devon Avenue, South Side barbecue, Pilsen and Cicero taquerias, Polish and eastern European delis up and down north Milwaukee Avenue. Perhaps that was what had left us in such a pickle—having cooked more than 250 dinners as X-marx, offering in excess of seven courses per dinner and rarely repeating menu items, there was just way too much out there to choose from.

We knew things would skew Asian. Abe grew up in Lowell, Massachusetts, a blue-collar town known best for being at the center of the American industrial revolution and the home of the famous rambler Jack Kerouac. But lesser known is that Lowell has a large population of Southeast Asian refugees, an influence that gave Abe an early taste for exploring

new flavors that he didn't find on the tables of his Portuguese-American upbringing. Adrienne grew up in a Chinese-American household in Chicago, where food and family were always at the forefront, and from an early age she could be found at the kitchen table making *jiao zhe* (dumplings).

It wasn't just Asian flavors we were after; we wanted hot and hearty meals to battle the long, frigid Chicago winters. We knew the cooking had to be home-style, and a reflection of us. But how would all of those pieces fit together? Looking through X-marx menus past gave us various dumplings and *bao* (stuffed Chinese buns), homemade sausages and noodle soups, spicy curries and abundant family-style dishes. The food we produced was interesting and delicious—but it didn't give us a clear direction in which to proceed, nor did we have a concise pitch for the press or potential guests. If we could've gotten away with leaving our place unnamed, or just naming it "Restaurant," we would have. At the end of the day, we just wanted a simple restaurant, reflective of our cultures and the food we loved cooking and eating. We just didn't know exactly what that was.

We pressed on. We pored over cookbooks, looking for an inspiration for our name. It had to be easy for people to say: "Hey, have you been to ___ " or "I just ate at ___ and it was awesome." There were brainstorming sessions every day for six months. Chalkboards full of candidates. Votes to cement it. (LoCo Kitchen, Rhinoceros, and Little Devil barely missed the cut.)

We looked through book after book in our library and found ourselves gravitating toward the Macanese book that Dona Aida had presented us in Macau the previous year. We saw the hearty, rustic, shareable dishes; intriguing Asian and Indian elements; a clear reflection of our cultures and interests. But this Macanese food was way out there—no one would recognize it, and no one would get it. Right?

We remembered Dona Aida, who had shown us not only how delicious Macanese cuisine was, but also how it was disappearing and how difficult it was to find. We always joked that our kids would be

"Macanese," and this restaurant was as close as we'd planned on coming to having kids anytime soon, so we went with it a bit. The name game went in a new direction: Caravel (the boats used by the Portuguese on their expeditions), Prester John (a mysterious, legendary Christian king from the West who was said to rule deep in Asia), even Bird's Eye (for the chilli pepper) entered (and quickly left) the conversation.

We got more books on Macanese food and other Portuguese-influenced cuisines, and the name of one of Macau's most famous dishes kept popping up: *arroz gordo*. The translation? Fat rice. The name was simple; it was bold; the dish looked delicious. But we'd never cooked it before. If it was a name that was going to make our list, we knew we'd have to start cooking it, and we'd have to make it *awesome*.

We tested and retested the *arroz gordo*, and at the same time, we dove deeper into the Macanese culinary pantheon. And it just had so . . . many . . . influences. Which was great, because that convinced us that we could do Chinese food, Portuguese food, Southeast Asian food, Indian food, and no one would ever be the wiser . . . because how do you explain Macau, its people, or its food? Most people don't even know where Macau is, let alone its history. And frankly, at the time, neither did we! But we loved the challenge, and settled on our "elevator pitch": Euro-Asian comfort food, and the name would be Fat Rice.

We set our focus on the food of Macau and other Portuguese-influenced Asian cultures. We learned that for centuries, the histories and cuisines of Portugal, Africa, Brazil, India, Malaysia, Indonesia, Japan, China, and beyond had melded to create utterly unique culinary languages. It wasn't so simple as "Lisbon-meets-Malaysia"; for hundreds of years, these cultures exchanged cooking techniques, ingredients, and styles. This spawned new cultures and traditions, not to mention flavor combinations that were unfamiliar to both Western and Asian palates. And the dish that led us in this direction in the first place–the dish we'd been working on and eating so much of as we built the restaurant–exemplified this amalgamation so well: the *arroz gordo*.

Eventually, we would create our own version of Arroz Gordo (page 69), but in all its incarnations, it exemplified what we wanted to cook: a dish that took root in Macau, the direct result of Portuguese unions, trade, and travel during the Age of Exploration, but had touched so many places along the way. We wouldn't just cook the food of Macau or Portugal; we'd explore everything in between, too. The name and the concept were born–or maybe they were simply remembered: Fat Rice.

THE AGE OF EXPLORATION AND MACAU

In 1453, the spice trade between Europe and Asia was brought to a screeching halt by the fall of Constantinople, with the Ottoman Empire effectively ending the rule of the Roman Empire. The powerful Ottoman army blocked overland trade routes and forced Europeans to turn to the sea. This began the Age of Exploration and the spice race was on. In 1494 the Treaty of Tordesillas was signed by the main players in Europe's nautical exploration game, splitting the world of exploration into two hemispheres divided by a line bisecting South America: travels to the west of Brazil would belong to Spain; Brazil and the east, to Portugal. With the Suez Canal shortcut nearly four hundred years away, Vasco de Gama led his Portuguese mission around South Africa's Cape of Good Hope in 1498, opening up an eastern sea route to the spices of Asia, and thus the gateway that would change the world's flavors forever.

In the years that followed, foodways and traditions–not only of the Portuguese but also of the people they encountered along the way–started to change. Chillies from Brazil found their way into India. In Malaysia, cooks began blooming turmeric, native to India, in vinegar. Malaysia's fermented shrimp paste and coconuts made the voyage to China. Techniques were adjusted and developed in new ports as well; Portugal's *carne de vinha d'alhos* (vinegar-braised meat) was infused with Indian spices, and ultimately evolved into *vindaloo*, one of the most widely recognized curry dishes in the world.

Macau is an SAR (Special Administrative Region) of China, but for the five hundred years before Macau returned to China in 1999, it was governed by Portugal. Portuguese sailors first gained land access to Macau in 1557, when they struck a deal by paying tribute to local authorities and acting as liaison in Japanese-Chinese trade (direct contact was forbidden by both sides). On their way to Macau during the Age of Exploration, the Portuguese made many stops–in

Mozambique and Angola in Africa, Goa on the west coast of India, Penang and Malacca in Malaysia, the southern islands of Japan, and more. Borne out of necessity, new techniques were developed at every stop by people who simply needed to satisfy the taste of home with the unfamiliar ingredients they encountered. This virtual larder of ingredients and knowledge traveled with the explorers and was compounded with each landing: each new port both grew and aided in the exchange.

This last fact is important to understand–it wasn't as though the travelers were sailing on a one-way course. After all, they were looking to set up trade; ultimately, the goal was to get the goods back to Portugal and other Portuguese trade ports and colonies. That said, old dishes continued to evolve into new as they made their way across waters and generations of combined culturalism. And the Portuguese weren't the only Europeans in Asia; remember, later on the Dutch and English had a large stake in this part of the world, and they weren't without influence. But if you look closely at Macanese food, you see the mark of the Portuguese: the already-comingled dishes they brought with them, and how the Chinese natives interpreted, adapted, and built upon those dishes. It's the food of oral tradition passed from generation to generation; the mother lode of union, history, and soul on a plate.

It would be nuts to think we could really cover it all. Instead, we learn all we can through everything we can lay our hands on, in English, Portuguese, or otherwise, including books, magazine articles, fictional stories where a character might talk about one of these dishes, family and church cookbooks, and connecting with people through social media and the Internet–fully knowing that for every recipe or technique, there's another one out there, just as legitimate. Part of the thrill of cooking is learning, and we are embracing that quest for knowledge and realizing that what we know is a small amount of what's actually out there. But there are those who do seem to know everything there is on this topic: especially the author and cultural preservationist Cecília Jorge; writer Annabel Jackson; one of the last remaining Macanese chefs, Dona Aida de Jesus; and the many other people who helped us along the way, whom you will soon meet in this book. These are the experts. Us? We're amateur historians, but we do our best to apply much of this knowledge and history in our roles as professional cooks.

A NOTE ON LANGUAGE

The recipes in this book reflect a cuisine that at once combines and contrasts aspects of the many cultures it has grown from. As such, many words and names will be foreign to you; others will seem familiar but might have different meanings than you are used to. A daunting aspect of our study of Macanese cooking and its related cuisines is the sheer number of countries and people that have left their mark on how we interpret the food today. Each has contributed ingredients, techniques, equipment, and names. Deciphering not only the pronunciation but also the meaning of these words has been an exciting if difficult challenge. We've had to look beyond literal meanings and keep an eye out for puns or colloquialisms that are often only known to local, native-speaking populations.

In this book you will find theories about the origins and etymology of many of the dishes we cook, and we draw from the linguistic traditions of Portugal (including the Azores and Madeira), China (and languages including Hokkien, Fukkien, Cantonese, and Mandarin), Malaysia, Burma, Thailand, Singapore, Indonesia, Japan, India (including Goa, Kerala, and Mangalore), Sri Lanka, Africa (including Angola, Mozambique, Cape Verde, and Cape Malay), Brazil, England, the Netherlands, the Philippines, and many more–plus, we contributed our own names to some of the dishes as well! This cultural richness is what makes our study of Macanese food so interesting. Plus, it makes it easy if aliens landed and asked what the best representation of our combined world cuisine is–Macanese food would definitely be the best answer!

THE FAT RICE MISSION

Fat Rice is more than a restaurant. Fat Rice is a center for the study, exploration, and sharing of global Portuguese cuisine.

Portuguese traders, sailors, and missionaries from the fifteenth to eighteenth centuries greatly influenced the way we eat today. The exchange of ideas, cultures, and traditions that occurred during the Age of Exploration changed the course of history—and most importantly for our purposes, foodways around the globe. Imagine Sichuan cuisine without the chillies, or pad Thai without the peanuts. Unthinkable!

Of course, this was also an era of brutal colonialism, of conflict and oppression that cannot be glossed over. Our mission at Fat Rice is to better understand the cultures and cuisine that were borne of this era: the unique yet Portuguese-related traditions of song, religious practice, and regional dialects (patuas) in regions like Goa, India; Malacca, Malaysia; East Timor, Indonesia; and of course, Macau. In Portugal's large cities, even today you find people who have emigrated from these territories. At Fat Rice, we seek to learn about the culinary traditions of these regions, and share our own interpretations to guests in our restaurant, and now, readers of our book.

It can be very difficult to trace some of these forgotten recipes; they were rarely written down and certain dishes, techniques, and ingredients have crisscrossed the globe, making it challenging to the pinpoint their source. Only recently in Macau—as the people see their culture disappearing—are they using their beloved foods as a means of heritage preservation. We have gone to great lengths to tap into this diminishing trove of knowledge by obtaining every

Macanese cookbook we are aware of; digging through libraries in Lisbon and Macau searching for things like small, self-published or photocopied recipe packets; even befriending unassuming folks via the internet, who would then let us into their homes to learn their recipes. Most of the dishes in this book are adaptions of recipes from passionate cooks who felt compelled to preserve their heritage through cuisine. Some may be an amalgamation of a few recipes and traditions, and not exactly how the originals were written, but they will be familiar to Macanese people.

As with any culture, the pride and conviction surrounding the cuisine leads one to feel their family's recipe is the right one. Our advantage as outsiders is that we're not bound to cook a dish one way or another for fear of being ridiculed by Auntie Maria. That being said, faithful accuracy is very important to us, and we make every effort to stay true to the dishes we've learned, interpreting them in a way that pays homage to their origins but also brings them into a more modern light.

In this book, we focus mostly on Macau, but we can't help but be curious about how the culinary practices used there developed and evolved. Macau was the last established territory in the Portuguese empire; therefore, its cuisine had influences from all of the places Portuguese travelled along the way.

This has truly been an adventure for us, an adventure that stemmed from a willingness take risks, to say "yes," "why not?" and "let's try it out." We are eternally grateful to all of the people who have let us into their lives and kitchens, graciously filling our bellies with heirloom recipes and our spirits with friendship. And thus, this book is dedicated to them. In that same spirit, please join us—this adventure is just beginning.

CHANG · BUTSCHER · Encyclopedia of **CHINESE FOOD AND COOKING** · Crown

HONG KONG COOKBOOK · ARTHUR LEM · DAN MORRIS

ROBERTS · LING · BRADSHAW · Historical Dictionary of **HONG KONG & MACAU**

Traditional Macanese Recipes *from my auntie Albertina* · CINTIA CONCEICAO SERRO

Cozinha de Macau · Maria Celestina de Mello e Senna

História Oral / Oral History · 8 · 從家傳的土生菜說起 · Receitas e Tesouros de Famílias Macaenses / *Family Macanese Recipes and Treasures* · 澳門堂大學公開學院同學會 出版

Cecília Jorge · MACANESE COOKING

Cuzinhia Cristang: A MALACCA-PORTUGUESE COOKBOOK · *Celine J. Marbeck*

A COZINHA DE MACAU DA CASA DO MEU AVÔ
THE CUISINE OF MACAO FROM MY GRANDFATHER'S HOUSE

CHINESE — ENGLISH · 香港點心 · **HONG KONG DIM SUM** · 區煒光編著・飲食天地出版社出版

Comé Qui Cuza? 食乜野? *What T...*

Saboroso

Culinária Macanese 澳門⋯⋯

Macau Portuguese Cuisine on the China Coast · Annabel J...

o Promotora da Instrução dos M...

Maria Celestina de Mello and Se⋯

A cookbook, simple printing, with many recipes of Chi⋯
date unknown edition, 60s or earlier, had its significan⋯
even today we speak of Income from Celestina. The ⋯
⋯alina Dias da Luz, and autographed by the auth⋯
⋯d on this portal. ⋯eal of the author, this initia⋯

EQUIPMENT AND TECHNIQUES

The equipment in the Fat Rice kitchen is quite different from that found in most Western restaurants. We focus on more elemental cookware—steel woks, cast-iron skillets, and clay pots—that was used in a time long before convection ovens and microwaves. These time-tested implements add an intangible element of soul to the food that nonstick pans and immersion circulators just don't bring.

In the following sections, we outline the tools and techniques you'll need to cook from this book.

EQUIPMENT

Woks

Woks are the most important piece of equipment in the Chinese kitchen. Wide and shallow, the wok helps foods cook evenly due to their concave base—flat-bottomed woks are not recommended. This tool is essential for quick stir-fried dishes and is also very handy for deep-frying because its tapered sides can prevent boiling over when a large amount of food is placed in the hot oil. Steaming and smoking can also be done in a wok with the help of a bamboo or metal steamer that fits inside.

PROCURING Most Chinese and Asian stores have a variety of woks to choose from. Size, shape, material, and method of manufacture all matter.

Generally speaking, we use carbon-steel woks as opposed to cast-iron woks, because steel conducts heat quickly and efficiently. Stainless steel, electric, or Teflon-coated woks are definitely not recommended and should be avoided for a number of reasons, including durability, practicality, cost, and health concerns. Both carbon steel and cast iron can be hand-hammered (identified by round hammer marks) or machine-pressed (identified by concentric lines on

the wok's surface). Both are good, but we prefer the hand-hammered woks.

STYLE Double-handled or loop-handled woks are typical in Southern China and preferred in our restaurant. This style provides two points of contact for lifting; however, it does require some practice to hold and handle when it comes to actually cooking and stir-frying. A single-handled wok (Northern style) is easier to stir-fry with and get the action needed to cook small items over high heat, but can be difficult and dangerous to lift when full of oil or boiling water.

SEASONING When you purchase an uncoated carbon-steel wok (either hand-hammered or machine-pressed), your new wok will be coated with machine oil to prevent rust from forming. You need to get rid of that machine oil and create a protective, rust-resistant coating that will become virtually non-stick over time. First, wash your new wok inside and out with hot soapy water. Rinse and dry well with paper towels or clean, lint-free rags (you may see some gray residue on the paper towels or rags; this is just residual machine oil, so continue on).

Place your wok over a full-blast open flame on your stove. As it heats, the gray metal will start to turn blue, then amber. This process burns off any residue left from manufacture and opens up the metal to better absorb the oil you are about to season it with. Once hot and lightly patined, it is time to start the seasoning process. There are many schools of thought here, but generally when seasoning a wok we use lard or peanut oil (about 4 to 5 tablespoons, depending on the size of the wok) and aromatics (Chinese chives, or a combination of scallions and ginger). It's hard to believe that the chives or aromatics impart any flavor into the wok; it's just a traditional way to help spread the oil in a thin layer and to act as an abrasive to remove any rust or metal dust. If at any time you feel the wok is absorbing the fat and looks dry, add a bit more. Once the oil is heated just below the smoking point, add the aromatics (make sure they are dry to prevent splattering) and use your wok ladle to move them around, spreading the oil to the furthest edges of the wok. Continue to stir over the flame until the aromatics are dry and crispy, always keeping the oil moving so that it evenly coats the wok at all times. This could take up to 20 minutes. Discard the oil and aromatics, then use a lint-free rag or paper towel to wipe out the inside of the wok. Wipe some of that residual oil on the outside and base of the wok (be careful as this still may be hot). Rinse thoroughly with warm, clean water. Your wok is now seasoned and ready to go–make sure that you don't use soap on it from now on.

It will help if you cook fatty things the first few times you use your wok, steering clear of acids or boiling water. The steel needs time to cure and you want to prevent pitting or corrosion. If you find that oil is unevenly solidifying on the bottom of the wok, you can use a stainless steel scrubby to "sand down" the solidified oil and return it to a thin, nonstick coating.

PREPARING YOUR WOK BEFORE USE It is important to always have a paper towel or clean, lint-free rag at the ready when using a wok to wipe out any dust or residual oil. To prepare your wok for use, start by giving it a quick wipe. Place it on the stove over the flame, add a tablespoon or so of fat, and rub with a rag to coat thoroughly. Rinse with warm water, then dry the wok over the flame and rub with another tablespoon of fat. Now you have a prepared wok. This should be done each time you use your wok.

CLEANING BETWEEN JOBS After you've cooked something in the wok, remove as much leftover food, sauce, or carbon as possible by wiping out the wok, then return it to the heat and add a couple of cups of water (depending on the size of the wok). Using a wok brush, scrub out any particles or buildup on the wok until the wok is clean. Place back over the flame to dry and kill any bacteria and rub with fresh oil–you now again have a prepared wok.

DEEP CLEANING Over time, carbon buildup can occur and little black flakes of previously cooked food or residual solidified oil will form and can potentially get in your food. At this point, you need to burn all of that off. Most home stoves do not have the firepower to do this, so we recommend doing it in a 500°F oven or over a grill set to full blast. Essentially, you want all those carbon bits to burn off and turn into ash–this process may take 30 to 60 minutes. After the wok has been in the oven or on the grill and the bits in question have turned to ash, carefully use a towel or metal scrubby to remove any stubborn pieces, then follow the steps in Seasoning (page page 19), minus the aromatics, to get back to square one.

Wok Accessories

Be sure to invest in these few handy tools to keep your wok in good working order.

WOK BRUSH A small, wooden wok brush is handy for cleaning woks and cast-iron skillets. It is firm enough to remove particles, but gentle enough not to scratch the seasoning.

WOK LID The lid is useful for steaming and steadying the temperature for foods that need longer cooking times. It can also be used as a splatter guard when things get popping.

WOK RING This will help stabilize your round-bottomed wok on the stove top and provide a sturdy place to set the wok when plating. Not completely necessary, but quite helpful.

WOK SPATULA (*CHUAN*) AND LADLE (*HOAK*) Wok cookery requires a good metal spatula (*chuan*) and ladle (*hoak*). Look for ones made of stainless steel with wooden handles; in total they should be a little bit longer than the diameter of your wok. Use the *hoak* to stir-fry and measure ingredients before going into the wok. Use the *chuan* to help remove items that are sticking to the cooking surface of the wok. Use them in tandem to pick up food for plating.

Other Equipment

You don't absolutely need all of these tools to cook from this book, but we use them in our kitchen every day, and they will help you achieve successful results.

BAMBOO-HANDLED STRAINER/SPIDER A bamboo-handled strainer or spider is an essential tool for frying and blanching. We refer to it a lot in this book, so get one that fits in your pots or wok at home.

CAST-IRON SKILLET From the get-go, cast-iron skillets have been indispensable in our kitchen. They hold heat well and are super versatile; you can sear meat, make potstickers, and bake cakes in them. We seek out antique cast iron made by Wagner and Griswold. These pans were made with a dual polishing process that creates a smoother surface than the single polished cast iron of today–if you can find them, you will never use a Teflon-coated pan again. They are virtually indestructible and will provide many, many years of use, if cared for properly.

Here are some basic tips for caring for your cast-iron skillet, which is similar to caring for a carbon-steel wok:

- Do not wash your cast-iron cookware in the dishwasher.

- If you rescued one from a barn or bought it on eBay, clean it before using with hot soapy water, wipe it dry, then wipe the inside with coarse salt and oil. Place it on a medium-high flame to heat

for 10 minutes, carefully wipe out the excess salt and oil, and you should be good to go.

- Never use soap to clean cast iron–just scrub it with hot water and a wok brush after each use. To dry, give it a quick wipe with a clean lint-free rag and heat it on the stove to rid it of any excess moisture and to prevent rust from forming. Give it another light coat of oil once dry and store upside down. If rust does form, just scrub it off with warm water. Then rinse it, oil it, and reheat it again.

- Don't "shock" a hot cast-iron pan with cold water because this can cause warping or cracking.

- Don't soak your pan in water for extended periods of time. This will remove the seasoning and encourage rust. If you have caked-on food that you want to get rid of, bring some water to a boil in the pan and scrub it with a wok brush.

BAMBOO CHOPSTICKS There are several uses for chopsticks–they're great for picking up small items when plating and garnishing, testing oil for frying temperature, and testing the doneness of braises, fish, and cakes. Use them in lieu of tongs while grilling or sautéing to grip, flip, or stir food. Chopsticks! Not just for eating anymore.

CHINESE CLAY/SAND POT We use these a *lot* at the restaurant–they provide a great stove-to-table presentation that retains a great amount of heat. They work well for slow-cooked stews and curries, too.

Look for pots without cracks that are fully glazed on the inside. We like the 2-quart size with a lid and a single handle for most dishes, readily available in your local Chinatown (except in Chicago–we've bought them all!) or online.

To season the clay pots before using the first time, soak in cool water overnight so that they swell, then carefully simmer in a mixture of water and a small handful of rice for one hour so that the starch in the rice can fill any microscopic cracks. Then rinse them with clean water, dry, rub with a bit of oil inside and out, and bake in a 400°F oven for thirty minutes. Rub in oil once more and it is ready to go.

CHINESE CLEAVER A quintessential tool of the prep and line cooks at the restaurant, the cleaver is the ultimate versatile tool for slicing, dicing, chopping, scraping, and scooping–Chinese cleavers are the best! Once you are comfortable with a cleaver, you will realize that it can perform tasks that a whole knife kit could. We source our cleavers from Chan Chi Kee in the Kowloon district of Hong Kong; they make a variety of sizes using a variety of metals. Stainless steel are available, but we prefer carbon steel, as they are quicker to sharpen; however, they do tend to rust, so be sure to keep oiled when not in use.

DIGITAL SCALE This was an important tool for us when creating this book, giving precise weights, especially for the baked goods and spice blends. A good digital scale will prove useful in many recipes beyond those in this book.

FINE/ULTRA-FINE MESH STRAINER Look for a fine-mesh strainer that is at least 8 inches in diameter so that you can easily filter your oil after deep-frying and a smaller, ultra-fine mesh strainer for skimming particles during deep-frying and stock making.

FRY/CANDY THERMOMETER This is an essential tool to ensure that you are deep-frying at the right temperatures–find one that is durable and can reach at least 500°F. In a pinch, we put a bamboo chopstick into hot oil–rapid bubbles will appear when the oil is at about 350°F to 400°F–but the thermometer is *way* more accurate.

RICE COOKER Rice cookers are the best, most consistent way to cook rice. The timing is precise, and you don't have to open the lid to see if things are going well, because they always will be. Just get a simple one with a "cook" and "warm" setting.

ROLLING PIN A wooden rolling pin is one of the most versatile tools in our kitchen. It's not just used to roll pastry, bread, and dumpling doughs–you can also use it to pound things flat, or to pack pickles in jars. Look for a sturdy, heavy one without handles.

SHARPENING STONE Find a stone with at least two grit counts–one fine, the other even finer–and keep your cleaver extra sharp. Few things in a kitchen are more dangerous than a dull knife.

SILICONE SPATULA An indispensable tool in the kitchen, a silicone spatula will help you scrape every last bit from mixing bowls, and it works great to use for stirring while cooking easily scorchable things like thick sauces and custards, or while blooming curry pastes and masalas. The silicone these spatulas are made out of is very sensitive, and you can feel through the handle if particles are sticking even if you can't see the bottom of the pot. Look for spatulas that are heat-resistant up to 500°F, with a rigid handle that won't bend when heated.

STEAMER SET You can achieve many things with a steamer set for your wok. As a general rule, bamboo steamers "breathe" better and allow condensation to escape, resulting in a finer product than the metal versions, but either works. Just place your steamer in the wok, fill the wok with water until it comes up to about 1/2 inch under your steamer, and fire up the wok. Look for the largest one that will fit in your wok.

WOODEN SPOON A tool of love that can help develop flavor in your sauces and curries without scraping the heck out of your metal cookware.

TECHNIQUES

Think of the techniques that follow more as philosophies than hard-and-fast directions. Free your mind from timing and temperature cues, and focus instead on the ideas we're presenting.

Blanching

We define the technique of blanching as quickly cooking an ingredient in a large quantity of boiling water (sometimes salted). Blanching is usually followed by shocking, wherein the blanched ingredient is quickly cooled in ice water before serving or cooking further.

WOK BLANCHING FOR GREEN VEGETABLES Woks can recoup boiling temperatures quickly after cold vegetables are dropped in. As a general rule you should use about 8 parts water to the volume of your to-be-blanched ingredient. The water should be salted to taste like the ocean—which means a 2 to 3 percent ratio of salt to water by weight.

BLANCHING STARCHY OR WOODY ROOT VEGETABLES We blanch starchy vegetables, such as lotus root, taro root, jicama, and malanga, to remove exterior starch and prepare the vegetables for their next phase of cooking, whether that be poaching, stewing, or stir-frying. Generally, we use the same 8 parts water to 1 part vegetable ratio.

BLANCHING RAW BONES AND MEATS Blanching raw bones and meats is essential to Chinese gastronomy. With bones, it helps remove impurities that can impart off flavors and reduce clarity if making a stock. Blanching meat helps remove bloody flavors and firms up the protein strands of a product for ease of cutting before stir-frying and to reduce cooking times. When you blanch bones or meat, it generally takes more time than for a green vegetable—it is important to take the protien to a place that is just about fully cooked, without going over (you don't want to release too much flavor and/or collagen into the blanching water).

BLANCHING CHINESE CURED MEATS When cooking with Chinese cured meats—for example, dry-cured sausages, duck, ham, pork skins, or fish maw—we always blanch them first, which can help remove external bacteria and off flavors that come from long-term aging and degredation of oils and fat, which become rancid over time.

Poaching

Poaching is a method of low and slow cooking in a minimal amount of liquid. We suggest you poach vegetables in a wok or pot at temperatures just below a simmer. Cover in just enough cold, filtered water with a healthy pinch of sea salt. Bring to a boil over high heat, then cover with a tight-fitting lid and simmer gently until tender. Test occasionally with a toothpick until cooked through but still intact.

Frying

Frying can occur in a little or a lot of oil, cooked at a low or an explosive temperature. Chinese gastronomy has more than twenty specific names for different frying techniques. We prefer all oil cookery be done in a wok. It's crucial to use all precautions when handling hot oil and fire—it can be dangerous if you are careless. We always use peanut oil for frying because of its high smoke point. When it comes to reusing frying oil, use your best judgment—if it's dirty and stinky, don't do it; if it's clean, just give it a strain through a fine-mesh strainer and you are good to go. To dispose of frying oil, let it cool, put it in a sealed container, then simply throw it away.

Stir-Frying

Stir-frying is high-heat cooking in a wok over an open flame with a small amount of oil or fat. Always keep your ingredients moving, either by shaking the wok or tossing with a spatula. In these recipes, we often refer to wok "hei": the prized smoky fragrance and flavor that comes from quick cooking in the dry

HOW TO COOK VEGETABLES

BLANCHING

	Leafy Green Vegetables	Hearty Green Vegetables	Hearty Non-Green Vegetables	Delicate Green Vegetables
Varietals	Bok choy, cabbage, Swiss chard, water spinach	Green beans, okra, longbeans, celery, English peas, broccoli	Jicama and water chestnuts	Small chois (tatsoi, pak choy, baby bok choy), lettuces, pea shoots, snow peas
Cook time	30 to 60 seconds, until vibrant green and tender	60 to 90 seconds, until vibrant green, cooked through but still crisp	45 to 60 seconds, until cooked through but still crisp	Do not pre-blanch these vegetables.
How to cool	Shock in ice water; remove when cool and gently squeeze out excess water	Shock in ice water; remove when cool and gently squeeze out excess water	Shock in ice water; remove when cool and gently squeeze out excess water	N/A

POACHING

	Carrots	Whole White and Sweet Potatoes	Cut Sweet Potatoes	Daikon, Turnip, Rutabaga, Radish	Taro and Malanga	Lotus and Sunchoke
Cook time	6 to 10 minutes, until cooked through but still firm	25 to 45 minutes in water with garlic and thyme; simmer until easily pierced with a chopstick	6 to 10 minutes, until easily pierced with a chopstick	First blanch for 30 seconds to remove some funk, then poach for 8 to 15 minutes until tender but not falling apart	15 to 20 minutes, until tender but not falling apart	8 to 12 minutes, until crunchy but fully cooked through
How to cool	Drain and place on wide sheet pan to cool	Drain and place on wide sheet pan to cool	Drain and place on wide sheet pan to cool	Drain and place on wide sheet pan to cool	Drain and place on wide sheet pan to cool	Drain and place on wide sheet pan to cool

DRY-FRYING

	Eggplants	Cauliflower	Hearty Green Vegetables
Varietals	Chinese, Japanese, or other slender varieties (not Thai eggplants)		Okra, green beans, longbeans, asparagus, broccoli
Cook time	30 to 45 seconds	30 to 45 seconds, until golden on the outside and tender on the inside	30 to 45 seconds, until slightly blistered and golden on the outside and tender on the inside
How to cool	On a wire rack, or submerge in a flavorful liquid to absorb the flavor and stop carryover cooking	On a wire rack to stop carryover cooking	On a wire rack to stop carryover cooking

environment of a hot, open wok over a screaming open flame. It takes practice, quick hands, and finesse to get that elusive smokiness without actually burning your food. Seek understanding . . . and someday, wok *hei*, my friend.

Braising

Much of Macanese cuisine is based on long, slow-cooked braises and curries. In most cases, we define braise in the classical French sense of browning the ingredient we are working with in fat and then gently simmering, about two-thirds covered in liquid, until the meat or poultry has reached its desired doneness. The cooking time for each cut will vary depending on the type and toughness of meat–have your chopsticks handy, and you can use them to poke the meat as a doneness tester. A braise can be tricky to get just right–and despite the fact that so much liquid is involved, a braise can be overcooked. We recommend fully cooling the braise in its cooking liquid, which allows the flavors to meld and deepen as the cooking liquid redistributes back into the meat. Making the braise a day ahead of serving is always a good idea.

Live Fuel Cooking

Sure, you could use a gas grill, but there really is no substitute for live fuel cooking, whether your fuel is hardwood or charcoal. We skewer up and grill our Galinha à Africana and sardines, and occasionally grill meats before braising them, to sear them and add a smoky element. Even the Arroz Gordo (page 69) hits our wood-fired grill, which gives the rice a wonderful smokiness. We use natural lump charcoal along with a mixture of oak and apple or other fruit wood for all of our grilling needs.

Love and Flavor Development

This is less a specific technique, more a general philosophy. We do not believe in love at first sight. Love must develop with time and patience, and that's exactly what you need for many of the recipes in this book. The ingredients need to interact with each other on a molecular level. Whether you are placing a pork chop in brine and waiting for osmosis to occur, or you are gently cooking the water out of your curry pastes so that the oil-soluble compounds come into contact with the fat and mellow the sharpness of the aromatics and harmonize the dish, or you are blanching, soaking, and squeezing your puffed pork skins for Tacho (page 209), you are applying your senses and engaging your will to make the best possible bite. Give it time, don't rush it, and make sweet, sweet love to the food you are cooking.

Knife Work

It is always best to use a sharp knife that you are comfortable with, and we recommend placing a wet paper towel strategically under your cutting board for stability and safety. Knife work is best done with both feet planted squarely on the ground shoulder-width apart. A small bowl used as a trash bin on your cutting board can help you save time and energy. Always wash your own knives, don't put them through a dishwasher, and never put knives in the sink! Keep a first-aid kit handy. For specific knife cuts, please refer to the photograph opposite.

Steaming

Steaming is a woefully underused cooking technique. We set up a bamboo or metal steamer in our woks to cook noodles, dumplings, and *bao*; to cook meat without the dilution of flavor that poaching and braising can cause; to cook delicate custards; and to gently cook whole fish and shellfish. When long-term steaming in a wok, be sure to add water occasionally so that it doesn't boil away. And, as always, be careful–steam burns are *mean*.

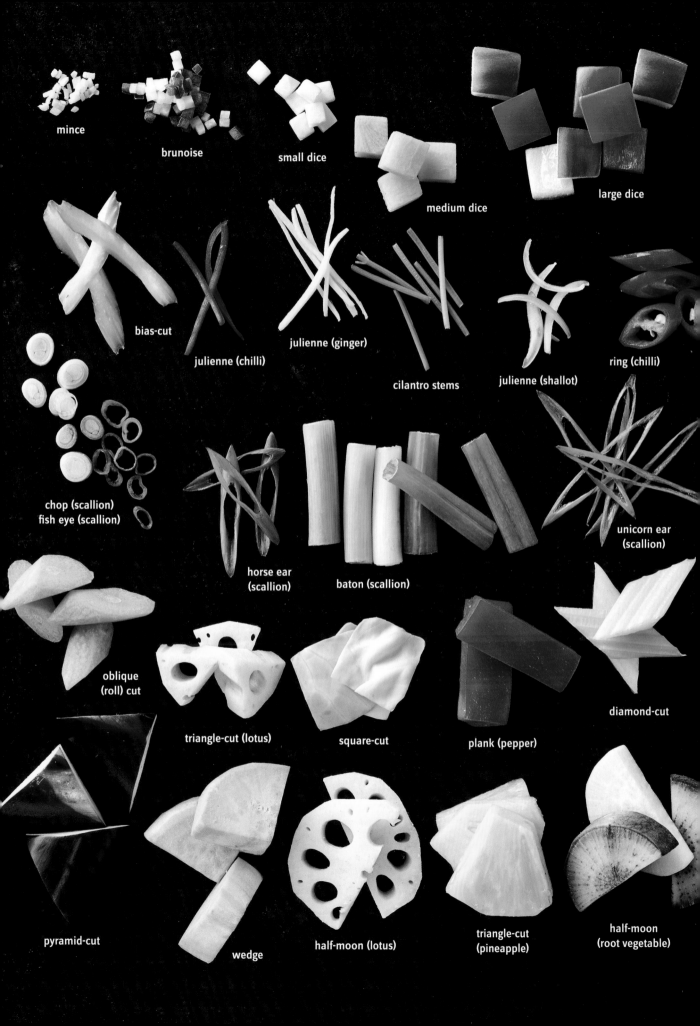

mince

brunoise

small dice

medium dice

large dice

bias-cut

julienne (chilli)

julienne (ginger)

cilantro stems

julienne (shallot)

ring (chilli)

chop (scallion)
fish eye (scallion)

horse ear
(scallion)

baton (scallion)

unicorn ear
(scallion)

oblique
(roll) cut

triangle-cut (lotus)

square-cut

plank (pepper)

diamond-cut

pyramid-cut

wedge

half-moon (lotus)

triangle-cut
(pineapple)

half-moon
(root vegetable)

1

ACHAR E CONSERVAS

PICKLES AND PRESERVES

Across the globe, cooks use preservation techniques to suspend food that would otherwise rot in a state of time-defying brightness–a remembrance of seasons past. Preserves are a beautiful confluence of necessity and art; if you had cucumbers or cabbage or carrots popping up faster than you and yours could eat them, you bet you were going to figure out a way to keep them around longer, especially without the advantage of refrigeration. In the case of Portuguese explorers, preserving food to transport it–both for sale and for consumption–between Asia, Africa,

Brazil, and Europe made long voyages possible. Preservation didn't just work for vegetables, but also for meat and fish: salting hams or cod created that bad-for-bad-bacteria environment that allowed them to be carried around the world. In their travels, the Portuguese came across new preservation techniques in India, Malaysia, and Macau, where the warm climates meant that things had an especially short life span after harvest.

In Asian cooking, preserved vegetables are served with rice dishes to add vibrancy, crunch, and acid.

At Fat Rice, preserved foods are often light snacks or an introduction to a meal or an accompaniment to richer foods.

We use a lot of items preserved in salt and vinegar in our cooking, too: Lemon Achar (page 38), which is simply lemons preserved with salt and aromatics, and Esmargal (page 33), a pickle that uses vinegar and tamarind to preserve fish.

Generally speaking, a cook can follow one of two paths to get a pickle: using salt or using vinegar. But neither route works without the magic of fermentation.

Most of us who grew up in the States are used to pickles made with vinegar. A strong brine of hot vinegar, garlic, and spices is poured over cucumbers, which absorb the flavors and acidity of the brine, creating crunchy, well-preserved pickles. When we pickle with vinegar, much of the heavy lifting has already been done for us. In fact, this method actually controls any additional fermentation, creating a shelf-stable environment.

Fermenting using salt, on the other hand, requires a bit more finesse. We make a brine with a specific ratio of salt to water, or we salt vegetables directly, in order to prevent the growth of "bad bacteria"–microbes that we don't want on the pickles because they will make the pickles squishy or smelly or downright dangerous to eat. Fortunately for us, this process also creates an environment in which "good bacteria" can thrive. These good bacteria, usually lactic acid bacteria, serve not only to give pickles their characteristic sour taste, but also to preserve the pickles by setting up camp before the undesirables arrive.

When making pickles, remember to work as cleanly as possible–that shoe can wait to be tied, that open sore can wait to be itched. Just keep things clean. It's all you can do to provide a good environment for the microbes to do their thing.

ESMARGAL (MACKEREL PICKLE)

In addition to coming across esmargal in Macau, we've seen similar techniques for preserving fish used all over the Portuguese-speaking world (*paŕa* in Brazil, *piexe tamarindo* in Goa, and the simply named "fish pickle" at Mary's Café in Singapore), and done with fish ranging from salmon to sawfish to freshwater fish. At the restaurant, we reach over to the Atlantic Ocean and use mackerel. Esmargal enriches dishes such as our Stir-Fried Greens with Green Papaya, Mushroom, and Mackerel Pickle (page 110), but it can play the star when fried and spooned over plain steamed rice or spread on Papo Seco (page 264) as well.

1 pound fresh Atlantic mackerel fillets, boned

1/4 cup salt

16 dried red chillies, stemmed

2 tablespoons cumin seeds, toasted and cooled

1/4 cup minced garlic

1/4 cup minced fresh ginger

2 1/2 tablespoons Tamarind Extract (page 285)

3 tablespoons Filipino cane vinegar

Extra-virgin olive oil, for covering

First, dry the mackerel: lay the mackerel skin-side down on a parchment paper-lined sheet pan. Cover evenly with half of the salt. Wrap the pan with plastic wrap and refrigerate for 12 hours.

After 12 hours, transfer the fish, still skin-side down, to a clean parchment paper-lined sheet pan. Cover evenly with the remaining salt. Wrap the pan with plastic wrap and refrigerate for another 12 hours.

After 12 hours, transfer the fish, still skin-side down, to a clean parchment paper-lined sheet pan. Leave out at room temperature and let dry for 24 hours. At this point, the fillets are dry enough to use for the esmargal.

Cover the mackerel in cold water and soak for 20 minutes to remove excess salt. Drain the water and repeat the process. Drain again, rinse the fish in cold water, and pat it dry. Remove the skin and discard, then cut the flesh into 1-inch squares and place in a bowl.

In a blender, grind the chillies (seeds and all) and cumin seeds into a fine powder. Add the garlic, ginger, tamarind, and cane vinegar and blend until smooth. Pour over the fish and mix well to ensure even distribution. Pack into a pint-size mason jar, pressing down firmly to remove any air bubbles. Top off with olive oil to keep the esmargal covered. Cover tightly and store at room temperature for 1 month.

After 1 month, put the esmargal into a standing mixer fitted with the paddle attachment and beat, adding a bit of olive oil as necessary to allow the fish to reach a thick, pastelike consistency. Alternatively, you can do this by hand with a wooden spoon, old-school style. Pack the esmargal back into a clean mason jar, top off again with oil, and store in the refrigerator for up to 3 months.

SWEET SOY BURDOCK

Here's another greatest hit taught to us by Adrienne's dad, Charlie. Also known as *gobo*, burdock root has a pleasantly fibrous and crunchy texture and is widely used in Chinese cooking and medicine. Here it soaks up a sweet, salty, and slightly numbing soy reduction, making it a great starter, side dish, or salty snack with a cold beer.

2 tablespoons salt

1 pound burdock root, peeled, split lengthwise, and cut on a bias into 1-inch pieces

2 tablespoons peanut oil

2 whole star anise

1 tablespoon minced ginger

¹/₃ cup sugar

³/₄ cup tamari or soy sauce

1 teaspoon ground Sichuan peppercorn

In a large saucepan, bring 3 cups of water to a boil and season with the salt. Add the burdock and blanch for 5 minutes, then transfer to an ice water bath to cool. Drain the burdock and dry well with paper towels.

In a large sauté pan or wok over medium heat, add the oil, star anise, and ginger, and sauté until fragrant, about 2 minutes. Add the burdock and increase the heat to high. Add the sugar and tamari and stir to incorporate the ingredients. Continue to stir and toss until the burdock has developed a glossy sheen, about 5 minutes. Once the liquid has reduced to form a glaze and the burdock appears dark brown, remove from the heat, season with pepper, and serve warm or at room temperature.

RAMP PICKLE

In the Midwest, the appearance of ramps marks the true arrival of spring after a long, frigid, nasty winter. This recipe is one example of our many attempts to apply Midwest seasonality to Macanese cuisine. The ramp comes close to the small, Southern Chinese onion called rakkyo or kin tau, and is traditionally pickled and added to Diabo (see page 40). Eat as an accompaniment to curries or on our Dry-Fried Asparagus with Minchi and Peixinhos Fritos (page 107).

1 cup Filipino cane vinegar

1 cup water

¹/₂ cup sugar

¹/₂ teaspoon salt

1 pound (1 bunch) ramps, trimmed, green tops removed and reserved for another use

Combine the vinegar, water, sugar, and salt in a small pot and bring to a boil over high heat. Add the ramp bottoms, return to a boil, then remove from the heat and cool completely. Store refrigerated, in the cooking liquid, for up to 1 month.

CHARLIE'S PEANUTS

These peanuts are Adrienne's mainline to nostalgia. Just smelling the soy sauce, cinnamon, and star anise of the marinade transports her back to early morning breakfasts before school. The crunchy, salty peanuts would go on the Chinese congee (rice porridge) known as *xi fan*, creating the ideal warming and nourishing food on a cold Chicago morning.

The peanuts of Adrienne's youth were simpler than what we offer here. Blame her father, Charlie, who bumped up the initial recipe with a slew of extra vegetables like burdock and lotus roots, shiitake mushrooms, carrots, and daikon radish, making an already great thing greater. When cooked, these vegetables all have slightly different textures: super-crisp lotus roots, absorbent shiitakes, and soft and unctuous daikon take the nuts to the next level.

The recipe originally came from Adrienne's paternal grandfather, James Lo, but Charlie was the one always tinkering with the recipe, and thus we've named the nuts after him.

1¹/₂ cups raw, shelled Spanish peanuts

¹/₂ cup dried shiitake mushrooms

¹/₂ cup peeled and sliced burdock root (¹/₃-inch-thick slices)

¹/₂ cup peeled and cut lotus root (¹/₃-inch-thick bite-size pieces)

¹/₂ cup peeled carrot, oblique cut (see 27)

¹/₂ cup peeled and diced daikon

¹/₂ cup diced extra-firm tofu

SOY MARINADE

1¹/₃ cups soy sauce

1 tablespoon palm sugar

2 whole cinnamon sticks

1 teaspoon whole Sichuan peppercorns

3 whole star anise

3 (¹/₄-inch) slices unpeeled ginger

1 tablespoon Chinese black vinegar

Cover the peanuts by 2 inches cold water, soak overnight, and drain. Soaked the dried shiitakes in 3 cups warm water overnight. Then strain, reserving the liquid for the soy marinade. Remove and discard the stems and dice the caps.

To make the soy marinade, combine 1¹/₂ cups of the shiitake soaking liquid, the soy sauce, palm sugar, cinnamon sticks, Sichuan peppercorns, star anise, ginger, and balsamic vinegar in a large saucepan. Bring to a boil. Cool, then strain and reserve.

To prepare the peanuts and vegetables, bring a large pot of water to a rapid boil over high heat. Add the peanuts, reduce the heat to a simmer, and cook for 15 to 20 minutes, until crisp with a tender crunch, similar to a fresh pea. Add the burdock and lotus roots and cook for an additional 5 minutes. Add the carrot, daikon, mushrooms, and tofu and cook for 3 to 4 more minutes, until the carrot is tender but still crunchy. Remove from the heat and drain immediately in a colander. Transfer the nuts and vegetables to a shallow container, add the soy marinade, and soak overnight, or for at least 4 hours. When the peanuts are flavored to your liking, drain them, leaving a bit of the juice to keep the peanuts moist. They are ready to serve immediately, or store tightly covered and refrigerated for up to 1 week.

LEMON ACHAR (PRESERVED LEMON PICKLE)

MAKES
2 POUNDS

In many South Asian regions, the Hindi word *achar* refers to pickles. Some achars can be served to open or accompany meals; others, like this lemon achar, are used as actual ingredients in more complex dishes, like Po Kok Gai (page 181). Add any leftover juices to cocktails, salad dressings, and even pasta sauces.

2 pounds lemons, quartered from pole to pole

1 tablespoon coriander seeds

1 tablespoon cumin seeds

2 teaspoons fennel seeds

2 cinnamon sticks, broken in half

8 whole green cardamom pods

2 whole black cardamom pods

3 dried bay leaves

1 cup salt

1/3 cup sugar

1/4 cup extra-virgin olive oil

2 tablespoons Filipino cane vinegar

Mix together the lemons, coriander seeds, cumin seeds, fennel seeds, cinnamon sticks, green and black cardamom pods, bay leaves, salt, sugar, olive oil, and cane vinegar in a large bowl, then divide evenly among 3 pint-size mason jars, using a wooden rolling pin to mash some of the juice out of the lemons and really get them packed down tightly. Make sure that the juice and oil rise to the top of each jar–if the lemons are exposed they might grow mold.

Store in a sunny spot at room temperature for 1 month. The salt and acid will soften the rind, rendering it soft and yellow all the way through when sliced. If there is still a raw white band of pith, let the whole operation soak for another couple of weeks.

To use, brush away and discard the seeds, then chop the lemon up. For a bit more refined approach, remove the lemon's flesh and finely julienne the rind.

SINGAPORE SOUR CABBAGE

This cabbage pickle is a great accompaniment to have on hand to give any dish a crunchy tang. We use a 2 percent salt-to-water brine ratio for all of our pickles. The finishing touches of this recipe are inspired by the flavors of a stir-fried cabbage dish at our friend Quentin's Eurasian restaurant in Singapore.

MAKES ABOUT 6 CUPS

FERMENT

2 quarts water

1¼ ounces (2 tablespoons plus 1½ teaspoons) salt

1 head (2 pounds) green cabbage

4 fresh red Fresno chillies, stemmed and thinly sliced

FINISH

2 tablespoons peanut oil

2 cloves garlic, minced

1 (½-inch) piece fresh ginger, peeled and minced

1 tablespoon black mustard seeds

1 tablespoon yellow mustard seeds

12 whole curry leaves

1 teaspoon ground turmeric

1 tablespoon sambal oelek

¾ cup Tamarind Extract (page 285)

2 tablespoons sugar

To make the ferment, combine the water and salt in a pot, stir well, and bring to a boil. Cool to room temperature. You've now made a 2 percent brine solution.

While the brine cools, cut the cabbage into quarters through the fibrous core. Lay the cabbage on a flat side and, cutting at an angle, cut out the core and discard. Cut the cabbage into 1½-inch squares.

Pack the cabbage and chillies into a clean, 2-quart mason jar. Pour the cooled brine over to cover by an inch or two. Fill a 1-quart zip-top bag halfway with the remaining brine, squeeze out all of the air, seal the bag, and put it on top of the cabbage to ensure that the cabbage stays submerged beneath the surface of the brine. Loosely cover the jar, allowing the gasses formed during fermentation to escape. Leave at room temperature until lightly fermented and sour, 2 to 3 days, skimming off any mold that forms on top. (Note: White mold is normal and fine; any darker colors or slime are undesirable–throw it all out and start over.) When the

desired sourness is achieved, cover tightly and refrigerate. The cabbage is great to eat as is (and can be stored in the fridge for up to 2 weeks), or continue to the next step to give it the Eurasian flavors we experienced at Quentin's.

Drain the cabbage well and set aside. To finish, heat the oil in a large heavy pot over high heat. Add the garlic and ginger and stir until fragrant, about 30 seconds. Add the mustard seeds and stir until they begin to pop, about 30 seconds. Add the curry leaves and stir until they become fragrant and begin to sizzle, about another 30 seconds. The leaves should be brittle and dry but retain their integrity, and the seeds should be golden brown. Add the turmeric and stir for another 30 seconds as it colors the oil, then add the sambal, tamarind, and sugar and bring to a boil. Add the fermented cabbage to the pot and stir well, then remove from the heat. Cool fully and store tightly covered in the refrigerator for up to 2 weeks, if not using immediately.

DIABO PICKLE

MAKES ABOUT 1 QUART

We developed this for our Diabo (Devil's Curry, page 221), and it was a challenging pickle to perfect. We reached back to less convenient times, beyond the past one hundred years of Macau, before the advent of prepared mustard and store-bought sweet piccalilly and chowchow-type pickles, and used whole mustard seeds and a variety of vegetables. Note–this may be your first introduction to asafoetida–so when storing it, be sure to keep it in its original container and in a zip-top bag–it's extremely strong-smelling and will invade your entire pantry otherwise!

MASALA

2 cups Filipino cane vinegar

10 dried red chillies

1 tablespoon black mustard seeds

1 tablespoon yellow mustard seeds

2 teaspoons ground turmeric

2 teaspoons cumin seeds

1/2 teaspoon fenugreek seeds

5 cloves garlic

1 (4-inch) piece fresh ginger, peeled and sliced against the grain

PICKLE

3/4 cup peanut oil

1/4 teaspoon ground asafoetida

1 tablespoon black mustard seeds

1 tablespoon yellow mustard seeds

2 cups water

3 cups sugar

Salt

8 ounces carrot, peeled and cut on the diagonal into 1/4-inch-thick slices

1 pound cauliflower florets, cut into bite-size pieces

12 fresh red chillies

1 pound green tomatoes, skin on and seeds intact, cut into bite-size pieces

1 red bell pepper, seeded and cut into bite-size pieces

To make the masala, bring the cane vinegar to a boil in a saucepan. Meanwhile, place the chillies and mustard seeds in a heatproof bowl. Once boiling, pour the vinegar overtop to soften the chillies. Let cool, then add to a blender with the turmeric, cumin, fenugreek, garlic, and ginger. Blend until a paste is formed, adding a bit of water if necessary to make the paste thin enough to be blended.

To make the pickle, heat the oil in a wide, heavy pot over medium heat. Add the asafoetida and stir with a wooden spoon until you're hit by its funkiness, 10 seconds. Add the mustard seeds and stir until they start to pop, 20 to 30 seconds. Add the masala to the pot and lower the heat to medium-low. Paying close attention, cook slowly, giving it a loving stir now and then. Slowly, the oil will begin to interact with the spices and take on their colors, the heat releasing all of their aromatic loveliness and blooming the flavors of the masala. This process will take anywhere from 5 to 15 minutes, but more importantly, trust your senses. Carefully add the water and sugar and bring to a simmer. Taste and adjust the seasoning. It should be sweet, sour, aromatic, and highly seasoned because you will be putting a large quantity of veggies into the liquid and you want to maximize the flavor that goes into them. Add the carrots and cauliflower, and return to a boil.

Put the chillies, green tomatoes, and bell pepper into a baking dish and pour everything from the pot into the baking dish. Cool in the refrigerator. When cool, put in an airtight container and refrigerate for up to 6 months.

GINGER ACHAR (GINGER PICKLE)

MAKES
ABOUT
2 CUPS

The sweet and sharp combination of this achar makes it an indispensable addition to the Lacassà (page 86) and the Diabo (Devil's Curry, page 221).

It will remind you of the sliced pickled ginger (*gari*) on a sushi plate, or the less commonly seen bright-red strips of pickled ginger known as *beni shoga* in Japan. *Gari* is pickled in vinegar, which causes very young ginger to produce a faint pink color. More industrial versions bypass the sourcing of young ginger and keep things cheap by adding food coloring. *Beni shoga*, however, is julienned and pickled in umezu, the liquid resulting from the production of the famous Japanese salted plums known as umeboshi– plums packed in salt with the addition of red shiso leaves. If your supply of umezu is short because you've been putting it in your gin and tonics (which is quite delicious), we've written this recipe using beet juice to color the ginger and add some sweetness.

8 ounces fresh ginger, peeled and julienned

1 1/2 teaspoons salt

8 ounces red beets, peeled and coarsely chopped

2 cups water

2 cups Filipino cane vinegar

1 cup sugar

Toss the ginger with 3/4 teaspoon of the salt in a medium bowl and set aside. Put the beets in a blender and set aside. Combine the water, cane vinegar, sugar, and remaining 3/4 teaspoon of the in a small saucepan over high heat. Bring to a boil, then pour over the beets. Blend carefully, covering the top of the blender with a towel and cracking the lid slightly to let steam escape safely, until smooth. Strain through a fine-mesh sieve back into the original saucepan and set aside.

Pat the ginger dry of excess moisture and place in an appropriately sized storage container, such as a clean mason jar. Bring the beet liquid to a boil over high heat, cook until reduced by half, then pour over the ginger. Let cool. Use immediately or cover tightly and refrigerate for up to 1 month.

JUMPWATER PICKLE

MAKES
1 POUND

This is a method for naturally fermenting vegetables into pickles that we picked up in Sichuan province. The term "jumpwater" was taught to us by "Old Chao," our chef-instructor at the Sichuan Higher Institute of Cuisine, because once you have an established, acidic brine, the pickles only take a short time: they jump in and jump out!

These pickles are great next to dumplings or alongside Arroz Gordo (page 69), or to cut through anything rich, really. We usually use a mix of vegetables including turnips and carrots, but most firm-fleshed vegetables can be fermented in this brine. Note that some vegetables–such as beets or red-fleshed radishes (which will dye everything), or okra (which should be rinsed free of its mucilaginous goo)–should be fermented separately, then added into the batch. When you're comfortable with the fermenting process, keep the jumpwater going throughout the year, adding seasonal vegetables as they arrive at the market or in your garden, adjusting the salt content and aromatic elements as necessary. Amounts and ratios are fairly important here, especially for the vegetables, water, and salt, so measure those carefully, and remember: cleanliness, especially when fermenting, is next to godliness.

YES JUMPWATER: CARROT, CELERY, CAULIFLOWER, RADISHES, TURNIPS, BOK CHOI, RAMPS, CUCUMBERS, SUMMER SQUASHES, GREEN BEANS

No JUMPWATER: TOMATOES, FRUITS, EGGPLANT, GREEN BELL PEPPERS

1 pound seasonal mixed vegetables, washed, peeled, and cut into bite-size chunks

4 cups water

3³/₄ teaspoons salt

4 whole dried red chillies

1 tablespoon clear spirits (vodka, strong rice wine, gin)

5 whole star anise

¹/₄ cup firmly packed light brown sugar

1 (1-inch) piece unpeeled fresh ginger, sliced ¹/₄ inch thick

2 cinnamon sticks

2 teaspoons whole Sichuan peppercorns

Put the vegetables in a 2-quart mason jar. Combine the water, salt, chillies, spirits, star anise, brown sugar, ginger, cinnamon sticks, and Sichuan peppercorns in a pot, stir well, and bring to a boil. Cool to room temperature. When cool, pour the brine over the vegetables to cover by an inch or two. Fill a 1-quart zip-top plastic bag half full with the remaining brine, squeeze out all air, seal the bag, and put on top of the vegetables to ensure that they stay submerged beneath the surface of the brine. Loosely cover with cheesecloth or a dish towel, allowing gasses formed during fermentation to escape. Leave at room temperature until lightly

fermented and sour, 2 to 3 days, skimming off any mold that forms on top. (Note: White mold is normal and fine; any other darker colors are undesirable–throw it all out and start over. Ditto for slime.) When the desired sourness is achieved, cover tightly and refrigerate for up to 3 months, making sure to keep the vegetables fully submerged. As you become more familiar with the pickling process, you may add more vegetables at any time; just be sure to add 2 teaspoons of salt along with every 8 ounces of vegetables that you add to the mix.

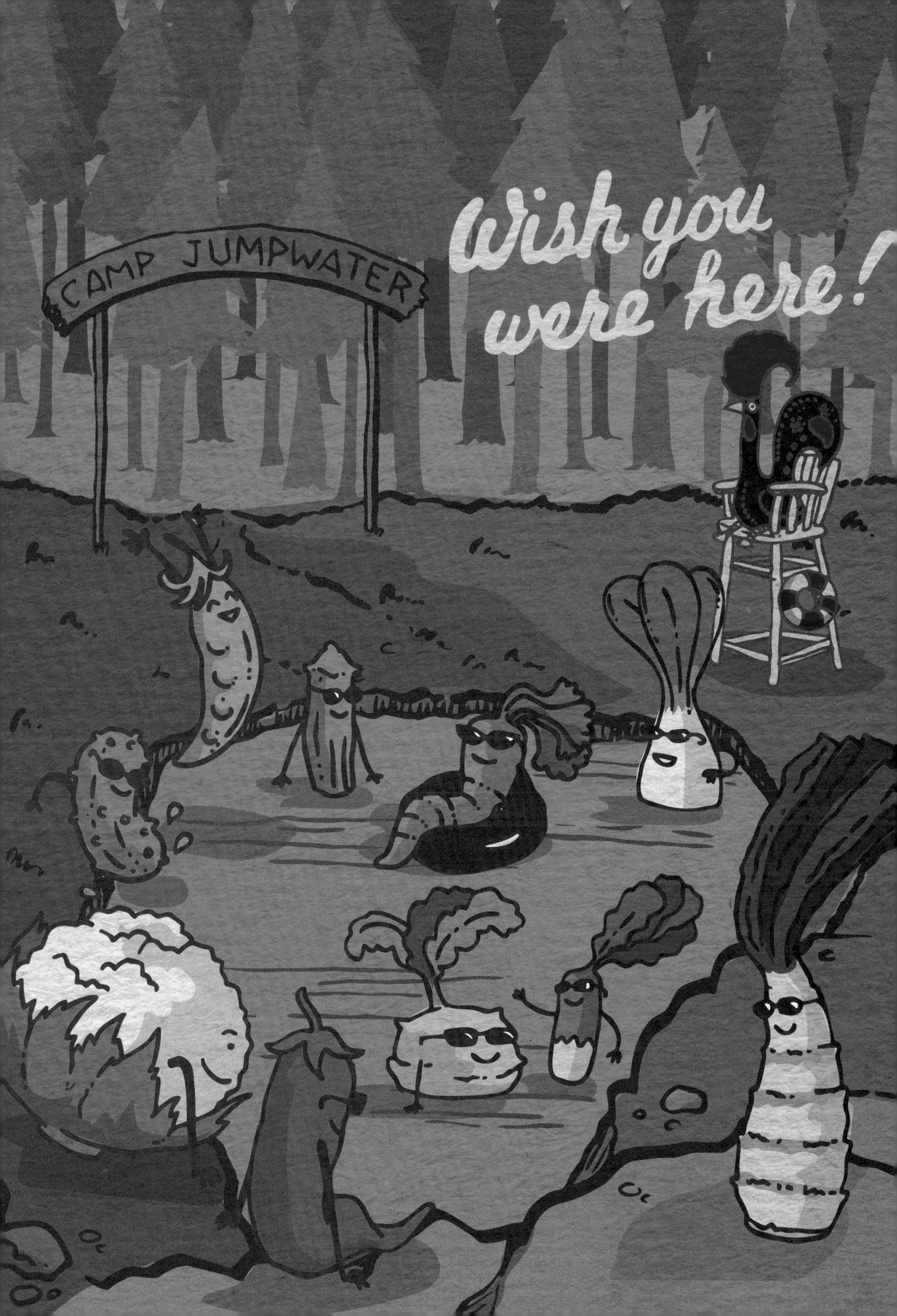
CAMP JUMPWATER
Wish you were here!

2

ENTRADAS

APPETIZERS

The recipes in this section are for serving at the ever-important opening of a meal. It's the warmth of something like the Portuguese-style fried Minchi Croquettes (page 53) that welcome guests into your kitchen, bringing them into the comfort zone for the approaching meal. When you invite people into your space, hand them a drink and offer a plate of Curried Vegetable Chamuças (page 49); it's an act of nurturing, loosening the mood (not to mention giving people something to do during those first few, possibly awkward moments) as they cross over into the world you've created for them.

In Macau, you generally find these items served Western-style, laid out on the table with olives and perhaps some of the pickles to be eaten before the main meal; at a smorgasbord-like *cha gordo* (literally, "fat tea") service, they'd be part of the composition of a table full of several other dishes to be picked at throughout the course of the meal. Keep in mind, these dishes may seem a bit prep heavy: hand-forming potstickers (page 60) doesn't happen in a flash–but once formed or prepped, these dishes can be finished as your guests arrive, leaving you free to join in the cocktail hour.

CURRIED VEGETABLE CHAMUÇAS

Fried savory pastries are found all over the world: India has bubbly, cone-shaped samosas, while Burmese samusas are usually flatter and smaller like these tiny, multilayered, and crispy chamuças from Macau. You might be curious about the wheat starch in the recipe–you could substitute all-purpose flour, but the wheat starch and water combo that we lovingly refer to as "Japanese cement" provides the strongest seal ever known to man. Pay close attention to the diagram when folding–this method completely seals the filling in while creating several layers of pastry.

6 dried wood ear mushrooms

2 tablespoons peanut oil, plus more for deep-frying

1 yellow onion, coarsely grated

1 teaspoon salt

2 tablespoons Macau Hot Curry Powder (page 279)

¼ head green cabbage, grated

2 carrots, peeled and grated

1 large russet potato, peeled and grated

½ cup wheat starch (or substitute all-purpose flour)

Approximately 30 wheat spring roll wrappers

Fragrant Tamarind Chutney (page 51), for serving

Place the mushrooms in a small bowl and cover with 2 cups of room temperature water. Soak until hydrated, about 20 minutes. Drain, then mince the mushrooms and set aside.

Pour the 2 tablespoons oil into a heavy pot or a wok over medium-high heat. Add the onions and salt and cook until slightly caramelized, about 5 minutes. Add the curry powder and stir until fragrant and copper in color. Don't burn it! Add the cabbage, carrot, and reserved mushrooms and cook until soft, about 5 more minutes. Add the potato and cook, stirring from time to time, until the potatoes are fully cooked and binding the mixture together, another 5 minutes or so.

➤➤ continued

Remove from the heat, adjust the seasoning as needed, and cool completely in the refrigerator.

Mix the wheat starch with enough water to form a loose, rubber cement-like paste. Follow the steps in the graphic on page 50 to fold the chamuças.

When you are ready to cook the chamuças, heat about 3 inches of oil for deep-frying in a wok to 350°F. Working in batches, fry a few chamuças at a time until golden brown and heated through, about 1 minute, turning with a spider as needed so that both sides brown. Transfer to a paper towel-lined plate and season with salt. Serve immediately with the chutney.

FOLDING CHAMUÇAS

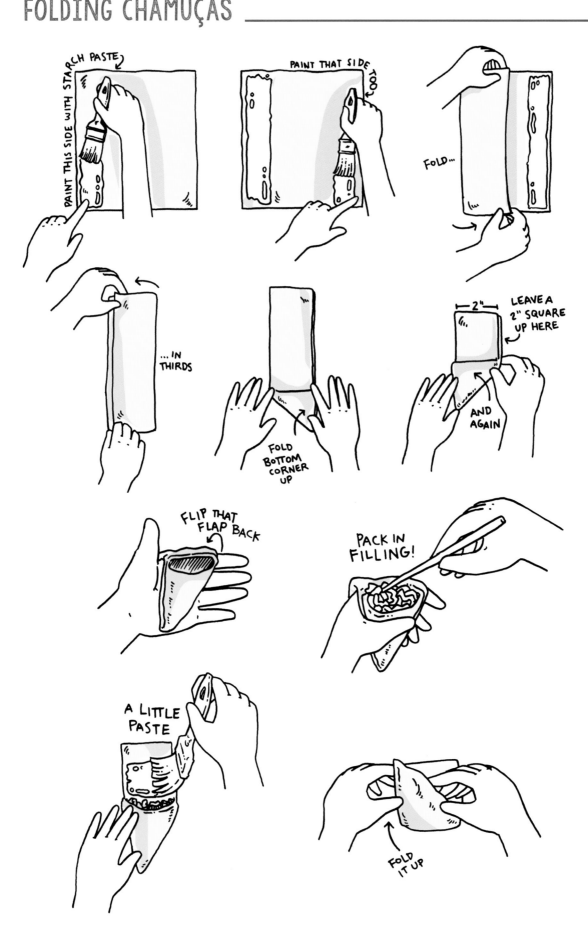

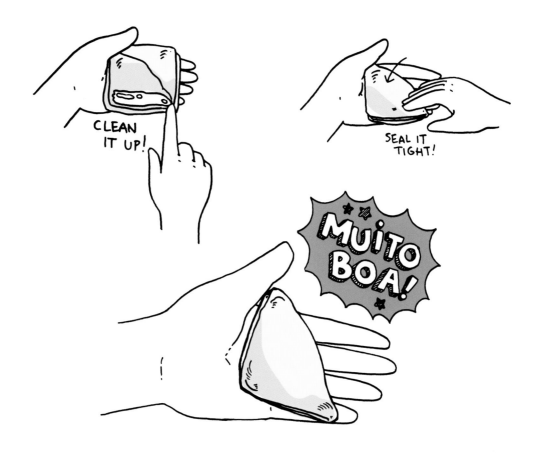

FRAGRANT TAMARIND CHUTNEY

2 tablespoons peanut oil

2 cloves garlic, minced

1 (½-inch) piece fresh
ginger, peeled and
minced

1 tablespoon black
mustard seeds

1 tablespoon yellow
mustard seeds

3 whole curry leaves

1 teaspoon ground
turmeric

1 tablespoon
sambal oelek

¾ cup Tamarind Extract
(page 285)

2 tablespoons sugar

MAKES
1 CUP

Heat the oil in a small, heavy pot over high heat.
Add the garlic and ginger and stir until fragrant,
about 30 seconds. Add the mustard seeds and stir until
they begin to pop, about 30 seconds. Add the curry
leaves and stir as they become fragrant and begin to
sizzle, about another 30 seconds. The leaves should
be brittle and dry, but maintain their integrity, and the
seeds should be golden brown. Add the turmeric and
stir for another 30 seconds as it colors the oil, then add
the sambal, tamarind, and sugar and bring to a boil.
Stir well, adjusting the texture with water as needed if
it gets too thick—you want the sauce to coat the back
of a spoon and hold a line when you stripe your finger
through it. Remove from the heat and cool completely.

Store tightly covered in the refrigerator for up to
1 month if not using immediately.

MINCHI (MINCED BEEF AND PORK) CROQUETTES

These little meat and potato pillows have been a staple at our brunch menu from the get-go. In this recipe, the outer-dough (made pliable by the addition of potato starch) holds the meat inside and keeps it moist and distinct, providing a two-toned texture. We like serving them on a doily with a saucer of Sweet Plum Sauce.

MAKES ABOUT 16 PIECES; SERVES 4

DOUGH

2 pounds russet potatoes, peeled and cut into 2-inch pieces

5 tablespoons potato starch

1 teaspoon salt

FILLING

1 cup Minchi (page 230)

BREADING

1 cup all-purpose flour

3 eggs

1 tablespoon water

1 cup panko bread crumbs

FINISH

Peanut oil, for deep-frying

Salt

Sweet Plum Sauce (page 56)

To make the dough, place the potatoes in a large pot and cover with cold, salted water. Bring to a simmer over high heat, then lower the heat and cook until the potatoes are knife-tender, about 20 minutes. Drain in a colander and let sit for 3 minutes to drain well, then mash, preferably with a potato ricer. Place the hot mashed potatoes in a large bowl and evenly sprinkle with the potato starch and salt. Gently combine using a wooden spoon and set aside to cool to room temperature.

To make the filling, place the Minchi in a bowl and add ¼ cup of the dough to bind it. Set aside.

On a 24 by 12-inch piece of plastic wrap, spread half of the remaining potato dough into a 4 by 12-inch strip on the bottom half of the plastic wrap. Fold the top half of the plastic wrap over the potato mixture and use a rolling pin to gently roll the dough into a 6 by 16-inch rectangle about ¼ inch thick. Fold back the top layer of plastic wrap and use a bench scraper to trim any rough edges. Form half of the minchi mixture into a line about ¾ inch wide across the bottom third of the potato dough lengthwise. Starting with the side closest to you, and using the edges of the plastic wrap as a handle of sorts, roll the potato dough away from you and around the minchi mixture to form an even

log, wrapping in the plastic as you go. Repeat this process with the other half of the dough and minchi mixture. Place the logs in the freezer for at least 1 hour, then remove the plastic wrap and slice each log into 1-inch croquettes and set aside.

To set up a three-step breading station, place the flour in a bowl, beat the eggs with the water in another bowl, and place the panko in a third bowl. Gently toss a croquette in the flour. Using your left hand, shake off any excess flour and toss the croquette in the egg wash, being sure to fully coat it. Using your right hand, shake off any excess egg and toss the croquette into the panko. Using your left hand, roll the croquette in the panko until it is thoroughly coated. Shape into a cylinder a little bigger than a tater tot and place on a baking sheet. Repeat with the rest of the croquettes. Once they are all breaded, freeze them for at least 4 hours.

To finish, when you are ready to cook, prepare a wok for deep frying and heat about 2 inches of the oil to 350°F. Working in batches, fry a few croquettes at a time until golden brown and heated through, about 1½ to 2 minutes. Transfer to a paper towel-lined plate and season with salt. Serve immediately with the plum sauce.

▶▶ continued

SHAPING THE CROQUETTES

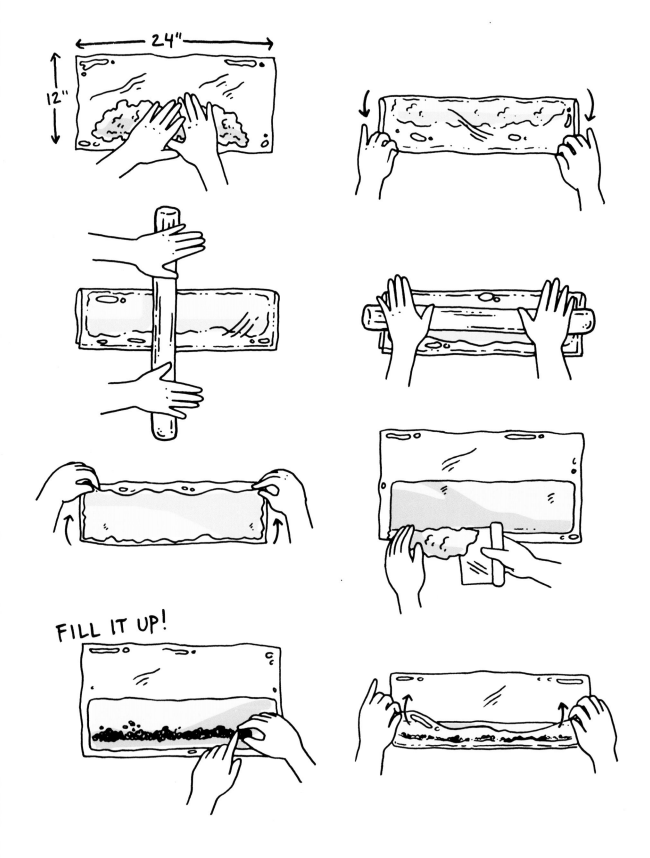

FILL IT UP!

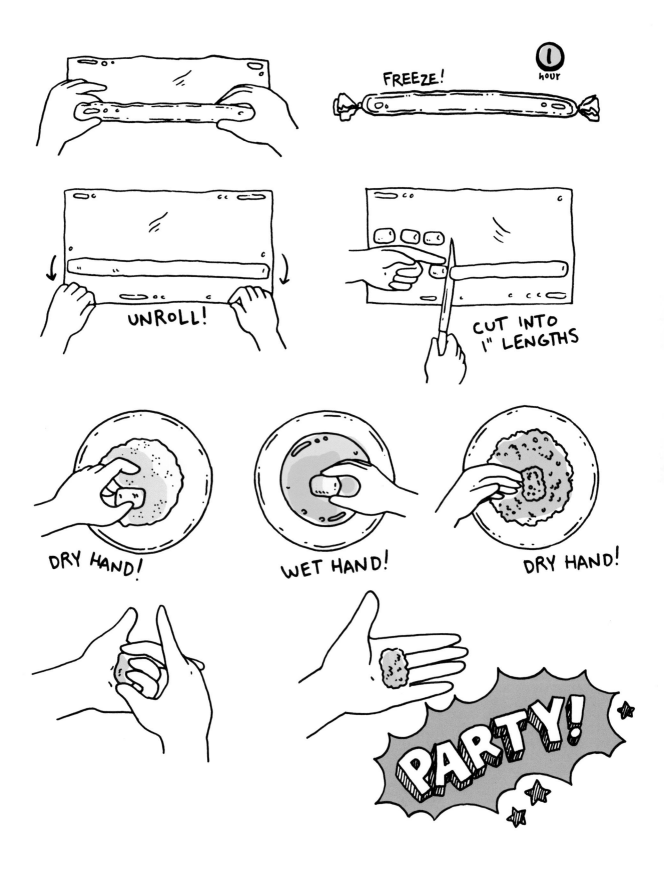

FREEZE! 1 hour

UNROLL!

CUT INTO 1" LENGTHS

DRY HAND!

WET HAND!

DRY HAND!

PARTY!

SWEET PLUM SAUCE

MAKES 1 PINT

2 tablespoons peanut oil

1 tablespoon fermented bean paste (pixian, see page 293)

1/2 teaspoon whole Sichuan peppercorns

1/2 small onion, diced

2 teaspoons minced garlic

1 (1-inch) piece fresh ginger, peeled and minced

6 ripe plums, pitted

1 tablespoon sugar

2 tablespoons Filipino cane vinegar

Salt

Heat the oil in a small heavy pot over medium heat. Add the *pixian* and Sichuan peppercorns and cook until fragrant and the oil becomes slightly red, about 2 minutes. Add the onion and cook until translucent, about 5 minutes, then add the garlic and ginger and cook until fragrant, about 30 seconds. Add the plums, sugar, and vinegar, cover, and cook until the plums are tender, about 15 to 20 minutes, stirring occasionally. Let cool slightly, then puree in a blender until smooth. Add salt to taste, if needed, and store in an airtight container in the refrigerator for up to 1 month.

POTSTICKERS ROYALE WITH CRISPY CREPE

Adrienne has a strong childhood memory of hand-forming dumplings of various shapes and sizes with her family. Their potstickers contained an ingredient that isn't often found in dumplings much outside of northern China: dill, added by Adrienne's grandparents' caretaker, Li Na. Despite initial skepticism, Adrienne's grandparents came to appreciate the strange addition, and a taste for dill trickled down to the recipe we use at Fat Rice. Li Na also introduced the light, eggless crepe that adorns our potstickers, one reason people love the potstickers at Fat Rice; the extra crispy bits can be the best part.

The crepe batter is a pretty precise recipe, and therefore will yield better results if measured by weight rather than volume. And know now what many a cook at Fat Rice have learned the hard way: the crepe is super difficult to master! There is a certain relationship between you, the pan, the potstickers, the crepe batter, and the universe that has to be in line, and there's no way to learn that other than by just giving it a go (after you've read the instructions, of course–always be careful when flipping a hot, heavy pan containing oil). This recipe makes a lot, so you've got some room for failure. And remember, you aren't selling these in a crowded restaurant (you aren't, right?), so even the ones that don't pop out under a perfect crepe will still taste delicious.

CREPE BATTER

1³/4 ounces (about 6 tablespoons) cornstarch

1 ounce (about 4 tablespoons) all-purpose flour

25¹/3 ounces (about 3 cups plus 2 tablespoons) water

DUMPLINGS

4 green onions, white and green parts, fisheye-cut (see page 27)

2 stalks celery, minced

1 bunch fresh dill, finely chopped

1 (1-inch) piece fresh ginger, peeled and minced

3 teaspoons toasted sesame oil

8 ounces shrimp, peeled, deveined, and chopped into ¹/4-inch chunks

1 tablespoon Shaoxing wine

2 teaspoons tapioca starch

8 ounces ground pork

1 teaspoon salt

¹/2 teaspoon ground Sichuan peppercorns

¹/2 teaspoon Five-Spice Powder (page 280)

1 egg, beaten

2 teaspoons soy sauce

36 dumpling wrappers

1 tablespoon peanut oil

Salt and ground Sichuan peppercorns

1¹/2 cups Potsticker Sauce (page 63), for serving

Place a large metal mixing bowl in the freezer for 20 minutes.

To make the crepes, combine the cornstarch and flour in a medium bowl. While whisking, add the water and incorporate thoroughly. Place ³/4 cup of the crepe batter in a squeeze bottle and set aside. (Always make sure the batter is well whisked right before measuring to ensure proper distribution of the ingredients.)

>> continued

SHAPING POTSTICKERS

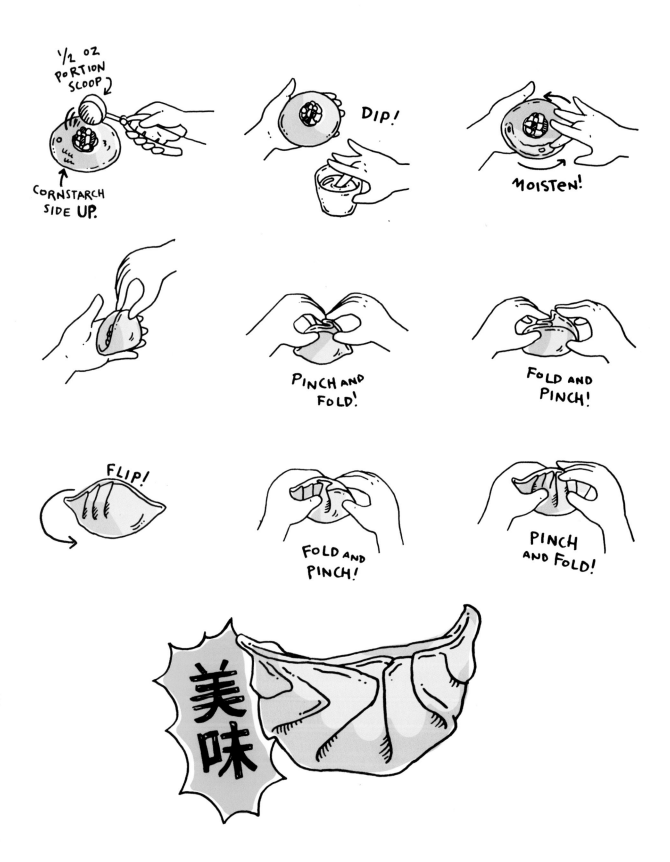

COOKING POTSTICKERS

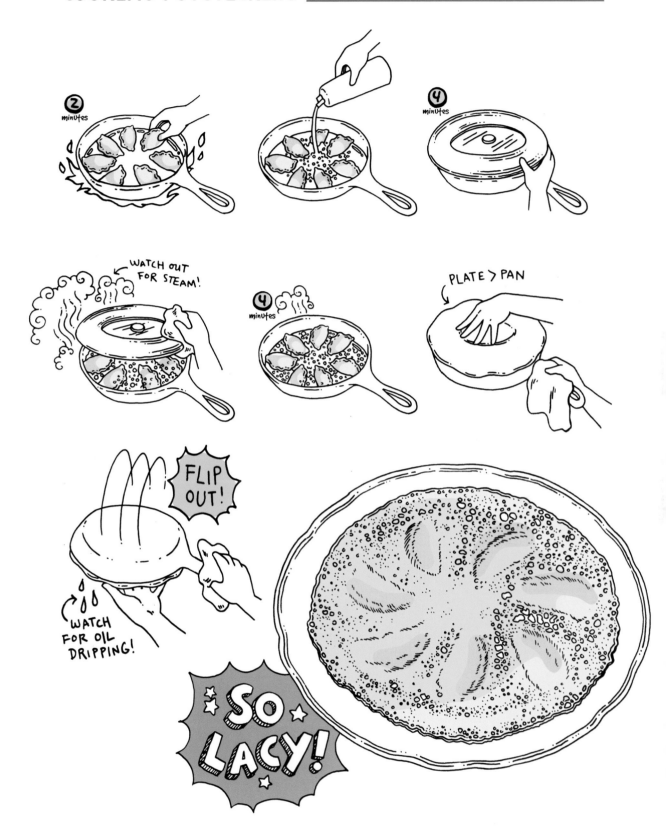

To make the dumplings, combine the green onions, celery, dill, ginger, and 2 teaspoons of the sesame oil in a separate bowl and toss thoroughly. Set aside in the refrigerator.

In another bowl, thoroughly mix together the shrimp, wine, and tapioca starch; set aside in the refrigerator.

Put the pork in the chilled bowl from the freezer. Put a glove on your hand and set all five fingers on the counter like Thing from *The Addams Family*. This is the position you need to hold your hand in while you're mixing the meat. Once you've mastered the Thing technique, use it to mix the pork in a clockwise motion, aggressively stirring about fifteen times around the bowl. Add the salt, Sichuan peppercorns, and five-spice powder and mix with Thing technique fifteen more times. Scrape the side of the bowl with the blade of your hand, Julia Child–style. Add the egg, soy sauce, and remaining 1 teaspoon sesame oil and mix fifteen more times, until incorporated. Add the chilled shrimp mixture to the pork mixture and mix fifteen more times, scraping as needed. Add the chilled vegetables and mix another fifteen times. Set aside and fill the potstickers (see page 60).

Using a 1/2-ounce portion scoop, place filling onto the center of the wrapper (the starchy side should face up). Wet your middle finger and moisten the rim of the wrapper.

Using your dry thumb and forefinger, draw the edges of the wrapper together and pinch the center, leaving the ends open.

Using a pinch and fold motion, pleat the side of the wrapper facing away from you with three folds.

Turn the dumpling around and finish the pleat in the same manner. You should have a completely sealed, crescent-shaped dumpling.

Do that again thirty-five more times. Good luck!

When all of the potstickers are formed, set yourself up with a well-seasoned, snugly lidded 10-inch cast-iron skillet and a plate that will fit comfortably inside the rim of said pan. Rub the peanut oil all over the pan to evenly coat it. Place seven potstickers in the pan in an evenly spaced pinwheel pattern and place over medium-high heat until they start to sizzle and become light brown on the bottom, about 2 minutes. Meanwhile, give the crepe batter a good shake to get it mixed up again. With the pan's lid in one hand and the crepe batter in the other, quickly and deliberately pour the batter over the potstickers in two circular motions and immediately cover the pan with the lid to capture the steam. Continue to cook, covered, until the potstickers start to swell and the top of the dough starts to become translucent, checking only after 4 minutes (be careful of escaping steam!). Remove the lid to allow the steam to evaporate and the bottom of the potstickers to crisp. At this point, rotate the pan as necessary to maximize evaporation and even browning, and lower the heat as needed. This process takes about 4 more minutes–things can burn easily, so pay attention! Gently lift each potsticker by its corner to be sure nothing is sticking. Give the pan a shake; everything will slide around freely when done.

At this point, turn the heat off. You have a couple of methods to get the potstickers out of the pan. You can take them out as cleanly as possible with a spatula and then invert them onto the plate or you can take the committed route we use in the restaurant and go for broke. *Fat Rice and all interested parties are not responsible for the scalding oil burns that can result if you do this improperly!* Place a plate that is larger than the pan upside down on top of the pan. With feet shoulder-width apart under springy knees, form the Thing with your nondominant hand, placing your fingertips in the center of the plate. Lift the pan from the stove with your dominant hand. Remembering that you are dealing with extremely hot food and even hotter oil, build a bit of momentum using a three-count bounce, then invert the pan so the plate is on the bottom, using an arclike motion. Make sure that the arm holding the plate is straight up and down to avoid any dripping oil. *That's really important!* Carefully remove the pan and ensure that all potstickers and crepe have come out uniformly. When you have produced flawless potstickers, season with salt and ground Sichuan peppercorns and serve immediately with the sauce. Of course, the ones that didn't come out so beautifully will still taste delicious–nibble on them while you perfect your technique.

POTSTICKER SAUCE

¹/₄ cup Chinese
black vinegar

¹/₄ cup balsamic vinegar

2 tablespoons sugar

¹/₄ cup water

¹/₂ cup soy sauce

1 (¹/₂-inch) piece fresh
ginger, peeled and
minced

3 cloves garlic, minced

¹/₄ cup coarsely chopped
fresh cilantro

1 tablespoon chopped
fresh chillies, pickled
chillies, or sambal oelek

**MAKES
ABOUT
1 ¹/₂ CUPS**

Whisk all of the ingredients together in a bowl. Store,
refrigerated, for up to 1 month if not using immediately.

BRINJAL SAMBAL
(SPICY SWEET-AND-SOUR EGGPLANT)

**SERVES 4
AS AN
APPETIZER**

If you don't like eggplant, it's because you haven't had it done right! Our dry-frying technique breaks down the rawness of the eggplant and allows the flavors of this sweet-and-sour bath to penetrate. This gives the eggplant an unctuous quality not unlike deliciously melting pork fat. This adaptation is inspired by a version we had in Singapore, and is a great room-temperature appetizer that can be made ahead of time and served with other pickles and achar before the meal. It's sweet and sour with spicy notes and greasy in a good way, and even if you hate eggplant, you'll love it. We add roasted peanuts at the end for crunch.

³/₄ cup Filipino cane vinegar

¹/₂ cup sugar

1 (1-inch) piece fresh ginger, peeled and minced

2 lime leaves

1 teaspoon salt

¹/₂ teaspoon ground turmeric

2 tablespoons Tamarind Extract (page 285)

1¹/₂ cups water

Peanut oil, for deep-frying

2 pounds (4 large) Chinese eggplant, cut into pyramids (see page 27)

3 tablespoons Sambal Tumis (page 275)

OPTIONAL GARNISHES

Handful of fisheye-cut green onions (see page 27)

1 teaspoon toasted sesame seeds

Handful of roasted peanuts

Handful of picked fresh dill leaves

Combine the vinegar, sugar, ginger, lime leaves, salt, turmeric, tamarind, and water in a medium pot and bring to a boil. Remove from the heat and set aside in a warm place.

Prepare the wok for deep-frying and heat the oil to 400°F. Working in small batches to maintain the oil temperature, fry the eggplant for 30 to 45 seconds per batch, just until the flesh turns golden brown and

the purple skin becomes vibrant. Remove the eggplant from the oil with a spider, let excess oil drain off, and place directly into the vinegar mixture. Repeat this process until all of the eggplant has been cooked.

After the eggplant has soaked for about 20 minutes, remove from the vinegar mixture (discard the mixture) and arrange on a plate. Top with the sambal and garnishes and serve immediately.

3

ARROZ

RICE

Rice is life. This versatile, life giving-grass has sustained humans around the globe for centuries–and for millennia in its native East Asia. As in Macau, no meal at our restaurant is complete without rice. Simple steamed rice acts a blank canvas to absorb flavors of rich curries and stews, and dressed up a bit, rice serves as a centerpiece in the aptly named Arroz Gordo, acting as a platform for myriad flavorful meats and garnishes. We use puffed rice as a crispy garnish or as a base for sweets. For long grain rice, as a rule we stick with jasmine varietals for their aromatic fragrance and fluffy texture. Treat rice gently so as not to break the individual grains, and take a moment to consider the important role it has played in the development of cuisines worldwide. In rice, we've found a common thread that unites people and lands; it fills our bellies and sustains our souls.

ARROZ GORDO

("FAT RICE")

First things first: the fact that this rice is *gordo* doesn't mean that the dish is full of fat; rather, it implies that the dish is substantive and full of goodies. Our "Fat Rice" is similar to paella (perhaps due to common ancestry in the Iberian Peninsula, and connection to Persian pilaus and Indian biryanis), garnished with myriad proteins and other toppings. Of course, versions of arroz gordo vary from household to household and cookbook to cookbook. Some use medium-grain rice, others long-grain rice. Our arroz gordo uses our housemade linguiça, but the Filipino *arroz valenciana* uses longaniza sausage. Crucial to all versions is the *refogado*: onions, garlic, and sometimes sweet red peppers and tomato cooked down to achieve a smoky, robustly caramelized taste and aroma that flavors the entire dish. Traditionally this *refogado* scents the rice in the dish, which is then topped with stewed chicken, Portuguese sausage such as chouriço or linguiça, pig trotters, hard-cooked eggs, croutons, fried shallots, pickles, and olives. During our travels and research, we've also come across recipes including roast pork, veal, or beef, and even some with prawns. We add clams to ours—not common, and solely our addition because we love clams and the extra little briny sweetness that they give to the dish.

Rice and meat dishes of this nature, such as paella, arroz con pollo, and biryani, are a bit temperamental. The rice is full of secrets. The main challenge is keeping the rice moist and fluffy, not sticky and mushy, so pay attention to the liquid-to-rice ratios and do not stir the rice!

Considering how many rich elements are in this dish—char siu, chilli prawns, turmeric chicken thighs, tea eggs, chicken fat-fried croutons, and Manilla clams—you need some acidity for flavor balance. That's where the sherry-soaked raisins come into play. Raisins are a traditional aspect of arroz gordo, but soaking them in sherry is our way to add brightness and freshness.

Traditionally this dish was made for large parties and reserved for special occasions such as christenings, weddings, and birthdays. In the restaurant, we serve a smaller portion, generally for 2 to 4 people, which comes in a clay pot. This was inspired by the charcoal stove-cooked clay pot rice we ate in Hong Kong. Sometimes, the best part of those dishes in Hong Kong was the crusty, almost burnt part of the rice, which we call *cara* (pronounced with a hard *r*), most likely a cousin of the word *soccarat*—the rice-crust calling card of an experienced paella cook.

The following recipe serves about 6 to 8 people, so we recommend a cast-iron Dutch oven about 12 inches in diameter, but whatever you use, make sure there is enough surface area to get that crispy *cara* and generate enough steam to cook the rice fully. We've actually made this in a large rice cooker for large groups—in that case, steam the rice in the cooker one time, then turn it on a second time to create the *cara*, heating the meats separately and arranging all the rice on a large serving platter, with the meats artistically arranged around and on top of the rice.

Arroz gordo, our namesake and most popular dish, is a great source of pride for us, and we're happy to pass it on through this book.

>> continued

ARROZ GORDO

ARROZ GORDO RICE

1 cup golden raisins

½ cup sherry vinegar

2 salted, preserved duck legs (see page 296)

1 (4-inch) piece fresh ginger, sliced into ¼-inch chunks

4 green onions, both white and green parts, cut into 2-inch sections

3 cups jasmine rice, rinsed well (see illustration, page 75)

⅔ cup Refogado (page 273)

Salt

MEATS

8 pieces Turmeric Baked Chicken (page 184)

2 cups "Portuguese" Curry Sauce (page 272), warmed and whisked

1 pound Char Siu (page 205)

½ cup Char Siu Glaze (page 206)

2 links Portuguese linguiça sausage

RICE FINISH

1 tablespoon lard

4 ounces dried Spanish chorizo

½ cup Chicken Stock (page 282)

1½ cups Chicken Fat Croutons (page 261)

PRAWNS

2 tablespoons extra-virgin olive oil

8 filled but uncooked Chilli Prawns (page 136)

¼ cup white wine

CLAMS

3 tablespoons Molho de Aziete, aka Mojo (page 270)

24 Manilla or littleneck clams, purged

⅓ cup white wine

GARNISHES

4 Tea Eggs (page 277), thinly sliced

Handful good Portuguese olives (see page 296)

12 cornichons

1 long red finger chilli, thinly sliced

3 green onions, horse-ear cut (see page 27)

2 lemons, quartered from pole to pole and dusted with Korean chilli flakes

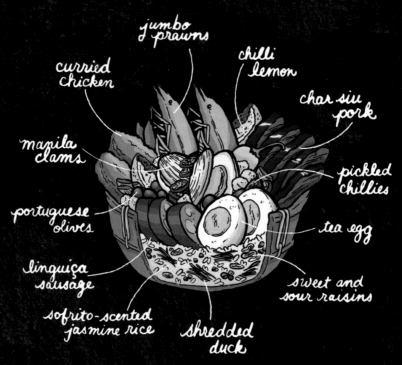

To make the arroz gordo rice, cover the raisins with the sherry vinegar and 1 cup water and refrigerate overnight. Put the salted duck leg in a large pot and cover with water. Bring to a boil, then discard the liquid. Add the ginger and green onions to the pot and cover with 12 cups cold water again. Bring to a boil, reduce the heat, cover, and simmer for 1 hour. Strain and reserve the liquid, discard the ginger and green onions, and pick all the meat and fat from the duck. Finely chop and set aside.

Bring the reserved duck water to a boil, add the rice, and stir well, cooking it like pasta for 4 minutes. Drain well, discard the liquid, and spread the rice out on a sheet pan, and cool completely.

When the rice is cooled, transfer to a bowl. Drain the raisins (reserving the liquid for another use, if desired) and add to the rice along with the duck and Refogado. Season to taste with salt and gently stir to incorporate all ingredients. Use immediately or refrigerate for up to 3 days.

To prepare the meats, preheat the oven to 400°F. Put the chicken thighs on one side of a baking sheet and evenly coat with the curry sauce. Put the char siu on a plate and brush with the glaze. Place the linguiça on the plate next to the char siu. Set the pan and plate aside for now.

To finish the rice, grease a large, shallow Dutch oven with the lard. Put the rice in an even layer in the pan and make a 2-inch-diameter hole in the center of the pan, exposing the bottom of the pan. Stud the rice with the chorizo. Place over medium-high heat for about 5 minutes, until the rice begins to sizzle–it's crucial that the rice is sizzling here. With the lid handy, add the stock to the pot through the hole you made in the rice and immediately cover with the lid. Cook for 3 to 5 minutes to generate steam, then transfer to the oven. Bake for approximately 30 minutes, until the rice is steamed, fluffy, and fully cooked.

Approximately 10 minutes after putting the rice in the oven, put the chicken in the oven and cook until bubbly, slightly browned, and heated through, about 20 minutes. About 15 minutes after putting the rice in the oven, transfer the char siu to the pan with the chicken and return to the oven, heating until bubbly and glazed, about 15 minutes. About 20 minutes after putting the rice in the oven, transfer the linguiça to the pan with the chicken and char siu and cook until heated through, about 10 minutes.

When everything in the oven is ready, remove and hold in a warm place to rest. Slice the linguiça 1/2 inch thick and the char siu 1/3 inch thick. Sprinkle about half of the croutons on top of the rice, then arrange the chicken, linguiça and char siu on top of the croutons. Reduce the oven temperature to 300°F and return the rice pan to the oven without its lid.

To prepare the prawns, heat a large lidded pan over high heat and add the olive oil. When the oil is smoking, carefully lay the prawns in the oil and cook until the shells start to brown and the flesh starts to turn pink, about 1 minute. Carefully add the wine to the pan–it will spatter–and immediately cover with the lid. Steam the prawns until fully cooked, about 4 minutes. Set aside.

To prepare the clams, put the mojo in a large pot over high heat. When the mojo becomes fragrant and starts to sizzle, after about 2 minutes, add the clams and wine and cover tightly. Cook until all the clams open, checking after 3 minutes, and remove from the heat. Discard any clams that have not opened.

To serve, remove the rice pan from the oven and arrange the prawns, then the clams, around the rice. Return the clam pot to high heat and reduce the liquid to about 1/2 cup, then drizzle over the clams. Scatter the remaining croutons, eggs, olives, cornichons, sliced chillies, and green onions on top of the rice, then place the chilli lemons all around the pot. Serve immediately.

COCONUT RICE

The marriage of rice and coconut makes magic: they both grow in the same climates/areas (India, Southeast Asia, and Sri Lanka, to name a few), many of which are influences in Macanese cuisine. That said, coconut rice isn't widespread in Macau, but it is found in sweet *baji* (rice pudding made with sticky rice and coconut milk), the Macanese answer to rice pudding.

Don't be deceived by rice's simplicity. Steamed rice is an integral ingredient to so many cultures, and it seems so effortless to cook. But to cook it right—resulting in light, fluffy, separate grains—can be extremely difficult. Be gentle handling the rice so it doesn't break, releasing more starch than you want and resulting in a gummy end product. And measure carefully—the proper liquid-to-rice ratio is key.

| 24 ounces (about 3 cups) jasmine rice | 1 (13.5-ounce) can full-fat coconut milk, shaken well | 13.5 ounces water (use coconut milk can to measure) | 1/2 teaspoon salt |

Rinse the rice: Put the rice in a fine-mesh strainer and put that into a large bowl. Place under cold running water. Gently stir clockwise with a slightly cupped hand, taking care not to break the rice. Discard the water as it becomes cloudy, then repeat the process a few times until the water runs clear. Drain in the fine-mesh strainer for at least 10 minutes prior to cooking.

To cook the rice using a rice cooker, put the rice, coconut milk, water, and salt in a rice cooker and stir gently to combine. Proceed to cook following your rice cooker's instructions. When done cooking, leave

the rice alone for at least 10 minutes before serving to allow it to absorb any residual moisture in the cooker.

To cook the rice on the stove top, put the rice, coconut milk, water, and salt in a heavy, 3-quart pot and stir gently to combine. Bring to a simmer over high heat, then cover and decrease the heat to low to maintain a low simmer. Cook for 9 minutes without uncovering. Don't open the pot! Don't stir it! Turn off the heat and leave the rice alone for at least 10 minutes before serving to allow it to absorb any residual moisture in the pot.

WASHING RICE

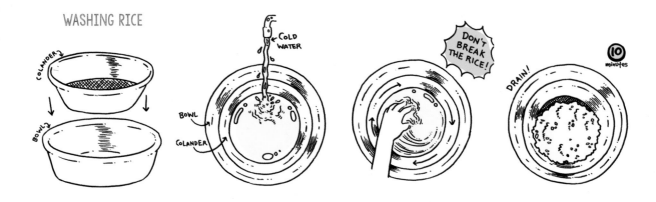

BASIC FRIED RICE

SERVES
2 AS A
MAIN, 4 IN A
MULTI-DISH
MEAL

So many bad versions of fried rice slip by the masses out there. Here's our
10 Commandments of Fried Rice. Well, really just seven, but you get the idea:

1. Less is more! As with pizza, too many toppings can overwhelm the integrity
   of the dish.

2. Keep things dry! Dryness is crucial to achieving successful wok *hei*, that special
   "essence" that the wok imparts to food when stir-frying. Added moisture will cool
   the wok down and make things stick. Trust that the Fried Rice Rice (page 261)
   you've prepared for this recipe will have retained enough moisture to rehydrate
   itself and don't add any more.

3. You want individual grains of rice when all is said and done, not big clumps.
   This is attained by proper cooking and drying of the rice, and by manually
   separating the rice using your finger tips as described in Fried Rice Rice (page 261).

4. Keep the vegetables bright and vibrant, and the egg light and fluffy, both done
   by avoiding overcooking.

5. Don't drown it in soy sauce! Season with *some* soy sauce at the end, along with
   salt, sugar, sesame oil, and white pepper.

6. Add the green onion whites in the beginning, with the aromatics, then add the
   greens at the end for lift, crunch, and verdant flavor.

7. Whenever possible, use the puffed rice as we describe below and in the Fried
   Rice Rice section (page 261). This adds the extra delicious dynamic of a new,
   crunchy texture.

1 tablespoon peanut oil,
plus more for deep-frying

2 cups Fried Rice Rice
(page 261)

Salt

1/4 cup diced meat or fish
(optional), raw or cooked

2 eggs, beaten

1/4 cup diced red
bell pepper

1/4 cup diced green
bell pepper

1/4 cup diced red onion

2 king trumpet
mushrooms, diced

2 cloves garlic, minced

1 tablespoon preserved
mustard green
stems (suimi ya cai,
see page 296)

1/2 teaspoon sambal oelek
or your favorite chilli
garlic sambal

1/4 cup fisheye-cut green
onion (see page 27),
white and green parts
separated

1/4 cup mung bean
sprouts, trimmed to
1-inch lengths

1 teaspoon soy sauce

1 teaspoon toasted
sesame oil

1 teaspoon sugar

Pinch of ground white
pepper

>> continued

Arroz

Prepare a wok for deep-frying by heating about 2 inches of peanut oil to 425°F. Take a small handful of fried rice rice (reserving the rest for later) and sprinkle it around the oil. The rice should sink to the bottom and immediately float back up and puff. You will see moisture leaving the rice in the form of bubbles, slowing down as more moisture departs, allowing the rice to start to brown. Use a fine-mesh spider to push the rice down beneath the surface of the oil. When the rice is light brown, after 30 to 45 seconds of total cooking time, scoop the rice out of the wok with the spider, transfer it to a paper towel-lined plate, season with salt, and set aside. If using, add any raw meats or fish to the oil and partially cook for a few moments (you will finish cooking them through in the final stages of the fried rice), then set aside.

Remove all the oil except about 1 tablespoon, or enough to coat the bottom, and place over medium heat. Add the egg and carefully swirl it about 3 inches up the sides of the wok, letting the egg set. Give the egg a scramble with the edge of your wok ladle, transfer to a plate, and set aside.

Clean the wok and prepare it (see page 20), then heat 1 tablespoon of oil over high heat. Just as the oil begins to smoke, add the peppers, red onions, and mushrooms. Stir-fry and cook for approximately 30 seconds. Add the garlic, preserved mustard greens, sambal, and green onion whites and stir-fry for another 30 seconds, then sprinkle the remaining fried rice rice into the wok so that the grains stay as individual as possible. Stir to incorporate, then let sit for approximately 10 seconds before stirring again. Repeat this process until the rice is hot and moist, about 3 minutes. Add the green onion greens, reserved egg, reserved meat, and bean sprouts and season with the soy, sesame oil, sugar, and white pepper. Stir to incorporate all of the ingredients. Add the reserved puffed rice and stir to combine. Taste and adjust the seasoning as needed and serve immediately.

POUR IN BEATEN EGG, AND CAREFULLY SWIRL WOK AROUND TO SET THE EGG.

GIVE THE EGG A SCRAMBLE WITH THE EDGE OF YOUR WOK LADLE.

REMOVE IT TO A PLATE AND SET ASIDE.

HEAT A TABLESPOON OF OIL IN THE WOK OVER HIGH HEAT.

JUST AS THE OIL BEGINS TO SMOKE, ADD PEPPERS, ONIONS, AND MUSHROOMS.

STIR-FRY, AND COOK FOR APPROXIMATELY 30 SECONDS.

30 seconds

ADD GARLIC, SUIMI YA CAI AND SAMBAL,
30 seconds
...AND STIR-FRY FOR ANOTHER 30 SECONDS.
SPRINKLE THE FRIED RICE RICE INTO THE WOK, KEEPING THE GRAINS AS SEPARATED AS POSSIBLE.
STIR-FRY IT UP!
LET SIT FOR APPROXIMATELY 10 SECONDS OVER HIGH HEAT...
10 seconds
...AND STIR-FRY AGAIN.
MUITO BOM!

ADD SCALLION, EGG, PARCOOKED MEAT, AND BEAN SPROUTS, AND SEASON WITH SOY, SESAME OIL, AND SUGAR.

ADD THE PUFFED RICE...

...AND STIR TO INCORPORATE ALL INGREDIENTS.

ADJUST SEASONING AND SERVE IMMEDIATELY!

BAKED PORK CHOP RICE

SERVES 2 AS A MAIN, 4 IN A MULTI-DISH MEAL

This dish seems so wrong and dirty in the most delicious way possible: a cookie-crusted, deep-fried pork chop over fried rice, covered in a rich sauce and melted cheese. It's a product of *cha chaan teng* (diner-like and tea restaurants) that were meant to appeal to the taste of visiting Westerners, offering Chinese-ified Western food (as opposed to the Americanized Chinese food found in the United States today).

2 tablespoons peanut oil, plus more for deep-frying

2 eggs, beaten

¼ cup diced red bell pepper

¼ cup diced green bell pepper

¼ cup diced red onion

2 king trumpet mushrooms, diced

2 cloves garlic, minced

1 tablespoon preserved mustard green stems (suimi ya cai, see page 296)

½ teaspoon sambal oelek or your favorite chilli garlic sambal

1½ cups Fried Rice Rice (page 261)

¼ cup fisheye-cut green onion, whites parts only, (see page 27)

1 teaspoon soy sauce

1 teaspoon toasted sesame oil

1 teaspoon sugar

1 Pork Chop in Brine (page 262)

¾ cup Po Bolacho Breading (page 219)

¾ cup Portuguese-style Tomato Sauce (page 271) or "Portuguese" Curry Sauce (page 272), gently warmed

½ cup grated cheese

2 tablespoons coconut powder (see page 293)

10 leaves flat-leaf parsley, tossed with a splash of extra-virgin olive oil and a pinch of salt

5 Portuguese olives, black or green, unpitted (see page 296)

Preheat the oven to 425°F.

Heat 1 tablespoon of the peanut oil in a prepared wok (see page 20) over medium heat, add the egg, and carefully swirl roughly 3 inches up the sides of the wok, letting the egg set, about 30 seconds. Give the egg a scramble with the edge of your wok ladle and cook until almost finished, but still a touch runny, another 30 to 60 seconds. Remove to a plate and set aside.

Prepare your wok again, then heat the remaining 1 tablespoon peanut oil over high heat. Just as the oil begins to smoke, add the peppers, onions, and mushrooms. Stir-fry for approximately 20 seconds. Add the garlic, preserved mustard greens, and sambal oelek and stir-fry for another 20 seconds, then sprinkle the fried rice rice into the wok so that the grains stay as individual as possible. Stir-fry again to incorporate and let sit for approximately 10 seconds before stirring again. Repeat this process until the rice is hot and moist, about 3 minutes. Add the green onion and reserved egg; season with the soy, sesame oil, and sugar and stir to incorporate all ingredients. Taste and adjust the seasoning as needed. Place in a baking dish.

Remove the pork chop from the brine and pat dry with paper towels. Coat liberally with the breading, pressing firmly to adhere the breading to the chop. To prepare for deep-frying, fill the wok with about 2 inches of peanut oil and heat the oil to 375°F.

Carefully add the breaded pork chop to the oil and fry for 20 to 35 seconds, until golden brown and nearly cooked through (it will finish cooking in the oven). Remove to a paper towel-lined plate, pat to remove excess oil, and let cool slightly. Using a cleaver, cut along the bone to separate the meat from the bone, then slice the meat into ¾-inch strips (6 to 8 strips) and place on top of the fried rice–throw in the bone section too, or gnaw on it while you finish the dish!

Smother the pork chop and rice with the sauce, cheese, and coconut powder and place in the oven for approximately 10 minutes.

"PLACE ON A PARCHMENT PAPER–LINED SHEET PAN IN CASE OF ANY BUBBLE-OVERS!"

Remove from the oven and top with the parsley and olives. Serve immediately.

4

MASSAS

NOODLES

Noodles are everywhere throughout Macau: *lojas de sopa de fitas* (ribbon soup shops) serve rich broths with wheat noodles, rice noodles, or a combination of both; makeshift side-alley *wonton mein* (wheat noodle) stands get commuters ready for their workday with steaming bowls to slurp down. In tea shops and *cha chaan teng* (see page 82), one can get springy ramen-like alkaline noodles topped with spicy curried beef brisket, and on street corners in the Three Lamp District, you can get a cone of steaming *chee cheong fun* (steamed rice noodles) with hoisin, sesame, and chilli sauces. If you are lucky, you can get yourself into the local spots cooking somewhat "Westernized" noodle dishes

like macaroni soup with black peppered chicken or oxtail, which the woman pictured is enjoying on Macau's neighboring island of Coloane.

But there are really only a couple of noodle dishes of the Portuguese-speaking Macanese that star in their own show, and they are based on thin rice vermicelli called *lacassà*, coming in both soup (page 92) and stir-fried (page 86) form. Otherwise, noodles made from various types of starches, including rice, sweet potato, and mung bean, play a supporting role in Macanese dishes such as Tchai de Bonzo (page 119), Tacho (page 209), and in our own creation, The Chilli Clam (page 154).

LACASSÀ (MACANESE RICE VERMICELLI STIR-FRY)

If you had to compare this dish to something, you could say that it's similar to a pad thai or Singapore noodle in form, but lighter and milder in flavor, with a garlic punch and sharp ginger achar.

The word *lacassà* always refers to a dish containing rice noodles, and most likely comes from a Cantonese phrase for rain, *loc-soei*, because the noodles, as they are extruded, resemble pouring rain. Solid technique will create the much-sought-after wok *hei* that gives this noodle dish its distinct flavor. And be sure to slice those vegetables thinly, so everything cooks at the same rate!

2 tablespoons light soy sauce

1 teaspoon salt

1/4 teaspoon freshly ground white pepper

2 teaspoons sugar

2 tablespoons water

3 ounces rice vermicilli

3 tablespoons peanut oil

3 eggs, beaten

1 small yellow onion, julienned

1 carrot, peeled and julienned

4 ounces Char Siu (page 205), julienned (about 1 cup)

5 green onions, white and green parts, shredded (see page 27)

5 ounces medium shrimp, peeled, deveined, and split lengthwise

3 cloves garlic, minced

Small handful of mung bean sprouts

1/2 teaspoon toasted sesame oil

3 tablespoons julienned Ginger Achar (page 41)

Small handful of chopped fresh cilantro

In a small bowl, mix together the soy sauce, salt, white pepper, sugar, and water; set aside.

Put the noodles in a bowl, cover with hot water, and soak for 2 minutes until soft, or as directed on the package. Drain and set aside.

Heat a prepared wok over medium heat. Add 2 tablespoons of the peanut oil and carefully swirl around to coat the wok. Add the beaten eggs to the wok and let sit until you start to see a ring of cooked egg on the bottom of the wok, about 5 to 10 seconds. Carefully tilt the wok in a circular motion to coat the sides with egg, approximately 8 inches in diameter. At this point you should be able to flip the egg–give it a quick season with salt and do so. Immediately turn off the heat and, using a wok ladle, fold the egg three times until you have a rectangular omelet of roughly 2 by 8 inches. Transfer to a cutting board, julienne into thin strips, season with salt, and set aside.

Wipe out the wok and return it to high heat. Add the remaining 1 tablespoon peanut oil and when smoking, add the onion, carrot, char siu, green onions, shrimp, and garlic. Stir-fry for about 1 minute, until the vegetables become vibrant and aromatic and the shrimp starts to turn pink. Add the noodles and continue to stir-fry until all of the ingredients are well distributed among the noodles, about 30 seconds. Then leave the wok alone and let the ingredients just hang for about 30 seconds to let the wok recover heat. Stir-fry for another 30 seconds; at this point the ingredients should be thoroughly softened and the noodles no longer wiry. Drizzle the soy mixture around the wok and stir-fry for about 15 seconds to ensure that the steam generated is being absorbed by the noodles. Add the cooked egg and bean sprouts, drizzle in the sesame oil, and stir-fry to incorporate.

Transfer to a large serving plate and garnish with the Ginger Achar and cilantro. Serve immediately.

➤➤ continued

HEAT A PREPARED WOK OVER MEDIUM HEAT.

ADD 2 TABLESPOONS OF PEANUT OIL AND SWIRL AROUND TO COAT THE WOK.

ADD THE BEATEN EGGS TO THE WOK...

5 seconds

...AND LET IT SIT UNTIL YOU START TO SEE A RING OF COOKED EGG ON THE BOTTOM — ABOUT 5 TO 10 SECONDS.

HOLDING THE EGG GENTLY IN PLACE WITH YOUR WOK LADLE,

...CAREFULLY TILT THE WOK IN A CIRCULAR MOTION TO COAT THE SIDES WITH EGG, UNTIL IT'S APPROXIMATELY 8 INCHES IN DIAMETER.

AT THIS POINT, YOU SHOULD BE ABLE TO FLIP THE EGG. GIVE IT A QUICK SEASON WITH SALT, AND DO SO.

IMMEDIATELY TURN OFF THE HEAT, AND USING THE LADLE, FOLD THE EGG THREE TIMES...

...UNTIL YOU HAVE A RECTANGULAR OMELET OF ROUGHLY 2 BY 8 INCHES.

JULIENNE INTO STRIPS, SEASON WITH SALT, AND SET ASIDE.

WIPE OUT THE WOK AND RETURN IT TO HIGH HEAT.

ADD THE REMAINING TABLESPOON OF PEANUT OIL, AND WHEN IT'S SMOKING...

...ADD THE ONION, CARROT, CHAR SIU, GREEN ONIONS, SHRIMP, AND GARLIC.

STIR-FRY FOR ABOUT A MINUTE, UNTIL THE VEGETABLES ARE VIBRANT AND AROMATIC.

1 minute

ADD THE NOODLES, AND CONTINUE TO STIR-FRY UNTIL ALL OF THE INGREDIENTS ARE WELL DISTRIBUTED.

30 seconds

LEAVE THE WOK ALONE, AND LET THE LACASSÁ HANG FOR ABOUT 30 SECONDS, FOR THE WOK TO RECOVER SOME HEAT.

STIR-FRY FOR ANOTHER 30 SECONDS.

ADD THE COOKED EGG AND BEAN SPROUTS, AND STIR-FRY FOR ANOTHER 30 SECONDS.

DRIZZLE THE SOY MIXTURE AROUND THE WOK AND STIR-FRY FOR ANOTHER 15 SECONDS TO ENSURE THAT THE STEAM IS BEING ABSORBED BY THE NOODLES.

滋 滋 滋

DRIZZLE IN THE SESAME OIL AND STIR-FRY TO INCORPORATE.

TRANSFER TO A LARGE SERVING PLATE...

DON'T FORGET THE GINGER ACHAR!

AND GARNISH WITH CILANTRO!

SOPA DE LACASSÀ
(RICE VERMICELLI SOUP WITH PRAWNS)

SERVES 4
AS A LIGHT
LUNCH OR
FIRST COURSE
TO A LARGER
MEAL

This soup is common in Macanese homes around Catholic holidays when meat is abstained from, especially on Christmas Eve day. Evolved from the laksas popular in Singapore, Malaysia, and Indonesia, this simple shrimp and rice noodle soup is elegant and refined. Laksa is sold streetside in Malaysia, and many *lojas de sopa de fitas* (ribbon soup shops) abound in Macau, selling soups usually made with beef or fish broth and sometimes using wheat noodles. However, Sopa de Lacassà is only found in Macanese homes and reserved mostly for special occasions; we've never come across this version on the street.

Balichão is essential to this dish; it provides an almost bisquelike flavor. We garnish with only caramelized shallots and shredded green onions, but we have found recipes that include crab, fresh tomatoes, and/or cilantro, so feel free to add these if you like. Use any type of rice noodle you want, as long as they are thin.

8 large head-on, shell-on shrimp

4 tablespoons lard, or more as needed

3 tablespoons unsalted butter

2 tablespoons balichão (page 260)

4 green onions, greens shredded (see page 27) and whites cut into 2-inch pieces and lightly crushed with the side of a cleaver

1 (1/2-inch) piece fresh ginger, thinly sliced

1 tablespoon minced garlic

10 small shallots, thinly sliced

2 ounces good Portuguese aged brandy

1/2 cup dry white wine

3 cups water

1/2 teaspoon sugar

Freshly cracked black pepper

6 ounces dry rice vermicelli

Salt and freshly ground pepper

Peel and devein the shrimp, reserving the heads and shells. Set the shrimp aside. Heat a heavy pot over medium-high heat and add 2 tablespoons of the lard and 2 tablespoons of the butter. When melted, add the Balichão and the reserved shrimp heads and shells. Use a wooden spoon to continually mash up the heads and sauté until pink and browned, about 5 minutes. Add the green onion whites, ginger, garlic and half of the shallots and sauté for 2 minutes. Raise the heat to high and deglaze with the brandy and white wine, scraping the bottom of the pot, and cook until the wine has reduced to a syrupy, nearly dry state. Add the water, sugar, and some fresh cracked pepper, return to a boil, and reduce the heat to a simmer. Cook for 30 minutes, taste and adjust the seasoning, then strain and keep hot.

Put the noodles in a bowl, cover with hot water, and soak for 2 minutes until soft, or as directed on the package. Drain and set aside.

Heat a cast-iron pan over high heat. Add the remaining 2 tablespoons lard, and when melted, season the shrimp with salt and pepper and lay evenly in the pan. Sear for 90 seconds, then flip and cook for an additional 60 seconds. Add the remaining 1 tablespoon butter and remaining shallots to the pan, reduce the heat to medium-low, and cook until lightly caramelized, about 60 seconds. Remove from the heat and set aside.

Divide the noodles among 4 bowls and top with the caramelized shallots and 2 shrimp per bowl. Garnish with the scallion greens and pour the steamy hot soup into the bowls tableside from an antique teapot (ooooh, fancy). Serve immediately.

FAT NOODLES

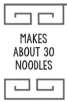

MAKES ABOUT 30 NOODLES

Chee cheong fun means a steamed and rolled rice noodle that resembles pig intestines (in appearance only!). In Macau, these noodles are sold in dim sum restaurants and by street vendors, where they are cut up with scissors and served in rolled paper cones slathered with hoisin and chilli sauces.

At first, making fat noodles can be a challenging process, and certainly it was for us at the restaurant; we'd often be steaming noodles as service started, adding chaos to the already hectic scenario. A key to success (aside from preparation and organization) is to keep the starch suspended in the liquid as much as possible, so we recommend mixing up the batter before steaming each noodle. Another important step is letting the batter sit out at room temperature overnight to a) let the starches hydrate to cook more evenly, and b) slightly ferment the batter for further flavor development. If you don't have a 6 by 10-inch pan (aka an eighth sheet pan), look for something similarly sized and/or shaped—a toaster oven pan, a Pyrex pan, a rectangular plate, even a round plate will work in a pinch—but don't sweat it too much. Again, it's a challenging process your first few times, so stick with it!

1 cup rice flour	1/2 cup potato starch	1/2 teaspoon salt
1/2 cup cornstarch	2 1/4 cups water	Oil, for greasing

In a bowl, combine the rice flour, cornstarch, potato starch, water, and salt with an immersion blender for 5 minutes. Let sit overnight, covered, at room temperature. Note that the mixture will separate overnight and form a rather hard layer on the bottom.

The next day, set up a wok half full of water with a steamer basket insert with lid and bring the water to a boil. Water should not enter the steamer basket. Remix your batter with an immersion blender starting toward the top, eventually working your way around to the bottom of the batter until all the starches are suspended throughout the liquid. Lightly grease a one-eighth sheet pan (or a round pan that fits in your basket) for steaming the noodle. Lightly grease a second sheet pan of similar size or larger to hold the steamed noodles.

Fill the one-eighth sheet pan with enough batter to make a thin, even layer, using 5 to 6 fluid ounces, about 2/3 to 3/4 cup, of the batter. Place the sheet pan inside the steamer basket, ensuring that everything

is level and the batter is evenly distributed. Cover the steamer basket and steam until the noodle is fully cooked and slightly translucent, 4 to 6 minutes. Remove the pan from the steamer basket and with the container positioned in a landscape view to maximize the length of the noodle, start from the farthest point away from you and peel the top edge of the cooked noodle toward you, rolling into a tight, even cylinder, about the size of a nickel. If it's over or under that, adjust the quantity of the batter you are using. Transfer the rolled noodle to the greased sheet pan and cover with plastic wrap while still warm before moving on to the next noodle. If you are having any sticking issues, wash the sheet pan with warm water (no soap!), dry completely, re-oil, and repeat the above process until all the batter is used.

When all the noodles are rolled, cut crosswise into 1 1/2-inch pieces (you'll get about 8 or 9 noodles) and store in an airtight container until ready to use. Refrigerate for up to 3 days if not immediately using.

MAKING FAT NOODLES

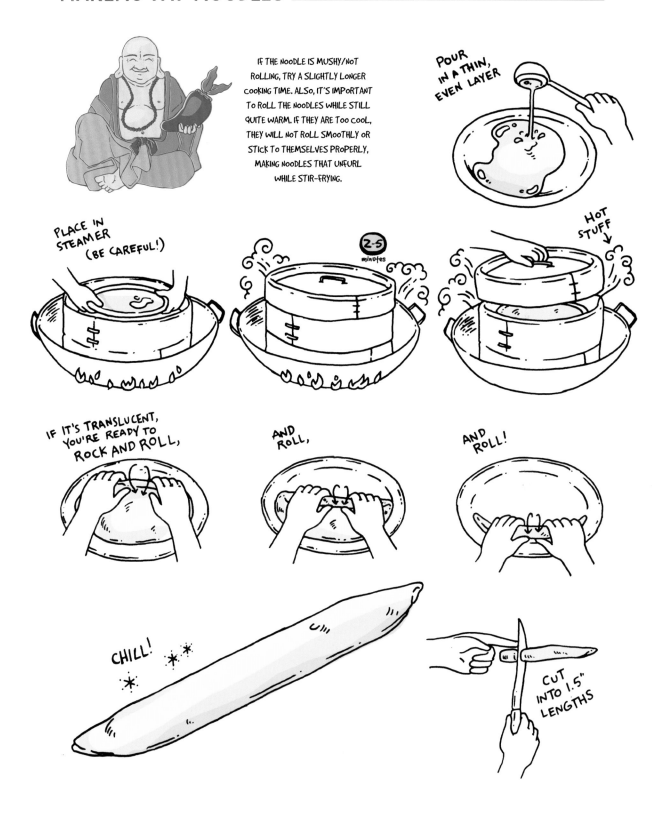

IF THE NOODLE IS MUSHY/NOT ROLLING, TRY A SLIGHTLY LONGER COOKING TIME. ALSO, IT'S IMPORTANT TO ROLL THE NOODLES WHILE STILL QUITE WARM. IF THEY ARE TOO COOL, THEY WILL NOT ROLL SMOOTHLY OR STICK TO THEMSELVES PROPERLY, MAKING NOODLES THAT UNFURL WHILE STIR-FRYING.

POUR IN A THIN, EVEN LAYER

PLACE IN STEAMER (BE CAREFUL!)

2-5 minutes

HOT STUFF

IF IT'S TRANSLUCENT, YOU'RE READY TO ROCK AND ROLL,

AND ROLL,

AND ROLL!

CHILL!

CUT INTO 1.5" LENGTHS

FAT NOODLES WITH XO SAUCE

This is a popular dish from our very first Fat Rice menu, and it even goes back to the X-marx days, when we called it the million animal noodle because of all of the umami-rich ham and copious varieties of tiny marine animals in the XO Sauce. The finished product isn't just about all that flavor, though. It's full of varying textures: snappy wood ear mushrooms, crunchy red peppers, crispy Peixinhos Fritos (page 276), and the chewy, soft Fat Noodles (page 94).

SERVES 2
AS A MAIN,
4 IN A
MULTI-DISH
MEAL

10 wood ear mushrooms

1 tablespoon peanut oil

12 to 14 pieces of Fat Noodles (page 94)

1 teaspoon peeled and minced fresh ginger

1 teaspoon minced garlic

1 teaspoon preserved mustard green stems (suimi ya cai, see page 296)

1 teaspoon sambal oelek or your favorite chilli garlic sambal

3 green onions, cut into 2-inch pieces, white and green parts separated

³/₄ cup Pork Wok Sauce (page 284)

¹/₃ cup Umami Juice (page 285)

¹/₂ red bell pepper, seeded and cut into ¹/₂-inch julienne

1 celery stalk, cut on the diagonal into ¹/₃-inch-thick slices

3 tablespoons (or more as needed) XO Sauce (page 268)

2 teaspoons tapioca starch mixed with 2 tablespoons water (optional)

Peixinhos Fritos (Tiny Fried Fish, page 276), for garnish

Place the wood ear mushrooms in a small bowl and cover with water. Soak until hydrated, about 20 minutes. Drain. Slice the mushrooms into thin strips and set aside.

Prepare a wok for stir-frying (see page 20) and place over high heat. When the wok begins to smoke, add the oil, then carefully add the noodles in one even layer. Let the noodles sear, unmoved, until slightly charred, about 1 minute. Use a wok ladle to gently flip the noodles so that they remain rolled up and sear the other side, about another minute. Add the ginger, garlic, preserved mustard greens, sambal, and green onion whites and stir-fry for about 30 seconds. Add the wok sauce and juice. Give the wok a gentle

shake to distribute the ingredients, taking care not to disturb the noodles too much, lest they unravel. After approximately 2 minutes, add the red pepper, celery, mushrooms, and green onion greens and give the wok another shake. As the sauce reduces and starts to thicken, add the XO Sauce and stir-fry to incorporate. You're looking for a rich amber sauce that has the consistency of a light, lump-free gravy. If necessary, stir in some of the tapioca slurry and bring to a boil to thicken more. Give it a final stir to coat all of the ingredients, then transfer to a serving platter and garnish with the fried fish.

➤➤ continued

PREPARE A WOK FOR STIR-FRYING AND PLACE OVER HIGH HEAT.

WHEN THE WOK BEGINS TO SMOKE, ADD THE OIL,

THEN CAREFULLY ADD THE NOODLES IN ONE EVEN LAYER.

LET THE NOODLES SEAR, UNMOVED, UNTIL SLIGHTLY CHARRED, ABOUT 1 MINUTE.

USE A WOK LADLE TO FLIP THE NOODLES TO SEAR THE OTHER SIDE, ABOUT ANOTHER MINUTE.

ADD THE GINGER, GARLIC, SUIMI YA CAI, SAMBAL, AND GREEN ONION WHITES

AND STIR-FRY FOR ABOUT 30 SECONDS.

30 seconds

ADD THE WOK SAUCE AND UMAMI JUICE.

GIVE THE WOK A GENTLE SHAKE TO DISTRIBUTE THE INGREDIENTS, TAKING CARE NOT TO DISTURB THE NOODLES TOO MUCH, LEST THEY UNRAVEL.

ADD THE RED PEPPERS, CELERY, MUSHROOMS, AND GREEN ONION GREENS AND GIVE THE WOK ANOTHER SHAKE.

AS THE SAUCE REDUCES AND STARTS TO THICKEN, ADD THE XO SAUCE AND STIR-FRY TO INCORPORATE.

YOU'RE LOOKING FOR A RICH AMBER SAUCE THAT HAS THE CONSISTENCY OF A LIGHT, LUMP-FREE GRAVY (SORRY, GRANDMA!).

IF NECESSARY, STIR IN SOME OF THE TAPIOCA SLURRY AND BRING TO A BOIL TO THICKEN MORE.

GIVE IT A FINAL STIR TO COAT ALL OF THE INGREDIENTS,

THEN TRANSFER TO A SERVING PLATTER AND GARNISH WITH THE PEIXINHOS FRITOS.

FAT NOODLES WITH MUSHROOMS AND EGG

Don't be fooled–this hearty vegetarian preparation of our Fat Noodles doesn't fall short on flavor. It's mushroom, it's egg, it's umami bomb productions! Feel free to add your favorite mushrooms, whether cultivated or wild.

SERVES 2
AS A MAIN,
4 IN A
MULTI-DISH
MEAL

3 tablespoons peanut oil

12 to 14 pieces of Fat Noodles (page 94)

1/2 cup bunapi mushrooms, separated into individual mushrooms and measured loosely

2 large king trumpet mushrooms, cut crosswise into 1/3-inch-thick slices

1 teaspoon peeled and minced fresh ginger

1 teaspoon minced garlic

1 teaspoon preserved mustard green stems (suimi ya cai, see page 296)

1 teaspoon sambal oelek or your favorite chilli garlic sambal

3 green onions, cut into 2-inch pieces, white and green parts separated

3/4 cup Vegetarian Wok Sauce (page 284)

1/3 cup Umami Juice (page 285)

5 shiitake mushrooms from Umami Juice (page 285), cut into bite-size chunks

1/2 red bell pepper, seeded and cut into 1/2-inch julienne

Slurry of 2 teaspoons tapioca starch mixed with 2 tablespoons water (optional if needed to thicken)

2 eggs, beaten thoroughly

Salt

BUNAPI ARE ALSO CALLED BEECH MUSHROOMS; IF YOU CAN'T FIND THEM, USE WHATEVER MUSHROOMS YOU CAN GET YOUR HANDS ON!

Prepare a wok for stir-frying (see page 20) and place over medium-high heat. When the wok begins to smoke, add 1 tablespoon of the oil, then add the rolled-up noodles in as even a layer as possible. Let the noodles sear, unmoved, until slightly charred, about 1 minute. Use a wok ladle to gently flip the noodles so that they remain rolled up and sear the other side, about another minute. Carefully add the bunapi and trumpet mushrooms and stir-fry to coat in oil for 30 to 60 seconds. When the mushrooms begin to develop a golden brown color and appear glossy, add the ginger, garlic, preserved mustard greens, sambal, and green onion whites and stir-fry for about 30 seconds. Add the wok sauce and juice. Give the wok a gentle shake to distribute the ingredients, taking care not to disturb the noodles too much, lest they unravel. After approximately 2 minutes, add the shiitakes, red pepper, and green onion greens and give the wok another shake. As the sauce reduces and starts to thicken, stir gently

to incorporate. You're looking for a light, coating sauce. If necessary, stir in some of the tapioca slurry and bring to a boil to thicken more. Give it a final stir to coat all of the ingredients and transfer to a serving platter.

Quickly prepare your wok again and heat over high heat. Add the remaining 2 tablespoons peanut oil and swirl around to coat the wok. Add the beaten eggs to the wok and let sit until you start to see a ring of cooked egg on the bottom of the wok, about 5 to 10 seconds. Carefully tilt the wok in a circular motion to coat the sides with egg, making a disk approximately 8 inches in diameter. At this point you should be able to flip the egg–give it a quick season with salt and do so. Immediately turn off the heat and, using a wok ladle, fold the egg three times until you have a 2 by 8-inch rectangle, more or less. Cut into 8 (1-inch-wide) sections, season with salt, and place on top of the plated noodles. Serve immediately.

Massas

5

LEGUMES

VEGETABLES

We love the brightness, textural contrast, and nutrition that vegetables bring to the otherwise protein-driven dishes of Macau. The main vegetables of the Macanese table are really those of Portugal: potatoes, carrots, onions, cabbage, tomatoes, and occasionally bell peppers. Still present but less common vegetables include daikon (which is often referred to as a turnip in Macanese cooking), pumpkins, sweet potatoes, and beans, both fresh and dried. Salads are rare, but a simple *salada Portuguesa* of lettuce, onion, tomato, green bell pepper, and zingy vinaigrette is a welcome addition to any Macanese meal.

The distinction between vegetable dishes and *vegetarian* dishes is often skewed in Macau (and much of China, for that matter); one finds things like balichão, oyster sauce, ground pork, or chicken stock in many of these original recipes. In Chinese culinary philosophy, a small amount of animal protein or fat added to vegetables during cooking releases the *xian,* or potential natural flavor within. The Chinese invented everything! Even the "everything is better with bacon" theory. Adapting Macanese vegetable dishes in a large metropolitan city like Chicago presents a challenge to us, as we encounter many fifth-level vegans (you know, those who won't eat anything that casts a shadow), and we have to accommodate their needs. So, for that reason, our Tchai de Bonzo (page 119), aka Buddha's Delight, is absolutely vegan and is the most satisfying vegetarian dish we have. With its array of flavors and satisfying textures, it is the arroz gordo of *our* vegetarian world.

DRY-FRIED ASPARAGUS WITH MINCHI AND PEIXINHOS FRITOS

SERVES 4
AS A SIDE

Everyone's had Sichuan green beans in their local Chinese joint—the beans' slightly wrinkled outsides with tiny smatterings of ground pork throughout, a good punch of garlic, and just greasy enough in all the right ways. The dry-frying technique ("dry-fried" denotes the lack of a batter) applies intense heat to the food, blasting and blistering the exterior and concentrating moisture within, all at the same time! We decided to take this basic preparation method and apply it to the delicious Midwestern asparagus that pops up every spring. That's why our lovely artist Sarah Becan created the Invasion poster to hang in our window for the month or so we serve it—it all pops up and it's here when it's here, and you gotta do something with it before it's gone and all that's left is that dry-bottomed, rubber band-strangled stuff that came on a third-class boat ride from Peru.

³/₄ pound (1 bunch) asparagus, in season, fattest and juiciest available

Peanut oil, for frying

Salt

2 tablespoons Chilli Oil (page 274)

¹/₄ cup whole dried red chillies

¹/₂ cup Minchi (page 230)

2 tablespoons oyster sauce

¹/₄ cup Pork Wok Sauce (page 284)

GARNISHES

¹/₄ cup chopped (1-inch pieces) Ramp Pickle (page 34)

¹/₄ cup Lemon Achar (page 38), julienned

Small handful Peixinhos Fritos (page 276)

Rinse and dry the asparagus well. Snap off the rough ends (about 1 inch off the bottom of the stems) and discard. Cut the asparagus into 3-inch pieces.

Pour about 3 inches of oil into a wok and heat over high heat to about 400°F. Carefully add a large handful of the asparagus to the oil and fry for 30 to 45 seconds, until wrinkled, blistered, and tender, but still green. Using a spider, transfer to a paper towel-lined plate and season lightly with salt. Repeat the process until all of the asparagus is cooked.

▶▶ continued

Remove excess oil from pan, and place over medium-high heat. When hot, add the Chilli Oil and chillies, cooking until the chillies are toasted and fragrant, but not burnt, about 15 seconds. Add the Minchi, oyster sauce, and wok sauce, stir, and increase the heat to high. Simmer briefly to meld the flavors, then add the asparagus, stirring to coat and heat through. Transfer to a serving platter and scatter the ramps and lemon over everything, finishing with the Peixinhos Fritos. Serve immediately.

THE ASPARAGUS WILL TELL
YOU HOW MUCH YOU SHOULD
SNAP OFF.

HEAT 3 INCHES OF OIL IN A WOK OVER HIGH HEAT TO ROUGHLY 400°F.

A WOODEN CHOPSTICK PLACED IN THE CENTER OF THE OIL WILL PRODUCE RAPID BUBBLES AT THIS TEMPERATURE.

30 seconds

CAREFULLY ADD A LARGE HANDFUL OF THE ASPARAGUS TO THE OIL AND FRY FOR 30 TO 45 SECONDS, UNTIL WRINKLED, BLISTERED, AND TENDER, BUT STILL GREEN.

USING A SPIDER, TRANSFER TO A PAPER TOWEL-LINED PLATE AND SEASON LIGHTLY WITH SALT. REPEAT THE PROCESS UNTIL ALL OF THE ASPARAGUS IS COOKED.

REMOVE EXCESS OIL FROM WOK, AND PLACE OVER MEDIUM-HIGH HEAT.

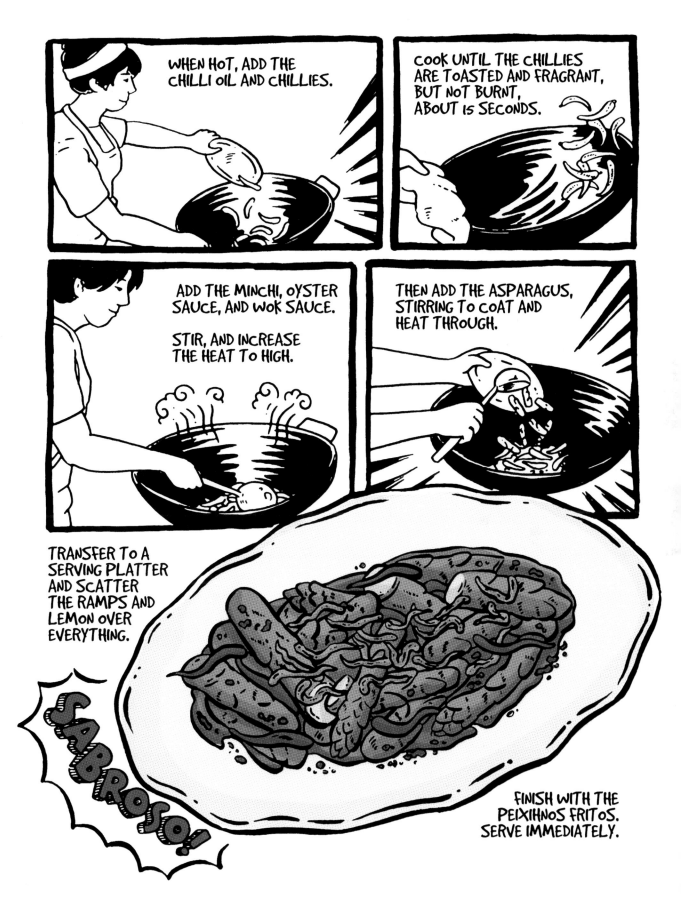

WHEN HOT, ADD THE CHILLI OIL AND CHILLIES.

COOK UNTIL THE CHILLIES ARE TOASTED AND FRAGRANT, BUT NOT BURNT, ABOUT 15 SECONDS.

ADD THE MINCHI, OYSTER SAUCE, AND WOK SAUCE.

STIR, AND INCREASE THE HEAT TO HIGH.

THEN ADD THE ASPARAGUS, STIRRING TO COAT AND HEAT THROUGH.

TRANSFER TO A SERVING PLATTER AND SCATTER THE RAMPS AND LEMON OVER EVERYTHING.

SABROSO!

FINISH WITH THE PEIXIHNOS FRITOS. SERVE IMMEDIATELY.

STIR-FRIED GREENS WITH GREEN PAPAYA, MUSHROOM, AND MACKEREL PICKLE

SERVES 4 AS A SIDE

In desperate and extensive searches for a Macanese vegetable side dish, we developed this recipe based on a little-known dish, bredo raba-raba. Bredo raba-raba is a stir-fry of various mixed greens—including amaranth (bredo), water spinach, and various chois—flavored with garlic, chillies, balichão, and *fula papaia* (the dried male buds of the papaya tree). Even Cecilia Jorge in her book *Macanese Cooking* substitutes mushrooms for the elusive and highly seasonal dried papaya buds. Here we've replaced the papaya buds with fresh green papaya, and furthermore, we bring our Esmargal (page 33) to the culinary crime scene rather than the more traditional Balichão (page 260). Our interperatation of bredo raba-raba can be seen as a somewhat inauthentic, mismatched hodgepodge, but it is, at the very least, crazy delicious.

1 green papaya

2 tablespoons peanut oil

5 cloves garlic, peeled and crushed

1 tablespoon Esmargal (page 33, optional)

7 wood ear mushrooms, rehydrated and hard bits removed

1 cup bunapi mushrooms (see note on page 103), separated into individual mushrooms and loosely packed

2 teaspoons tian jin preserved vegetable (see page 298)

8 cups mixed hearty greens (amaranth, Chinese water spinach, Swiss chard, napa cabbage, and various chois), leaves picked or cut into 2-inch strips and stems cut into 2-inch pieces (keep leaves and stems separate)

¹/₃ cup Vegetarian Wok Sauce (page 284)

Salt and white pepper

Sugar

To prepare the green papaya, peel it, then cut in half. Scoop out the seeds and discard. Split one of the halves in half lengthwise, then cut one of *those* halves in half crosswise. Slice one of *those* halves into ribbons as thinly as possible, preferably on a mandoline. You should have about 1 cup of sliced ribbons, each about 1 by 3 inches. Set the ribbons aside and reserve the unused papaya for another use.

Heat the oil in a wok over low heat. Add the garlic and stir just until it begins to brown, about 1 minute. Add the Esmargal and break it up with your wok ladle, allowing the Esmargal to bloom until the oil turns red,

about 30 seconds. Increase the heat to high and add all the mushrooms, the tian jin preserved vegetable, the papaya, and the stems of the greens. Stir-fry, cooking until the stems are vibrant in color and the mushrooms have begun to release moisture and appear slightly glossy. Add the leaves and give the wok a couple of flips to mix thoroughly. Add the wok sauce and stir well. When the greens have just started to wilt and become tender, and the sauce is slightly reduced and coats the vegetables, turn off the heat and season to taste with salt, white pepper, and sugar. Serve immediately.

➤➤ continued

HEAT OIL IN WOK OVER LOW HEAT.

1 minute

ADD GARLIC, AND STIR UNTIL IT BEGINS TO BROWN — ABOUT A MINUTE — AND TURN DOWN THE HEAT.

30 seconds

ADD THE ESMARGAL, AND BREAK IT UP WITH YOUR WOK LADLE, ALLOWING IT TO BLOOM UNTIL THE OIL TURNS RED, OR ABOUT 30 SECONDS.

TURN THE HEAT BACK ON, AND ADD ALL MUSHROOMS, TIAN JIN, PAPAYA, AND GREENS STEMS.

STIR-FRY, COOKING UNTIL THE GREENS STEMS ARE VIBRANT IN COLOR.

ADD THE GREENS...

...AND GIVE THE WOK A COUPLE OF FLIPS TO MIX THOROUGHLY.

ADD VEGETABLE WOK SAUCE AND STIR WELL.

WHEN GREENS HAVE JUST STARTED TO WILT AND BECOME TENDER, AND THE SAUCE IS SLIGHTLY REDUCED AND COATS THE VEGETABLES...

...TURN OFF HEAT, AND SEASON TO TASTE WITH SALT, WHITE PEPPER, AND SUGAR.

EAT YOUR GREENS

MALAY-STYLE VEGETABLE CURRY

SERVES 4 IN A MULTI-DISH MEAL

This Malay-inspired curry is flavored with Balichão (page 260), coconut milk, and Malacca Sweet Curry Powder (page 280), and with fried tofu puffs it is a perfect vehicle for seasonal vegetables. You have a lot of flexibility in the vegetables you can include. In the photos on pages 116 and 117, the left platter shows optional vegetables that should be roasted or poached; on the right are the vegetables that should be blanched or fried; and surrounding are last-minute additions and/or garnishes. Follow this visual guide and prepare your vegetables in advance so that you are simply heating them up in the sauce at go time. Serve the dish with Coconut Rice (page 75).

Peanut oil, for frying

1 large Chinese eggplant, pyramid-cut (see page 27)

1/2 teaspoon salt, plus more to season

1 handful longbeans, cut into 2-inch pieces

4 tablespoons coconut oil

1/4 Spanish onion, julienned

1/4 head green cabbage, cored and cut into 1-inch squares

2 tablespoons water

2 teaspoons Balichão (page 260)

3 cups Malay Vegetable Curry Sauce (page 115)

1 sweet potato, peeled, cut into 1/2-inch slices, and poached until tender

12 tofu puffs (see page 298), halved

1 cup whole okra, blanched and cut on the diagonal

6 triangle-cut pieces pineapple (see page 27)

OPTIONAL GARNISHES

Chopped fresh cilantro

Red onion, julienned

Fresh red finger chilli, thinly sliced

Oil, vinegar, salt, and fresh lime, for seasoning

Pour about 3 inches of oil into a wok and heat over high heat to about 400°F. Carefully add a large handful of the eggplant to the oil and fry for 30 to 45 seconds, until wrinkled, blistered, and tender. Using a spider, transfer to a paper towel-lined plate and season lightly with salt. Repeat the process until all of the eggplant is cooked, then repeat with the longbeans. Discard the frying oil and wipe the wok clean.

Heat 3 tablespoons of the coconut oil in a large, heavy pot over medium-high heat. When melted, add the onion and lightly brown until translucent, a few minutes. Add the cabbage and 1/2 teaspoon salt, stirring to coat the cabbage with the oil. Add the water, reduce the heat to low, cover the pot, and cook for 15 minutes, stirring as needed to keep the cabbage from sticking to the bottom of the pot. The goal is for the cabbage to soften but retain a slight crunch. Spread out on a clean sheet pan to cool while preparing the rest of the dish.

Preheat the oven to 450°F. In a clay pot or Dutch oven, melt the remaining 1 tablespoon coconut oil over medium heat, then add the Balichão. Bloom until the oil develops the color of the sambal and most of the moisture has been cooked out, 2 to 3 minutes. Add the curry sauce and stir until heated through.

Evenly distribute the remaining ingredients and the dry-fried eggplant and longbeans in the clay pot, cover with a lid, and place in the oven for 5 minutes. Give the pot a gentle stir to ensure that all of the ingredients are coated with the sauce and everything is heating through, and return to the oven until fully heated through, up to another 5 minutes.

Season the garnishes with oil, vinegar, salt, and lime, mix well, and use to garnish the curry. Serve immediately.

MALAY VEGETABLE CURRY SAUCE

6 cloves garlic, thinly sliced

1 large Asian shallot, julienned

1 lemongrass stalk, minced

PEEL AWAY THE ROUGH, WOODY, GREENER LAYERS AND USE ONLY THE SOFTER, LIGHTER PARTS OF THE LEMONGRASS.

1 (2-inch) piece fresh ginger, peeled and coarsely chopped

1 fresh Thai bird chilli, stemmed and minced

1 (1-inch) piece fresh turmeric root, peeled and coarsely chopped

2 tablespoons Filipino cane vinegar

5 teaspoons Malacca Sweet Curry Powder (page 280)

2 tablespoons coconut oil

2 cups Vegetable Stock (page 281)

7 ounces (¹/₂ can) coconut milk

¹/₂ cup Tamarind Extract (page 285)

1 ounce palm sugar (see page 296)

¹/₂ teaspoon salt

Set aside half of the garlic and half of the shallots. Combine the remaining garlic, shallots, lemongrass, ginger, chilli, and turmeric in a food processor and process into a chunky paste, scraping down the sides of the processor as necessary. Add the vinegar and curry powder and process to combine. Set aside.

Heat the coconut oil in a heavy pot over medium-high heat. Add the reserved garlic and shallots and fry, stirring constantly, until the garlic is almost golden brown, 1 to 2 minutes. Add the curry paste and stir well. Lower the heat to medium, stirring often and scraping the pan as needed to toast the spices and caramelize the aromatics without burning them, about 5 minutes.

Add the stock, coconut milk, tamarind, sugar, and salt and whisk until the sugar is dissolved completely. Taste and adjust the seasoning with additional salt, tamarind, or sugar as needed. Use immediately or store tightly covered and refrigerated for up to 3 days.

TCHAI DE BONZO (BUDDHA'S DELIGHT)

MAKES
AS MUCH AS
YOU LIKE

Translated as "meal of the Buddhist monk" (*tchai* is a simple Chinese word for "meal" or "vegetable," while *bonzo* is the Portuguese word for "Buddhist monk"), this adopted and adapted Chinese dish is the only truly vegetarian dish of the Macanese. It is composed of three categories of ingredients: items that absorb the sauce (tofu puffs, glass noodles, mock-duck roll), items that add texture (cabbage, various chois, snap peas, fresh mushrooms, fresh bamboo, mung bean sprouts, ginko nuts, lotus root, peanuts, pistachios, almonds, water chestnut, jicama, fat choy), and the flavor bombs (fermented bean curd, smoked shiitake mushrooms, dried lily bulbs, jujube dates), all of which are added to the sauce and noodles at various stages and finally topped with our seared mock duck to make for a truly divine, guilt-free meal.

It's important to include at least a few items from each category, but don't feel limited to just these ingredients–if you've got something out of this world growing in your backyard that you think could fit into one of the categories in the chart (see page 120), try it out!

**SWEET POTATO
STARCH NOODLES**

Sweet potato noodles
(see page 298)

Peanut oil

MOCK DUCK

1 tablespoon
tapioca starch

1 tablespoon water

1 tablespoon light
soy sauce

3 large sheets fresh yuba
(tofu skin, see page 298)

2 tablespoons peanut oil

TO FINISH

Ingredients of your
choosing (see page 120)

Tchai de Bonzo Sauce
(page 121), warmed

To make the noodles, bring a large pot of salted water to a boil. Drop the sweet potato noodles into the water and cook for approximately 5 minutes, until softened and stretchy. Shock in cold water, toss with a bit of peanut oil, and set aside.

To make the mock duck, whisk the tapioca starch, water, and soy sauce together in a small bowl. Lay out 1 sheet of yuba and brush with the soy slurry all over, then lay another sheet of yuba on top, repeating this process until all the sheets are layered. Fold any rounded edges of layered yuba sheets inward so you have straight sides, and proceed to roll tightly upward from the bottom. Place the yuba roll on a plate and steam for 5 minutes, following the instructions on page 94. Cool to room temperature and set aside.

To finish, arrange your chosen ingredients in an appropriately sized clay pot with the reserved sweet potato noodles in the center and all of the other ingredients evenly dispersed and equally visible. Pour enough of the warm sauce over the ingredients so that they are about three-quarters submerged and bring to a simmer.

Meanwhile, to finish the mock duck, heat a cast-iron pan over medium heat, then add the 2 tablespoons peanut oil. Sauté the steamed mock duck roll on one side until crisp and brown. Roll to the other side, repeat, and transfer to a paper towel-lined plate.

Continue to cook your Tchai de Bonzo until all the ingredients are heated through and the sauce has thickened and reduced a bit, about 5 to 10 minutes.

Slice the mock duck roll into 1/2-inch pieces and place on top. Garnish with the desired ingredients from line E (see page 120) and serve immediately.

▸▸ continued

EACH LINE IN THIS CHART REQUIRES A DIFFERENT PREPARATION:

- Lines A and B must be soaked in water to hydrate.
- Line C must be roasted or blanched.
- Line D should be added in the last minutes of cooking.
- Line E should be added at the very end.

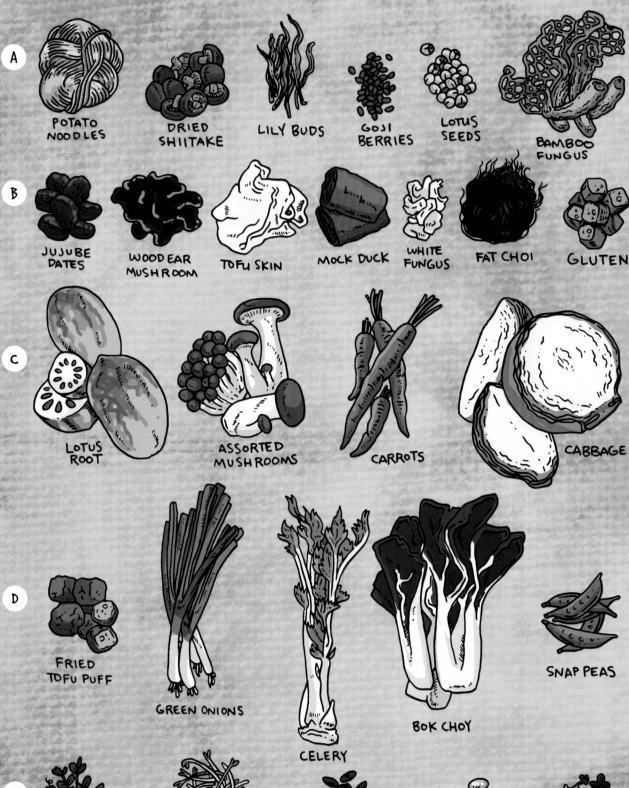

A
- POTATO NOODLES
- DRIED SHIITAKE
- LILY BUDS
- GOJI BERRIES
- LOTUS SEEDS
- BAMBOO FUNGUS

B
- JUJUBE DATES
- WOOD EAR MUSHROOM
- TOFU SKIN
- MOCK DUCK
- WHITE FUNGUS
- FAT CHOI
- GLUTEN

C
- LOTUS ROOT
- ASSORTED MUSHROOMS
- CARROTS
- CABBAGE

D
- FRIED TOFU PUFF
- GREEN ONIONS
- CELERY
- BOK CHOY
- SNAP PEAS

E
- PEA SHOOTS
- MUNG BEAN SPROUTS
- TOASTED ALMONDS
- GINKGO NUTS
- EDIBLE FLOWERS

TCHAI DE BONZO SAUCE

1 tablespoon peanut oil

3 cloves garlic, minced

1 (1-inch) piece fresh ginger, peeled and minced

¼ cup fermented bean curd (see page 293)

2 tablespoons juice from fermented bean curd

4 cups Umami Juice (page 285), mushrooms strained out before measuring

¼ cup soy sauce

2 tablespoons sugar

2 tablespoons tapioca starch mixed with 3 tablespoons cold water

MAKES ABOUT 4 CUPS

Heat the oil in a medium saucepan over medium-high heat. Add the garlic and ginger and cook until fragrant, about 1 minute. Add the fermented bean curd and cook until fragrant, breaking up with a wooden spoon, about 2 more minutes. Add the juice, soy sauce, and sugar and stir to incorporate all of the ingredients.

Bring to a boil and whisk in the tapioca starch slurry. Return to a boil, whisking, then remove from the heat. Puree using an immersion blender, then cool completely. Use immediately or refrigerate tightly covered for up to 1 month.

BEBINCA DE RABANO (XO DAIKON CAKE)

**SERVES
8 TO 10
AS A SIDE**

Throughout the Portuguese-speaking world, *bebinca* basically describes something that has been steamed or baked to set. Also known as Bebinca de Nabo, turnip cake, white carrot cake, and chai tow kway, this dish isn't really a cake per se, but more of a steamed loaf. Confusing as hell but absolutely delicious.

1½ pounds shredded daikon radish

1 teaspoon salt

1½ cups rice flour

¼ cup coconut oil

6 cloves garlic, minced

1 (1-inch) piece fresh ginger, peeled and minced

4 ounces fresh shiitake mushrooms, stemmed and coarsely chopped

1 cup fisheye-cut green onions, white part only (see page 27)

1 teaspoon tian jin preserved vegetable (see page 298)

3 tablespoons preserved mustard stems (suimi ya cai, see page 296)

1 teaspoon sambal oelek

3 tablespoons peanut oil

2 tablespoons Chilli Oil (page 274)

10 cloves garlic, thinly sliced

1 red onion, finely diced

1 green bell pepper, seeded and finely diced

6 green onions, white parts only, fisheye-cut (see page 27)

2 fresh red finger or fresno chillies, sliced into thin rounds

1 jalapeño, sliced into thin rounds

¼ cup Umami Juice (page 285), Vegetable Stock (page 281), or Chicken Stock (page 282)

1 cup XO Sauce (page 268), optional

2 tablespoons soy sauce

GARNISH

Small handful of cilantro, torn into pieces

Pinch of Peixinhos Fritos (page 276)

Toss the radish and salt together in a small bowl, then transfer to a strainer and set the strainer over a bowl. Let the liquid drain for 30 minutes, then squeeze any excess liquid from the radish and set the radish aside.

In a separate small bowl, whisk together the rice flour and 1 cup water to make a slurry. Set aside.

Heat a prepared wok (see page 20) over high heat. Add the coconut oil and when melted, add the minced garlic and ginger and cook until slightly brown and fragrant, about 1 minute. Add the mushrooms and green onions and cook until fragrant, an additional 2 minutes. Add the radish and mix well, then add the preserved vegetable, preserved mustard stems, and sambal and mix to incorporate. Whisk the slurry again and while stirring, add to the wok and thoroughly mix until thickened. Remove from the heat.

Pour the mixture into a standard 9 by 5-inch loaf pan and set aside. Set up a wok half full of water with a steamer basket insert with lid and bring the water to a boil. Place the loaf pan in the steamer, cover, and steam for 2 hours, making sure to add water to the wok as necessary.

After 2 hours, when the cake is solid and firm, remove from the heat and let fully cool. The cake can be wrapped tightly and refrigerated for up to 3 days.

When fully cooled, turn the cake out from the loaf pan. Cut into 1-inch slices, then cut each slice in half crosswise. Heat a large sauté pan over high heat, add the peanut oil, and when the oil starts smoking, carefully lay the squares in the pan (you may need to do this in batches, wiping out the pan and adding new oil each time). Allow to sit in the pan, untouched, until dark golden brown with a slight char, about 2 minutes. Flip and repeat, then remove to a serving platter and set aside.

Heat a prepared wok over high heat. Add the Chilli Oil, then the sliced garlic, and toast for 15 seconds. Add the onion, bell pepper, green onions, chillies, and jalapeño and stir-fry for 60 seconds. Add the juice and stir until most of the liquid has left the pan. Add the XO Sauce and soy sauce and stir to combine, then remove from the heat and top the cakes with the stir-fry. Garnish with the cilantro and Peixinhos Fritos and serve immediately.

6

PIEXE E MARISCOS

FISH AND SEAFOOD

The tie that binds the cuisines of Portuguese-speaking people around the world–especially in the regions touched on in this book–is the sea. Since the Portuguese were seafarers, most of the places they traveled to are coastal: Cape Verde on the west coast of Africa, Mozambique on the east; Goa on the west coast of India, Brazil on the east coast of the Americas; and, of course, the islands through southern Asia leading up to the Pearl River Estuary on which Macau lies.

The variety of crustaceans, shellfish, and finfish seem limitless–and so do their preparations.

At Fat Rice, we employ rich seafood curries of Indian origin (Shrimp Curry with Okra with Tomato, page 166), streetside hawker dishes of Malay influence ("Portuguese" Barbecued Clams, page 153) or the fire-roasting and grilling of the Portuguese (Portuguese Barbecued Seafood with Big Ben's Sambal, page 139). Preserved seafood plays a big role as well in our various *bacalhau* (salt cod) dishes, Balichão (page 260), and XO Sauce (page 268), reflecting the importance of not only what you can catch for that day, but also how you can preserve it for the future.

EMPADA DE PEIXE ("MACANESE" FISH PIE)

SERVES 4

Empada de peixe is one of the most intriguing dishes in the Macanese repertoire, and a wild stroll across the sacred garden of culinary rules: Cheese with fish? Yes! A sweet crust on a savory pie? Yes! Olives? Nuts? Lard? Yes, yes, yes.

Our friend, the Macanese chef Florita Alves, introduced us to empada de peixe. Just as she did, we mix the dough by hand biscuit-style, creating maximum opportunity for a moist crust with a crumby flake. For the filling, we use any firm-fleshed fish such as sea bass, halibut, or snapper. However, you must beware the elusive pili nut; it's commonly referred to as a pine nut, but it is actually the pit of the Chinese olive (see page 296), high in fat content and grown in the Philippines. We list it in the ingredients, but it can be hard to find; you can use a mixture of almonds or macadamia nuts with common pine nuts, as needed.

Serve empada de peixe as an appetizer, at brunch, or, for more intrepid guests, use its beguiling characteristics as a bridging course between a savory entrée and a sweet dessert. We like dusting it with a touch of confectioners' sugar to enhance the sweetness of the dough.

FILLING

1/3 cup pili nuts, or substitute pine nuts, almonds, macadamia nuts, or a combination

2 teaspoons ground cumin

2 teaspoons ground coriander

1 1/2 teaspoons ground turmeric

1 teaspoon salt

Juice of 1 lemon

8 ounces white ocean fish (sea bass, halibut, snapper, or other firm white saltwater fish), cut into 1 by 2-inch pieces

3 tablespoons extra-virgin olive oil

1 Spanish onion, diced

2 shallots, julienned

2 cloves garlic, minced

1/3 cup shredded Parrano cheese or other firm Dutch-style cheese with good melting characteristics

1/3 cup firm ripe black Potuguese olives (see page 295), pitted and chopped

1/3 cup chopped flat-leaf parsley

1 egg yolk

Salt and freshly ground pepper

DOUGH

1 1/2 cups pastry flour

1/2 cup granulated sugar

3/4 teaspoon baking powder

3/4 teaspoon salt

1/3 cup lard, cubed and chilled

4 large egg yolks, beaten

1 tablespoon brandy

1 tablespoon port

OPTIONAL GARNISH

Confectioners' sugar

Portuguese olives

Preheat the oven to 350°F.

To make the filling, put the nuts on a baking sheet and bake until toasted and aromatic, about 10 minutes. Let cool, then set 5 nuts aside for garnish. Chop the remaining nuts and set aside.

In a bowl, combine the cumin, coriander, turmeric, salt, and half of the lemon juice and stir well. Add the fish and toss to combine.

▶▶ continued

Heat a large cast-iron pan over high heat. Add 2 tablespoons of the olive oil, and when the oil is just starting to smoke, carefully lay the fish pieces in the pan to quickly sear, about 1 minute per side, using a fish spatula to flip. Do not worry about cooking the fish all the way through in this step—you just want a nice sear to remove some external moisture. Remove from the pan, place on a paper towel-lined plate, and set

aside. Add the remaining 1 tablespoon oil to the pan, then add the onions stirring and cooking until translucent, about 3 minutes. Add the shallots and garlic and continue to cook until aromatic and the shallots have softened a bit, about 1 more minute. Transfer to a bowl and set aside to cool slightly.

Combine the cheese, olives, parsley, egg yolk, onion mixture, remaining lemon juice, and half of the chopped nuts in a large bowl. Season to taste with salt and pepper and mix well to combine. Divide the mixture in half and set aside.

To make the dough, sift the flour, granulated sugar, baking powder, and salt into a large bowl. Add the lard, and using gloved hands, pinch, press, and thoroughly mix the lard into the dry ingredients until fully incorporated. Add the egg yolks and mix thoroughly again. Add the brandy and port and work into the dough. Take care not to work the dough any more than necessary. Wrap the dough in plastic wrap and chill for at least 20 minutes.

Preheat the oven to 375°F.

When the dough is chilled, cut into two pieces at a rough 60:40 ratio and form each piece into a ball. The larger piece will be for the bottom crust, the smaller piece for the top crust. Place the larger piece between two sheets of parchment paper and use a rolling pin to roll into a disk about 1/3 inch thick. Set aside and repeat the process with the smaller piece.

To assemble the pie, remove the top piece of parchment paper from the larger piece of dough and invert an 8-inch baking dish or cast-iron skillet onto it. Using the parchment paper to help you, flip the dish over and let the dough fall into the dish. Gently press the dough into the pan. Sprinkle in the remaining chopped nuts, and top with the seared fish. In an even layer, top with the cheese and onion mixture. Place the smaller piece of dough on top of the fish mixture and tuck the top dough in, leaving the bottom dough edge exposed. Using a rubber spatula, bring the edge of the bottom dough up and using an upward motion gently pull and spread to unify the two pieces of dough until smooth. Chill, uncovered, in the refrigerator for about 15 minutes.

When ready to bake, create a scale pattern on the crust using a wet spoon and gently press in the reserved whole nuts on top as garnish. Bake for 45 to 60 minutes, until the crust is golden brown and the filling has heated through. Let cool on top of the stove for a few minutes, then dust with confectioners' sugar, garnish with olives, and serve.

SHAPING THE EMPADA

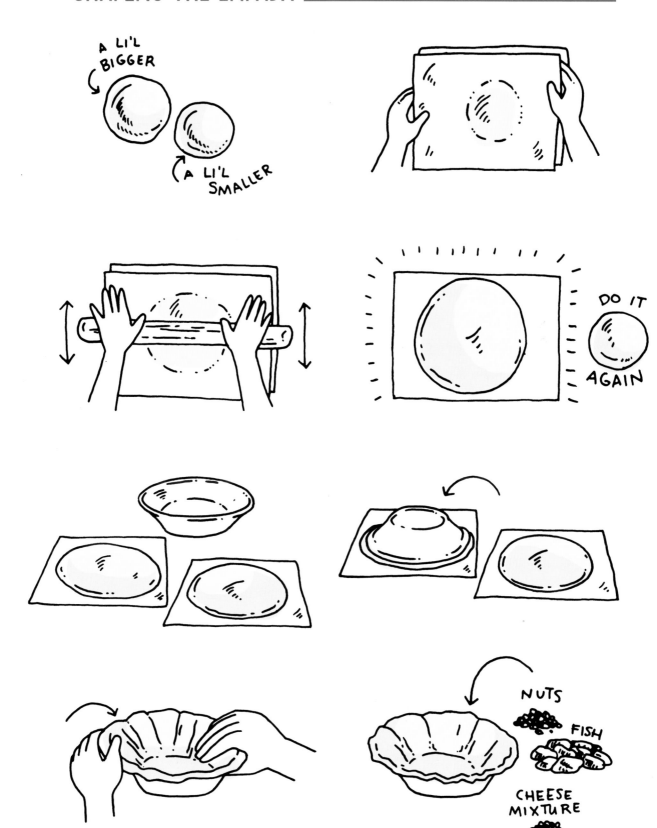

A LI'L BIGGER

A LI'L SMALLER

DO IT AGAIN

NUTS

FISH

CHEESE MIXTURE

SHAPING THE EMPADA

CRAZY SQUID RICE

SERVES 2

Early on in our research on Macanese cuisine, we came across *arroz de chocos*, a saucy tomato, squid/cuttlefish, and rice dish (frankly, more popular in Portugal than Macau), and also *sotong masak hitam*, a Eurasian recipe of squid cooked in its own ink with chillies and garlic. Inspired by aspects of both, we combined the two and added a large scoop of crazy, leaving the purple membrane on the outside of the squid to boost flavor and cutting it oddly, like bias-cut noodles. Texture adds to the cacophony as well—peanuts, crispy puffed rice, and bean sprouts provide varying levels of crunch. The key to this dish—aside from reading the recipe thoroughly and being completely prepared with ingredients chopped and ready to go—is high-heat cooking, to get that wok *hei* flavor on the rice and to keep the squid tender.

1 tablespoon peanut oil, plus more for deep-frying

1½ cups Fried Rice Rice (page 261)

Salt

4 ounces squid or cuttlefish, cleaned (see page 135)

1 clove garlic, minced

1 (½-inch) piece fresh ginger, peeled and minced

½ habanero, seeds and all, minced (more or less to taste)

¼ cup sliced garlic chives, cut into ½-inch segments

½ cup sliced mung bean sprouts (½-inch segments)

2 green onions, fisheye-cut (see page 27), white and green parts separated

¼ cup diced ripe tomatoes or halved cherry tomatoes

10 leaves Christmas basil, torn (substitute Thai basil, if needed)

3 tablespoons Crazy Squid Sauce (page 135)

Roasted peanuts, for garnish

OPEN THE WINDOWS! IT'S GONNA GET SMOKY AND HOT! WORK FAST!

Prepare a wok for deep-frying by heating about 2 inches of peanut oil to 425°F. Take a small handful of Fried Rice Rice (reserving the rest for later) and sprinkle it around the oil. The rice should sink to the bottom and immediately float back up and puff. You will see moisture leaving the rice in the form of bubbles, slowing down as more moisture departs, allowing the rice to start to brown. Use a fine-mesh spider to push the rice down beneath the surface of the oil. When the rice is light brown, after 30 to 45 seconds of total cooking time, scoop the rice out of the wok with the spider, transfer it to a paper towel-lined plate, season with salt, and set aside. Strain the oil, reserving for another use, and wipe wok out with a clean paper towel.

Heat the wok over high heat until it begins to smoke. Add the 1 tablespoon oil to the wok and swirl to coat. When smoking hot—which will happen quickly—add all of the squid to the wok in one shot but *do not move it*. Working quickly, add the garlic, ginger, habanero, and garlic chives at once, right on top of the squid. *Now* you can give the ingredients a quick stir, but then leave them alone again for about 30 seconds. Sprinkle the remaining unpuffed Fried Rice Rice over the squid. Give the wok another stir, then leave it alone once more for another 60 seconds. Add the bean sprouts, green onion whites, tomatoes, and Thai basil and give it another stir. Add the sauce and give the wok three or four more stirs to incorporate all of the ingredients, then transfer to a serving dish. Fold in the green onion greens and sprinkle the puffed rice and roasted peanuts over the dish, then turn off the smoke alarm.

▶▶ continued

CRASY SQUID SAUCE

¹/₄ cup sugar

¹/₄ cup Tamarind Extract
(page 285)

¹/₄ cup fish sauce

1 tablespoon squid or
cuttlefish ink (optional;
if you don't have any ink,
you *can* still make the
dish!)

MAKES
ABOUT
³/₄ CUP

Combine all of the ingredients in a small saucepan
and bring to a boil. It'll be stanky! Whisk well until
the sugar dissolves, remove from the heat, and cool
completely. Store tightly covered in the refrigerator for
up to a week.

PREPARING YOUR SQUID

At Fat Rice, we use "dirty squid," meaning it's been minimally processed, with all of
the good guts and ink still inside. Ultimately, this provides maximum flavor, but it also
means maximum effort. If you have a friendly fisherman nearby, use what he's pulling
out of the water every day. If this intimidates you, we suggest you get cleaned squid
with both bodies and tentacles, and don't forget to buy squid ink at the same time.
If you haven't cleaned squid before, here's our method:

Set up a clean cutting board, preferably in a sheet pan to catch all of the juicy
runoff from the squid. Working one at a time, gently pull the head and tentacles from
the body of the squid. Everything should come out clean and smooth, but put your
hand in the body of the squid to check for any straggling bits, including the long,
plasticlike quill or bits of the squid's last meal. With a sharp knife, cut the tentacles
off of the squid as close to the eyes as possible. Some ink may come out at this point,
but that's okay. Use the knife to separate each tentacle and set aside. Using the tip of
your knife, carefully remove the ink sac and reserve. Slide the knife into the squid's
body tube and slice from the inside out to make one flat sheet. Lay the sheet flat and
square with the cutting board and cut at a 45-degree diagonal into ¹/₃-inch-wide strips
(lengths will vary). Combine with the tentacles.

To harvest the ink, puncture the ink sac with the tip of your knife and squeeze the
ink into a small dish and reserve. Discard the empty ink sac.

CHILLI PRAWNS

MAKES 8 PRAWNS; SERVES 4 TO 6 AS A STARTER

Chilli prawns like these can be found all over Macau. At Fat Rice, they're served head-on and shell-on, stuffed with a mixture of garlic, chillies, cilantro, and fermented black beans. The word *prawn* can cause some unnecessary confusion–we use it here simply to describe large shrimp. Look for shrimp that are head-on, shell-on, extra jumbo-sized U-10 (meaning under 10 per pound) or bigger. We had one at Restaurante Litoral in Macau that probably weighed half a pound! Use your hands to peel and eat the prawns, and don't neglect the heads! Place the open end in your mouth, squeeze, and suck all that good stuff out. It's even better if you've got some good dry Madeira to pour inside the head for a boozy shot of bisquelike goodness.

GARLIC-CHILLI STUFFING

2 tablespoons fermented black beans, minced

1/4 cup seeded and minced fresh red chillies or sambal oelek

6 cloves garlic, minced

3 tablespoons minced cilantro stems

8 U-10 prawns, head-on and shell-on, thawed if frozen

1/4 cup extra-virgin olive oil

1/4 cup dry white wine

1 tablespoon unsalted butter

OPTIONAL GARNISH

Small handful of Portuguese olives (see page 296)

Small handful of horse ear-cut green onions (see page 27), green parts only

1 lemon, cut into wedges and dipped in Korean chilli flakes

To make the stuffing, combine the fermented black beans, chillies, garlic, and cilantro stems in a small bowl and mix well. Set aside.

Using a razor blade or kitchen shears, cut through the shell and flesh of each prawn along the back about halfway deep, starting at the base of the head through a quarter of the way from the tip of the tail. Remove the vein running along the back using the edge of the razor or shears and discard. Fill the space you just cleaned on each prawn with the stuffing.

Heat a large pan with a lid over high heat and add the oil. When the oil is almost smoking, carefully lay the prawns in the oil and cook until the shell starts to brown and the flesh starts to turn pink, about 1 minute. Flip the prawns and cook for another minute, browning the other side. Carefully add the wine to the pan–it will spatter–and immediately cover with the lid. Steam the prawns until completely pink and fully cooked, about 4 minutes. Remove the pan from the heat and transfer the prawns to a serving dish. Add the butter to the pan and swirl until melted by the heat remaining in the pan. Pour the sauce over the prawns. Garnish with the olives, green onions, and lemon and serve immediately.

IT'S BEST TO COMPLETE EACH STEP ON EVERY PRAWN BEFORE MOVING ON TO THE NEXT STEP, OTHERWISE YOU'LL GET THAT NASTY VEIN MIXED IN WHERE IT OUGHT NOT GO!

"PORTUGUESE" BARBECUED SEAFOOD WITH BIG BEN'S SAMBAL

MAKES
2 CUPS
SAMBAL,
ENOUGH FOR
ONE WHOLE
FISH OR
SEVERAL
FILLETS TO
SERVE 4 TO 6

Portuguese barbecued or baked seafood is very popular all along the coastal regions of the Malay Peninsula, but its epicenter is Malacca, on the southwest coast. A few miles from the city center lies the Perkampungan Portugis, literally translated as "The Portuguese Village" and popularly known as the "Portuguese settlement." There we met a huge, gruff chef who goes by the nickname "Big Ben." Benildus De Silva is a fourth-generation chef of Cristang (Malaccan-Portuguese) descent who proudly cooks and serves authentic Cristang dishes out of his tiny but efficient seaside kitchen. In Malacca, Portuguese barbecued seafood can be made from an array of species, including stingray, snapper, small mackerel, or squid. Of all that we tried, Ben's red snapper was the best, so we chose to include it here and on our menu at the restaurant. Malaccans probably call this preparation "Portuguese" because many Malaccans of Portuguese descent are fishermen. This dish is essentially just a "Catch o' the Day" preparation, so have the sambal ready to go for a quickly made meal after a long day of fishing.

Here's how to do it Big Ben style: Scale and butterfly a freshly caught fish. Rub it all over with this spicy, fragrant sauce, and place on a fresh banana leaf from a nearby tree. Wrap the fish and leaf in a tight aluminum foil envelope and throw the whole thing over hot coals to cook. When heated and charred, the banana leaf protects the fish and adds a great herbal, smoky note, and the foil envelope holds in the moisture and aromatic steam during cooking. You can use any whole fish or fillets, or you could use prawns or clams. Our recipe is written fairly loosely; it's really a recipe for the sambal and a technique for cooking the fish. The Balichão (page 260) is optional, but it'll really elevate the flavor of the dish, and the laksa leaf—also known as *rau ram* or Vietnamese cilantro—has a unique flavor worth scouring your Asian market for.

SAMBAL

1¼ cups water

½ cup Filipino cane vinegar

1½ teaspoons salt

¼ cup dried red chillies

6 cloves garlic, crushed

1 (1-inch) piece fresh ginger, peeled and thinly sliced across the grain

1 Asian shallot, sliced

1 (2-inch) piece galangal, peeled and minced

1 lemongrass stalk, rough outer layers removed and tender inner layers minced

2 lime leaves, center vein removed

1 fresh red chilli, seeded and thinly sliced

1 pinky-size piece fresh turmeric, peeled and minced

¼ cup peanut oil

1 tablespoon Balichão (page 260, optional)

¼ pineapple, peeled, cored, and cut into 1-inch chunks

10 laksa leaves or 3 whole sprigs cilantro

⅓ cup Tamarind Extract (page 285)

2 tablespoons sugar

Juice of 1 lime

FISH

About 3 pounds whole fish, scaled and butterflied, or filleted

Banana leaves (optional)

OPTIONAL ACCOMPANIMENTS

Cucumber, peeled and sliced

Asian shallot, peeled and thinly sliced

Fresh lime wedges

▶▶ continued

To make the sambal, combine the water with 6 tablespoons of the cane vinegar and $\frac{1}{2}$ teaspoon of the salt in a small pot and bring to a boil. Put the dried chillies in a bowl and cover with the boiling vinegar mixture, making sure the chillies are completely submerged. Let the chillies soak for 30 minutes, then add the garlic, ginger, and shallot, again making sure everything is submerged. Let soak for an additional 2 hours, then drain, reserving the liquid.

Combine the soaked chillies, garlic, ginger, and shallot in a blender and add the galangal, lemongrass, lime leaves, fresh chilli, and turmeric. Add enough of the soaking liquid to cover the ingredients by about 1 inch. Start blending on low speed, gradually increasing the speed to medium, then high. If at any point the machine isn't easily blending the ingredients, stop it and add a couple more tablespoons of liquid. You want the paste to be smooth, but not runny; shoot for the consistency of tomato paste. When you get to this point, stop blending.

Heat a heavy pot over medium heat and add the oil. Carefully add the chilli paste and stir with a wooden spoon—things will splatter and sputter, so use caution. Continue to work the paste with the spoon as the moisture cooks out. All told, this will take a very attention-filled 5 to 10 minutes, but be sure to use your senses and observe what is happening in the pan. The oil will begin to separate out from the mixture, and you will essentially be frying the paste to a rich red

color. Add the Balichão and cook for about 1 minute, then add the pineapple, cilantro, tamarind, remaining 1 teaspoon salt, remaining 2 tablespoons cane vinegar, and the sugar, along with $\frac{1}{2}$ cup reserved soaking liquid or water. Stir well. Bring to a simmer, then lower the heat to medium and cook to meld the flavors, about 5 minutes. Remove from the heat and allow to cool slightly, about 10 minutes. Add the lime juice and puree the sauce in a blender. If not using immediately, store in an airtight container in the refrigerator for up to 1 week.

To cook the fish, build a raging fire in a charcoal grill (or heat a gas grill to high) and let the coals ash over and glow a radiant red. On a work surface, lay down two pieces of aluminum foil large enough to hold the fish, then lay a slightly smaller banana leaf on the foil, leaving at least an inch or two of foil exposed around the edges. Spread a dollop of sambal into a thin layer on the banana leaf, then place your fish on top of the sambal. Coat the top of the fish with a generous amount of sambal. Put a third piece of foil directly on top of the fish and fold each side of the packet in a couple of times to make a nice tight pouch. Place on the hot grill and cook for about 8 minutes per pound, until the foil is fully puffed with steam and the fish is cooked through. Serve immediately with the accompaniments on the side, cutting open the pouch at the table to release all the wonderful aromas.

BACALHAU DE VÓVÓ (SALT COD SPREAD)

In Abe's hometown of Lowell, Massachusetts, he grew up knowing this dish simply as *bacalhau*–pronounced with the Porto-Massachussetts accent as buck-ee-yow–a preparation saved for special occasions and holidays. Our version is an homage to the families of Madeiran-Portuguese heritage, started with the recipe from Abe's great-grandmother, Beatrice Jardin Abreu. We use our house-dried salt cod, good extra-virgin olive oil, vinegar, olives, onions, smoked paprika, and fresh mint, simply served with Papo Seco (page 264). Buy good salt cod from a reputable fishmonger, European market, or fine grocer. Once dried, salt cod requires about three days of soaking and multiple changes of water to bring it back to the proper level of salinity.

MAKES 4 CUPS; SERVES 4 TO 6 AS AN APPETIZER

PAY ATTENTION TO THE EMULSION YOU ARE FORMING DON'T RUSH THINGS, AND MAKE SURE ALL THE INGREDIENTS STAY BOUND!

10 ounces salt cod

4 cups whole milk

1½ cups plus 2 tablespoons extra-virgin olive oil

½ small onion, diced and rinsed

10 Arbequina olives, pitted

Juice and finely grated zest of 1 lemon

¾ cup loosely packed minced parsley (about 1 bunch)

2 teaspoons sherry vinegar

½ teaspoon freshly ground black pepper

1½ teaspoons salt

GARNISH

½ fresh red chilli, seeds and all, sliced into thin rounds

Small handful of green Portuguese olives (see page 296)

10 mint leaves, torn into small pieces if large

Papo Seco (page 264) or crackers, to serve

Place the cod in a nonreactive container and cover with cold water by 2 inches. Cover and refrigerate for 12 hours. Discard the water, cover the cod with fresh cold water, and refrigerate for another 12 hours. Repeat this process over the course of 3 days, until the cod has had a total of 6 soaks.

Drain the cod and set aside. Pour the milk into a small pot with a tight-fitting lid and bring to a simmer, uncovered, over medium-high heat, being careful not to let the milk scorch (if it does, get rid of the milk and start over–you don't want the entire batch of *bacalhau* to taste burnt!). Cut the heat, place the cod in the milk, and cover the pot immediately. Set aside for 10 minutes. Drain the cod and let cool slightly, then shred the cod into rough 1-inch chunks, making sure to remove any bones, then set aside.

Put the cod in a standing mixer fitted with the paddle attachment and mix on low speed for about 1 minute. With the machine still running on low, slowly drizzle in 1½ cups of the olive oil to form an emulsion with the fish. The slower the drizzle the better! When the emulsion is formed, stop the mixer and add the onion. Mix on low until incorporated, about 1 minute, then stop the machine and add the Arbequina olives, lemon juice and zest, parsley, sherry vinegar, pepper, and salt, Mix on low until fully combined, another minute or so, then taste and adjust the seasoning as desired.

Spoon into a serving bowl, drizzle with the remaining 2 tablespoons olive oil, and garnish with the chilli, olives, and mint. Serve immediately with Papo Seco or crackers and store any leftovers tightly covered in the refrigerator for up to 1 week.

BACALHAU AL FORNO (OVEN-BAKED SALT COD)

Whereas the Bacalhau de Vóvó (page 141) results in an appetizer-ready spread, this Portuguese preparation is more of a complete one-pan meal, served straight from the oven with the fish left in large pieces next to chunky peppers, onions, and potatoes, all doused with roasted garlic and charred lemon. Don't shy away from the generous amount of olive oil in this rustic recipe—it's necessary to carry and mingle all the flavors in the dish and will result in an excellent sop-up for a good piece of bread. Don't forget to give the salt cod a good soaking.

1 pound salt cod

³/₄ cup extra-virgin olive oil

1 head garlic, top cut off to expose the individual cloves

1 green bell pepper, seeded and sliced into ¹/₂-inch rings

1 red bell pepper, seeded and sliced into ¹/₂-inch rings

1 Spanish onion, sliced into ¹/₂-inch rings

1 teaspoon salt

1 tablespoon soy sauce

2 tablespoons sherry vinegar

¹/₂ teaspoon smoked paprika

1 teaspoon freshly ground black pepper

1 pound Boiled Potatoes (page 184), sliced ¹/₂ inch thick

3 small tomatoes, halved

¹/₄ cup dry white wine

1 lemon, halved

4 ounces Portuguese linguiça, chouriço, or Spanish chorizo, sliced into ¹/₂-inch-thick coins

Small handful of green or black Portuguese olives (see page 296)

Put the cod in a nonreactive container and cover with cold water by 2 inches. Cover and refrigerate for 12 hours. Discard the water, cover the cod with fresh cold water, and refrigerate for another 12 hours. Repeat this process over the course of 3 days, until the cod has had a total of 6 soaks.

Preheat the oven to 400°F.

Heat ¹/₄ cup of the olive oil in a 10-inch cast-iron pan over medium-high heat. Add the garlic, cut-side down, followed by the bell peppers and onion. Cook, stirring occasionally, until the vegetables brown a bit, about 5 minutes. Remove from the heat and add the salt, soy sauce, sherry vinegar, smoked paprika, and black pepper and stir to combine. Pour into a bowl and set aside.

Add ¹/₄ cup of the olive oil to the same pan and place over medium-high heat. Lay down a bed of potatoes in the pan, then lay the fish on top, skin-side up. Arrange the onion and pepper mixture over and around the fish, making sure to use all the liquids in the bowl, and add the tomatoes, wine, and lemon to the pan. Transfer to the oven to roast. After about 10 minutes, scatter the sausage around the pan and return to the oven. Continue to roast until the peppers and onions have wilted down a bit and the fish is fully cooked, 15 to 20 minutes total. When done, remove from the oven, squeeze the warm lemon and garlic all over, and garnish with olives. Serve immediately.

SALADE DE TAU-FU COM CHATCHINI DE BACALHAU (SOFT TOFU SALAD WITH CRISPY GOLDEN SALT COD "CHUTNEY")

**SERVES 4
AS AN
APPETIZER
OR A LIGHT
SUMMER MEAL**

Usually referred to simply as chatchini, the golden, turmeric-infused chatchini de bacalhau dourado Maquísta (Macanese golden salt-cod chutney) is an interesting preparation similar to that of pork rousong (also called pork floss, see page 297).

When the salt cod is cooked correctly, the result is a light, feathery, flavorful floss. When the coconut water has evaporated from the coconut milk (which will take some time), the milk breaks, leaving behind its lovely coconut oil, in which the muscle fibers of the fish can fry as you stir and stir until they become separated and golden. The finished product should be slightly crunchy, and you should be able to pick it up with your fingers like a dip of chewing tobacco (only way tastier!). Generally, chatchini is a garnish for plain rice; here we serve it with a simple chilled tofu salad.

1 pound soft silken tofu

3 tablespoons Chinkiang black vinegar

4 tablespoons tamari

2 tablespoons dark soy sauce

1¹/₂ tablespoons honey

³/₄ cup water

1 whole seedless cucumber, halved and thinly sliced

¹/₄ cup Chatchini de Bacalhau (page 148)

1 bunch cilantro, stems and leaves, coarsely chopped into 1-inch pieces

1 fresh red chilli, seeded and julienned

2 green onions, unicorn-cut (see page 27)

1 tablespoon Ginger Achar (page 41)

¹/₂ cup roasted and salted Spanish peanuts

2 tablespoons extra-virgin olive oil

Salt

OPTIONAL GARNISH

Various fresh herbs and flowers

Small lettuces, torn into pieces

Cherry tomatoes, halved

Baby carrots, thinly sliced

Radishes, thinly sliced

Baby turnips, quartered or thinly sliced

Put the tofu in a small bowl and let sit to remove excess water. Set aside.

Combine the vinegar, tamari, dark soy sauce, honey, and water in a small bowl and mix thoroughly.

Use a spoon to divide the tofu among 4 plates or bowls. Distribute roughly two-thirds of the soy mixture over the tofu, then garnish with the cucumber, Chatchini de Bacalhau, cilantro, chilli, green onions, Ginger Achar, and peanuts. Drizzle with the olive oil, the remaining soy mixture, and any of the optional garnishes, then season to taste with salt. Serve immediately.

>> continued

CHATCHINI DE BACALHAU
(CRISPY GOLDEN SALT COD CHUTNEY)

MAKES ABOUT 3/4 CUP

8-ounce piece salt cod

1/2 cup coconut, olive, or peanut oil

1/2 small Spanish onion, diced

2 cloves garlic, minced

1 fresh red chilli, seeded and minced

2 teaspoons ground turmeric

1 tablespoon Filipino cane vinegar

1 (13.5-ounce) can coconut milk

Salt

Put the cod in a nonreactive container and cover with cold water by 2 inches. Cover and refrigerate for 12 hours. Discard the water, cover the cod with fresh cold water, and refrigerate for another 12 hours. Repeat this process over the course of 3 days, until the cod has had a total of 6 soaks.

Pour 2 quarts of water into a wok and bring to a boil over high heat. Add the fish and reduce the heat to a simmer. Poach until the fish begins to flake and is fully cooked through, about 5 minutes. Drain the water and let the fish cool. Remove all skin and bones from the fish and break up the flesh into flakes.

Heat a wok over high heat until it begins to smoke and add 2 tablespoons of the coconut oil. When melted and hot, add the onion, garlic, and chilli and cook, stirring, for about 30 seconds. Add the turmeric and stir for about 30 more seconds to bloom. Add the cane vinegar, coconut milk, and remaining 6 tablespoons oil and bring to a boil. Add the salt cod and return to a boil. Reduce the heat to medium-high and cook, stirring constantly with a wooden spoon. The mixture will begin to bubble (be careful that the sugars and the gelatin from the ingredients do not stick and burn to the bottom–they surely can, so use your wooden

spoon to scrape the bottom to keep things moving). After 15 to 20 minutes of stirring and scraping, the mixture will begin to separate and the oil will start to foam over. Continue stirring. When you see foam start bubbling on the surface you are getting close; the foam is an indicator that the moisture from within the ingredients is evaporating. Using a slotted spoon or spider, frequently check the status of your chatchini. This is where most people chicken out, but keep going! You should see more foam as you continue to use your wooden spoon to check for stiff and separate golden threads. When the chatchini is crisp and golden, immediately pour the oil and the chatchini through a fine mesh strainer into a heatproof container to prevent any risk of burning the chatchini. Press all the absorbed oil out of the chatchini with the spoon through the strainer. If you are nervous about the doneness you can always recombine the oil and chatchini to take it a bit further. Crispy is key! You are looking for crispy and golden; the color will deepen after drying a bit. Transfer the chatchini to a paper towel-lined sheet pan and spread out with chopsticks. Season with salt. Let cool fully, then store, tightly covered at room temperature, for up to 1 month.

IN A PREPARED WOK BRING 2 QUARTS OF WATER TO A BOIL.

PLACE SOAKED AND DRAINED SALT COD IN TO WATER AND TURN HEAT TO LOW. POACH UNTIL FISH BEGINS TO FLAKE AND IS FULLY COOKED THROUGH.

REMOVE FROM WATER TO COOL. DISCARD WATER.

REMOVE ALL SKIN AND BONES FROM COOKED SALT COD AND BREAK UP INTO FLAKES.

IN A PREPARED WOK ADD 2 TABLESPOONS OIL, ONION, CHILLI, AND GARLIC.

SWEAT BRIEFLY, THEN ADD TURMERIC, AND LET IT BLOOM

ADD COCONUT MILK AND REST OF THE OIL.

BRING IT TO A BOIL, THEN ADD THE SALT COD.

NOW IT IS TIME TO STIR! USE A WOODEN SPOON AND STIR CONSTANTLY.

THE MIXTURE WILL BEGIN TO BUBBLE. KEEP STIRRING!!

BE VERY CAREFUL THAT THE INGREDIENTS DO NOT STICK TO THE BOTTOM AND BURN. USE YOUR WOODEN SPOON TO SCRAPE THE WOK AND KEEP THINGS MOVING.

AFTER ABOUT 15 TO 20 MINUTES OF STIRRING AND SCRAPING, THE MIXTURE WILL BEGIN TO SEPARATE, AND THE OIL WILL RISE.

KEEP STIRRING! ONCE YOU SEE FOAM START BUBBLING ON THE SURFACE YOU ARE GETTING CLOSE.

USING A SLOTTED SPOON OR SPIDER, FREQUENTLY CHECK THE STATUS OF YOUR CHATCHINI.

HERE IS WHERE MOST PEOPLE CHICKEN OUT, BUT KEEP GOING! YOU SHOULD SEE MORE FOAM. KEEP USING YOUR SLOTTED SPOON TO CHECK FOR STIFF, SEPARATED GOLDEN THREADS.

 ONCE YOU ARE THERE, IMMEDIATELY POUR THE OIL AND THE CHATCHINI THROUGH A FINE-MESH STRAINER INTO A HEAT PROOF CONTAINER. DON'T LET IT BURN!

 WITH A SPOON, PRESS ALL ABSORBED OIL OUT OF THE CHATCHINI THROUGH THE STRAINER.

 TRANSFER CHATCHINI TO A PAPER TOWEL-LINED SHEET PAN AND SPREAD OUT THE PIECES WITH CHOPSTICKS.

SEASON WITH SALT AS DESIRED. IT SHOULD BE RELATIVELY SALTY.

"PORTUGUESE" BARBECUED CLAMS

This is our version of a plate of beautiful clams we found at the night market on Jonker Street in Malacca. They're simply steamed with a fiery, garlicky, smoky, slightly sour sambal that finds its way inside to coat each briny, plump clam. Crisp, fresh cucumbers provide a refreshing contrast to the heat. Served steaming on banana leaves, the dish has a beautiful fragrance that transports us right back to Malacca. Serve alongside Coconut Rice (page 75) or Papo Seco (page 264), with beer or a nice clean white Portuguese wine.

SERVES 2 AS A MAIN, 4 IN A MULTI-DISH MEAL

3 tablespoons Assam Sambal (recipe follows)

2 pounds Manila or littleneck clams, purged

GARNISH

1/2 English cucumber, seeds removed and cut into bite-size chunks

Small handful of laksa leaves (also known as rau ram or Vietnamese coriander)

Combine the Assam Sambal and clams in a covered wok or heavy pot with a lid and bring to a boil over high heat. Steam until all the clams are just opened.

Discard any clams that don't open. Transfer the clams to a serving bowl and reduce the sauce until thick and chunky, 2 to 3 minutes; pour over the clams. Garnish with the cucumber and laksa leaves and serve.

ASSAM SAMBAL

1/2 cup dried red chillies

1 cup water

1/4 cup peanut oil

1 tablespoon Balichão (page 260)

1 large onion, minced

6 cloves garlic, minced

1 tablespoon tomato paste

2 tablespoons sweet soy sauce

1/2 cup Tamarind Extract (page 285)

2 ounces palm sugar (see page 296), grated

2 tablespoons Filipino cane vinegar

1 teaspoon salt

MAKES 2 CUPS

Preheat the oven to 350°F.

Spread the dried red chillies on a baking pan and roast until darkly toasted, about 5 minutes. Transfer to a small bowl. Bring the water to a boil in a wok and pour just enough water over the chillies to cover them. Soak for 30 minutes, then puree in a blender or food processor using all the soaking liquid. Set aside.

Heat the oil in a heavy pot over medium heat. Add the Balichão and break up using a wooden spoon, cooking until the Balichão turns deep purple in color, about 1 minute. Add the onions and stir, cooking until

they begin to caramelize, about 3 minutes. Add the garlic and cook until fragrant, about 30 seconds. Add the reserved chilli puree and tomato paste and slowly work into the oil, letting the pastes bloom and the oil separate out, essentially frying the pastes, about 5 minutes. Add the soy sauce, tamarind, and palm sugar and stir, cooking until the sugar is dissolved, about 60 seconds. Add the cane vinegar and salt, stir to combine, and simmer until the sauce is thick. Remove from the heat and cool. Store refrigerated for up to 1 month if not using immediately.

THE CHILLI CLAM

Chinatown restaurants from Chicago through the Northeastern United States have various preparations of the enormous bivalve known as the surf clam. The disappointing fact of the matter, however, is that the clam is almost always overcooked and steamed to death, since the various parts of the clam cook at different rates. In our preparation, we break the clam down and cook the parts separately, reuniting them in the final dish. A single clam makes a nice appetizer for two–split between the shells, you each have your own little shell plates!

1 surf clam, purged and butchered (see below), shells reserved

2 teaspoons salt, plus more to taste

1 bundle dried mung bean noodles (about 1½ ounces)

1 clove garlic, minced

1 tablespoon fermented black beans in brine

¼ fresh red chilli, thinly sliced

¼ piece Lemon Achar (page 38), pulp and pith removed, julienned

3 green onions, white and green parts, shredded (see page 27)

Juice of ¼ lemon

2 tablespoons butter, melted

⅓ cup cornstarch

⅔ cup cornmeal

1 tablespoon extra-hot ground chilli or cayenne pepper

2 teaspoons freshly ground black pepper

2 teaspoons Sichuan pepper (see page 289), ground

1 large egg, beaten with 1 tablespoon water

Peanut oil, for deep-frying

Small handful of cilantro leaves

¼ lemon, dipped in Korean chilli flakes

PROCURING YOUR SURF CLAM You can go about this in one of two ways: put on your clam diggers and head straight for the Northeastern coastline, or go down to Chinatown and locate the store with the cleanest-looking tanks holding all the live shellfish. If you are lucky, you will see one of the biggest bivalves you have ever laid eyes on (unless, of course, you are experienced with the geoduck clam, which is a whole other story). If you don't see any, be brave and ask the shopkeeper if they ever get them, and when they come in. If you run out of luck, find a reputable fishmonger in town and ask them to order you some. When you do find them, alive and kicking is the name of the game–don't let anyone sell you clams with cracked shells, limp tongues hanging out, or a wretched odor. They should be on top of well-drained ice, not sitting in a bin of melted ice, and they should be tightly closed. If they are open, give the shell a tap and they should close up quickly–watch your fingers! Get it home immediately and begin.

PURGING YOUR SURF CLAM Make a cold water bath with a 2 percent ratio (by weight) of sea salt to water and a handful of ice cubes large enough to submerge the clam in. Give the clam a good rinse under running water to remove any debris and sand on the outside of the shell and then put it into the iced saltwater bath. Sprinkle a small handful of cornmeal into the bath (this is a point often debated–some believe that in the purging process the cornmeal will

HOW LONG DOES THIS TAKE?
ASK NOT ME, ASK THE CLAM.

be consumed by the creature, creating excess waste, and some believe it does nothing at all, but we like the cornmeal move because it acts as an abrasive to loosen and trap sand). Allow the surf clam to hang out for at least 30 or up to 45 minutes. And don't get creeped out if your new pet wants to come out and play–between the salt and the cornmeal, this guy will think he's back at Newburyport Beach, so he might thrash about, stick his tongue out at you, and try to spit in your face. Don't let this angry beast scare you, my friend; this vivaciousness is a good sign of the fresh and tasty meal to come.

KILLING AND BUTCHERING YOUR SURF CLAM

The goal here is to make the killing process quick and painless (to both parties). To get this clam open, you need a flexible boning knife, a couple of towels for gripping, a small sheet pan to catch the juices, and a new iced 2-percent saltwater bath for rinsing.

Grip the clam with a towel, making sure the part that opens is facing you. Starting at about the one o'clock position, insert the blade of your knife between the two shells and slice through the adductor muscle holding that side of the shell shut, rotating the clam counterclockwise and continuing to slice along its front lip until you slice through the other adductor muscle on the opposite side. Keep in mind you are not just sawing through the whole thing; rather, you are simply slicing along the seal of the clam and the knife should never disappear into the center of the clam. At this point the top shell should separate from the bottom half.

▶▶ continued

Next, slide your knife gently beneath the clam meat and totally remove it from the shell. Most of the clam is edible. Even though it doesn't look like it now, you will soon see that the individual parts naturally come apart at the seams. Separate the tongue, scallops, and collar and set aside.

Give your cutting board a wipe with the saltwater and place the tongue on the board. This large, meaty bit is the shape of Africa or Brazil, depending on which way you look at it, and has some fatty guts in the belly. This part can be delicious on smaller clams but can hold sand in a larger specimen; best not to chance it, so carefully run the back of your knife blade away from the tip of the tongue to remove the guts. Discard them and set the tongue aside.

Wipe your board with saltwater and place the collar on it. Remove and discard the brown membrane lining the collar and slice off and discard the siphon at the end of the collar.

The scallops should be good; simply inspect for sand and rinse in saltwater as needed.

Give all the clam parts a rinse in the salted ice water to remove any sand, then rinse the shells inside and out. It's super important to remove all traces of sand, as it will ruin the final dish.

Clean your cutting board well, eliminating all traces of sand and grit. Wipe with the saltwater, then place the collar back on the board. Slice horizontally and vertically into four even pieces and set aside. Slice the scallops into pieces similar in size to the collar. Set aside with the collar and tongue.

BUTCHERING THE SURF CLAM

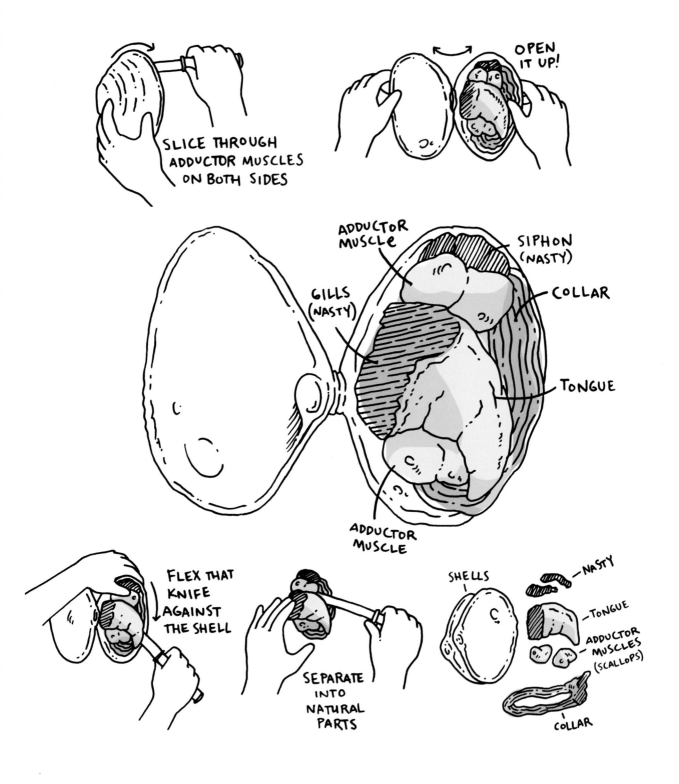

SLICE THROUGH
ADDUCTOR MUSCLES
ON BOTH SIDES

OPEN
IT UP!

ADDUCTOR
MUSCLE

SIPHON
(NASTY)

COLLAR

GILLS
(NASTY)

TONGUE

ADDUCTOR
MUSCLE

FLEX THAT
KNIFE
AGAINST
THE SHELL

SEPARATE
INTO
NATURAL
PARTS

SHELLS

NASTY

TONGUE

ADDUCTOR
MUSCLES
(SCALLOPS)

COLLAR

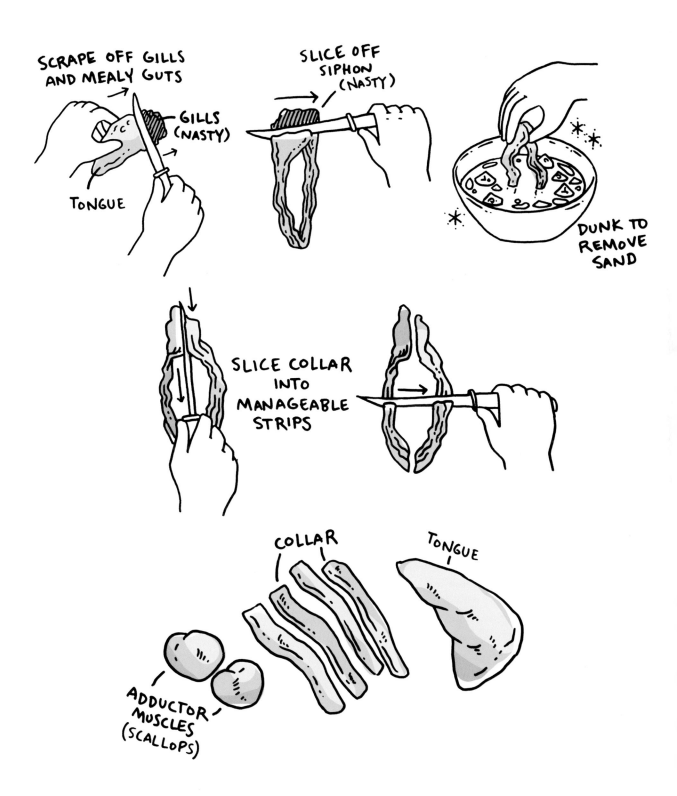

SCRAPE OFF GILLS AND MEALY GUTS

GILLS (NASTY)

TONGUE

SLICE OFF SIPHON (NASTY)

DUNK TO REMOVE SAND

SLICE COLLAR INTO MANAGEABLE STRIPS

COLLAR

TONGUE

ADDUCTOR MUSCLES (SCALLOPS)

ATTACK OF THE CHILLI CLAM!

COOKING THE CHILLI CLAM Fill a wok one-third full with water, add 1 teaspoon of the salt, and bring to a boil over high heat. Prepare an ice bath of fresh water.

Quickly blanch the mung bean noodles until tender, about 30 seconds, and shock in the ice water. Remove, drain well, and reserve in a small bowl.

Blanch the clam tongue for 10 seconds, then immediately shock in the ice water. Remove, pat dry, and transfer to a clean cutting board.

Blanch the clam shells for 1 minute, shock in the ice water, pat dry, and set aside. Reserve the blanching water.

Slice the blanched tongue diagonally into long thin strips and set aside on a cool, dry plate.

Combine the noodles with the garlic, black beans, chilli, Lemon Achar, green onions, lemon juice, butter and a pinch of salt in a bowl and mix well to incorporate. Divide the mixture between the two shells. Rub the sliced tongue in the bowl you used to mix the noodles to pick up the last bits of flavor and place on top of the noodles in the shells. Place the shells in a bamboo steamer and set aside.

In a medium bowl, combine the cornstarch, cornmeal, cayenne, remaining 1 teaspoon salt, black pepper, and Sichuan pepper and whisk to fully combine. Put the egg wash in a separate bowl. Dunk the clam collar and scallop slices into the egg wash. Shake off excess wash and toss the clam pieces in the cornmeal mixture, pressing firmly so the breading coats the clam pieces well. Shake off any excess and set aside.

Heat 2 inches of oil to 375°F in a small pot over high heat.

Bring the blanching water in the wok back to a boil over high heat.

Get ready, this is going to go fast!

Place the steamer basket in the wok (make sure the boiling water does not come through the bottom of the steamer basket) and steam for 45 to 60 seconds. You want to gently heat the tongue and the noodles through–do not commit bivalve sin of overcooking! Use your fingers to sense the heat inside the noodles.

While the tongue steams, drop the collar and scallop pieces into the hot oil and fry until golden brown and crisp, 30 to 45 seconds. Transfer to a paper towel-lined plate and season with salt.

Transfer the steamer basket with the shells and noodles to an attractive plate and top the shells with the fried collar and scallops. Top with the cilantro and chilli lemon. This dish should be enjoyed immediately, even if you are standing next to the stove with chopsticks and a beer–it will disappear quickly, but savor it–and reflect on all the hard work you just put in for a few bites of a damn good clam!

FILL THE WOK ONE-THIRD FULL WITH WATER, ADD SALT, AND BRING TO A BOIL OVER HIGH HEAT.

QUICKLY BLANCH THE MUNG BEAN NOODLES UNTIL TENDER (ABOUT 30 SECONDS).

30 seconds

SHOCK THEM IN ICE WATER. REMOVE, DRAIN WELL, AND RESERVE IN A SMALL BOWL.

BLANCH THE CLAM TONGUE FOR 10 SECONDS, THEN IMMEDIATELY SHOCK IN ICE WATER.

10 seconds

REMOVE, PAT DRY, AND TRANSFER TO A CLEAN CUTTING BOARD.

BLANCH THE CLAM SHELLS FOR 1 MINUTE, SHOCK, PAT DRY, AND SET ASIDE.

1 minute

SLICE THE BLANCHED TONGUE INTO LONG THIN STRIPS ON THE DIAGONAL AND SET ASIDE ON A COOL, DRY PLATE.

COMBINE THE NOODLES WITH THE GARLIC, BLACK BEANS, CHILLIES, LEMON ACHAR, SCALLIONS, LEMON JUICE, BUTTER, AND A PINCH OF SALT IN A BOWL AND MIX WELL TO INCORPORATE.

DIVIDE THE MIXTURE BETWEEN THE TWO SHELLS.

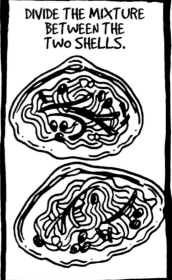

RUB THE SLICED TONGUE IN THE BOWL YOU USED TO MIX THE NOODLES TO PICK UP THE LAST BITS OF FLAVOR AND PLACE ON TOP OF THE NOODLES IN THE SHELLS.

PLACE SHELLS IN A BAMBOO STEAMER AND SET ASIDE.

DUNK THE CLAM COLLAR AND SCALLOP SLICES IN THE EGG WASH.

SHAKE OFF EXCESS WASH AND TOSS THE CLAM IN CORNMEAL BREADING, PRESSING FIRMLY SO THE BREADING COATS THE CLAM PIECES WELL. SHAKE OFF EXCESS AND SET ASIDE.

HEAT A COUPLE OF INCHES OF OIL TO 375°F IN A SMALL POT OVER HIGH HEAT.

BRING BLANCHING WATER IN WOK BACK TO A BOIL OVER HIGH HEAT.

GET READY, THIS IS GOING TO GO FAST!

PLACE YOUR STEAMER BASKET IN THE WOK (MAKE SURE THE BOILING WATER DOES NOT COME THROUGH THE BOTTOM OF THE STEAMER BASKET) AND STEAM FOR 45 TO 60 SECONDS.

45 seconds

YOU SIMPLY WANT TO HEAT THE TONGUE AND THE NOODLES THROUGH. DO NOT OVERCOOK!

30 seconds

WHILE THE TONGUE STEAMS, DROP THE COLLAR AND SCALLOP PIECES INTO THE HOT OIL AND FRY UNTIL GOLDEN BROWN AND CRISP, ABOUT 30 TO 45 SECONDS.

TRANSFER TO A PAPER TOWEL-LINED PLATE AND SEASON WITH SALT.

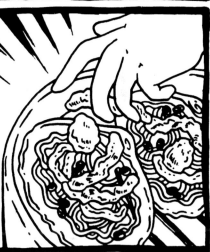

TRANSFER THE ENTIRE STEAMER BASKET BOTTOM WITH THE SHELLS AND NOODLES TO AN ATTRACTIVE PLATE AND TOP WITH THE FRIED COLLAR AND ADDUCTOR MUSCLES.

TOP WITH CILANTRO AND CHILLI LEMON.

CURRY CRAB

SERVES
4 TO 6

Curry crab is a popular item in coastal regions from Africa to Indonesia, but it is prized especially in Macau. There are variations in the types of curries employed, from the bright, thick "Portuguese" Curry Sauce (page 272) to thinner, darker, spicier Indian-style curries. We land in between with our adaptation of a crab curry we enjoyed from a Malaccan streetside stall. A coconut milk base, spiked with sweet curry powder, makes a rich, aromatic, and satisfying dish. Seek out the biggest, most lively, and handsomest Dungeness crabs for this recipe. Avoid small blue crabs because they don't have a ton of meat, and you will spend the entire evening swimming around in the sauce trying to find a piece of meat. And serve with cold beer, claw crackers, and gloves, or at least a big pack of travel tissues like they sell you tableside in Malaysia.

1 large Dungeness crab, still alive

1 Spanish onion, finely diced

1 (1-inch) piece fresh ginger, peeled and minced

2 cloves garlic, minced

^{1}/$_2$ cup plus 2 tablespoons peanut oil

2 whole star anise

1 tablespoon cumin seeds

6 dried red chillies

12 curry leaves

1^1/$_2$ tablespoons Malacca Sweet Curry Powder (page 280)

2 teaspoons ground turmeric

1 (13.5-ounce) can coconut milk

2 cups Chicken Stock (page 282)

2 teaspoons sugar

1 tablespoon fish sauce

Juice of 1 lime

4 small shallots, quartered

1 fresh green chilli, sliced into ^{1}/$_4$-inch pieces

1 fresh red chilli, sliced into ^{1}/$_4$-inch pieces

3 green onions, white and green parts, cut into 1-inch pieces

1 lime, cut into wedges

Start with a live crab. It must be alive! Leave the rubber bands on the claws.

Scrub with a clean brush to remove any sand or nasty bits from the top shell and underside of the crab. Rinse well under water. Place a cutting board in a sheet pan to catch all of the liquid from inside the crab (there is good flavor in there!). Place the crab on the board bottom-side up. Using a cleaver, cut straight through the crab shell right between the eyes to split the crab in two. Fast and hard, quick and painless is the name of the game here. Remove both pieces of the split abdomen flap, flip over, and remove both pieces of top shell. Underneath the top shell you will find some grayish brown gills; remove them by pinching them off with your fingers. Discard the abdomen flaps and gills and set the top shell pieces aside. You now have two halves of crab. Using the tip of your cleaver, cut through the main part of the body following the seams between the legs. Continue until you have separated all of the legs and claws with pieces of the body attached to them. Next, using the back of your cleaver, go through all the legs and claws and give the thick-shelled parts (that is, the bigger legs and claws) a quick crack to promote even cooking, sauce absorption, and easy eating. Remove the rubber bands from the claws and transfer the claws to a plate with the top shell pieces. Drain and strain the crab juices collected on the cutting board and pan and reserve.

Combine the onion, ginger, and garlic in a food processor and puree. Set aside.

Heat ^{1}/$_2$ cup of the peanut oil in a wok over high heat, then add the star anise, cumin, dried chillies, and curry leaves. Cook until the spices start to pop, about 30 seconds, then add the onion puree and cook, stirring constantly, until the moisture has been removed and things start to brown, about 5 minutes. Add the curry powder and turmeric and stir until the oil separates back out from the ingredients, about 3 minutes. Add the coconut milk and stock and stir to incorporate. Bring to a boil and stir in the prepared crab and any reserved crab juice; cover the wok to steam for about 8 minutes, until the meat is firm and opaque throughout.

Uncover the wok and transfer the smaller pieces of crab to a serving platter, leaving the claws and carapace top shell halves to cook longer as the sauce reduces over high heat to a coating consistency, about 5 minutes, stirring constantly. Transfer the claws and carapace top shell halves to the serving platter. Season the sauce with the sugar, fish sauce, and lime juice, and pour over the cooked crab.

Quickly wipe out the wok and return to high heat. Add the remaining 2 tablespoons peanut oil, then add the shallots, fresh chillies, and green onions. Stir-fry until the chillies and green onions have softened but are still vibrant, about 1 to 2 minutes. Pour over the top of the crab and garnish with the lime wedges. Serve immediately.

CAMARÃOES COM CARIL DE QUIABO E TOMATE (SHRIMP CURRY WITH OKRA AND TOMATO)

SERVES 2 AS A MAIN, 4 IN A MULTI-DISH MEAL

This classic Macanese curry was most likely borne of Goa, India, and brought along as okra made its way to South China and Southeast Asia. As with the empada (page 126), this recipe was inspired by a curried shrimp-daikon dish prepared for us by Florita Alves during a visit to Macau. Her expert technique and her husband Vitor's homemade curry paste made it one of our favorite dishes of that trip. In our version, we swap the daikon for okra, then make a robust and spicy broth from the shrimp shells, our rendition of Vitor's curry paste, and tomato, all cooked down to a rich gravy. In the wintertime, substitute poached daikon for the okra, just like we had at Florita and Vitor's house. Serve with Coconut Rice (page 75) or Papo Seco (page 264).

12 large head-on, shell-on shrimp

5 tablespoons extra-virgin olive oil

1¹/₂ cups water

2 teaspoons salt, plus more to taste

¹/₂ red onion, thinly sliced

1 clove garlic, thinly sliced

4 tablespoons Vitor's Curry Paste (page 278)

¹/₂ cup whole peeled tomatoes

8 ounces okra

Freshly ground black pepper

¹/₂ teaspoon sugar

5 cherry tomatoes, halved

Juice of ¹/₂ lime

Small handful fresh cilantro

Peel and devein the shrimp, reserving the heads and shells. Set the shrimp aside.

Heat a heavy pot over high heat and add 2 tablespoons of the olive oil. Add the reserved shrimp heads and shells. Use a wooden spoon to continually mash up the heads and sauté until pink and browned, about 5 minutes. Add the water, bring to a boil, and reduce the heat to simmer for 10 minutes. Remove from the heat, strain, and set aside.

Heat a wide sauté pan over high heat. Add 2 tablespoons of the olive oil, then the season the shrimp with salt and lay evenly in the pan. Sear on one side for 1 minute, then flip and cook on the other side for 1 more minute. Focus on a good sear–don't worry about cooking them all the way through here.

Remove to a plate and add the remaining 1 tablespoon olive oil to the pan. Add the onion and garlic and cook until lightly browned, about 3 minutes. Add the curry paste and reduce the heat to medium. Cook, stirring, to bloom the spices for 1 minute. Add the reserved shrimp stock, the salt, and the whole peeled tomatoes; smash the tomatoes up with a wooden spoon. Bring to a simmer, then add the okra and a couple cranks of black pepper. Stir and cook for 5 minutes, adjusting the heat as necessary to maintain a steady simmer, until the okra is tender but still vibrant. Add the sugar, cherry tomatoes, lime juice, and reserved shrimp and heat through, about 1 minute to finish cooking the shrimp. Taste and adjust the seasoning, then transfer to a serving platter, garnish with the cilantro, and serve.

7

AVES

BIRDS

Many of Macau's most famous dishes are built on poultry. It seems that there is a place of origin for every poultry preparation in Macau: Macanese chicken, Portuguese chicken, Malaysian chicken, and African chicken. As with meat, every piece of the animal is used, from the blood and *miudos* (giblets) to the feet, which are especially beloved by the Chinese mainlanders. You find chicken feet puffed and steamed with curry or soy-based master sauce in local *yum cha* (dim sum) houses in upper Macau. Down on Hac Sa Beach you can get a grilled bird and eat it while you relax seaside, drinking a beer and watching people windsurf. Poached and curried chicken wings are the base for sublime noodle soups in Coloane. The more upscale Macanese and Portuguese-style restaurants serve the world-famous

Galinha à Africana ("African" Chicken, page 171) and Pok Kok Gai ("Portuguese" Chicken Curry, page 181). Duck also plays a big role, with Pato De Cabidela (Duck Cooked in Blood, page 187) being the best known, along with Duck with Lotus, Duck with Tamarind, and Duck with Balichão–not to mention Salted Waxy Duck as a huge source of flavor in the heavy Tacho (Macanese Boiled Dinner, page 209). Roast pigeon and goose are quite popular, but other game bird preparations are fairly rare. However, there are chicken dishes made to taste like game, such as Galinha en Molho de Perdiz, literally translated as "chicken in partridge sauce," with a deep, gamey flavor coming from the use of the bird liver in the sauce. Even our heroic Galo can't get a better piece of chicken than the recipes that follow!

葡莱

THE ADVENTURES OF

FAT RICE

FIREBIRD

GALINHA À AFRICANA

("AFRICAN" CHICKEN)

Galinha à Africana is one of the original dishes from Fat Rice's opening menu, evolving from a simple plate of hot, skewered drumsticks to a more elaborate dish involving the whole smoky bird under a rich and spicy coconut-tomato sauce, garnished with herbs, cornichons, olives, and chilli lemons, and served with smoky thrice-cooked potatoes.

Galinha à Africana isn't from Africa per se (you'll see similar, related dishes elsewhere: *frango assado* in Brazil, chicken *cafreal* in Goa, piri piri chicken in Portugal, and peri peri chicken in South Africa), though this original recipe of Macau was heavily inspired by its creator's visit to Mozambique in the 1940s. While there, the Macanese chef Americo Angelo learned of piri piri chicken, a spicy grilled chicken dripping with a sauce made with *piri piri*, aka *peri peri*, aka bird's-eye chillies. Americo brought this inspiration back to Macau and created a version of his own with a coconut-rich sauce: Galinha à Africana. Its spicy and rich flavor was and still is wildly popular in Macau, and just before Americo passed on to that great spicy kitchen in the sky in the late 1970s, people clamored to get his recipe (Americo was good at keeping secrets—he had a special,

deeply yellow spice and herb mix blended specifically for this dish in a Macanese spice shop, the owner of which was sworn to secrecy). Luckily our friend Manuela Ferreira, the owner of Restaurante Litoral in Macau, was let in on the secret; Americo had trained under her grandmother at Pousada de Macau way back when, and in a gesture of appreciation and good culinary karma, he gave young Manuela his blessing to reproduce his secret dish in her future restaurant.

Back in Chicago—at the time, never having tasted Manuela's version—we needed to develop our own recipe, so we built on an Indian-style butter chicken sauce from our X-marx days as a basic foundation of flavor. We removed the cream and added coconut milk, along with more regionally appropriate spices, finely ground peanuts, and coconut powder. We take the dish back to its roots by grilling the chicken on our wood-burning grill before saucing it (rather than broiling, as is done in Macau). After finally getting to taste Manuela's version, we're happy to report that the flavor of ours isn't vastly different. So hopefully, you will enjoy and Manuela (and Americo!) will be proud.

>> continued

GALINHA A AFRICANA

SERVES 2
AS A MAIN,
4 IN A
MULTI-DISH
MEAL

1 whole chicken

1 cup Galinha à Africana
Marinade (page 175)

8 cups Galinha à Africana
Sauce (page 173)

GARNISHES

Generous handful of
chopped fresh herbs
(such as parsley, cilantro,
and mint)

Assorted olives
(Portuguese, of course!)

Lemon wedges dusted
with Korean chilli flakes

Cornichons

TO SERVE

Thrice-Cooked Potatoes
(page 173)

To prepare the chicken, using kitchen shears, cut the backbone out of the chicken. Reserve for Chicken Stock (page 282) or another use. Place the chicken flesh-side down on a cutting board and, using a cleaver or heavy knife, carefully split the chicken in half through the keel bone (breast bone). Rub the chicken with the marinade and refrigerate, tightly covered, for 24 hours.

Get a charcoal grill going hot and heavy until the flames burn down and you are left with raging white-hot coals. (Alternatively, you can heat a gas grill over high, we suppose.) Place the chicken on the grill, breast-side up, and cover with the lid. Cook until the bones on the bottom of the chicken are dark brown and starting to char, 10 to 15 minutes. Flip the bird and continue to cook until the skin is dark brown, crispy, and starting to char–but not burnt! This could take anywhere from another 10 to 20 minutes. When the chicken is done (inner-thigh area cooked to an internal temperature of 155°F), remove from the grill and let rest on a cutting board, about 5 minutes.

Heat the sauce while the chicken rests. Cut the chicken into 6 to 8 serving pieces and place on a heatproof serving dish. Coat generously with the sauce and broil for 5 to 10 minutes, until the sauce begins to brown, thicken, and become bubbly. Then, add the garnishes, and serve alongside the potatoes.

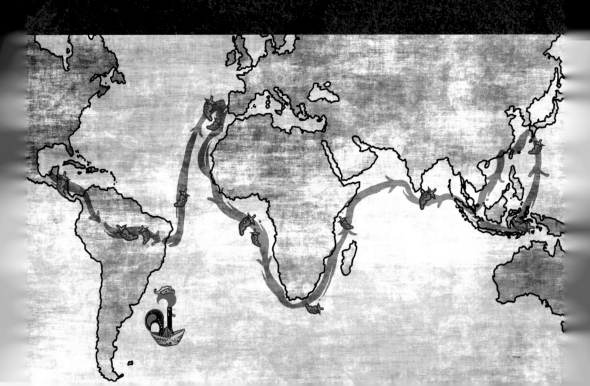

GALINHA À AFRICANA SAUCE

5 tablespoons
unsalted butter

2 bay leaves

1 Spanish onion, diced

1 (2-inch) piece fresh
ginger, peeled and
minced

8 cloves garlic, minced

½ stick cinnamon, ground

1 teaspoon ground
coriander

1 tablespoon
sweet paprika

2 tablespoons sambal
oelek, or more to taste

2 cups Chicken Stock
(page 282) or water

1 cup coconut milk

1 (14-ounce) can whole
peeled tomatoes

1 tablespoon sugar

2 teaspoons salt

2 cups roasted peanuts,
coarsely ground

⅓ cup coconut powder
(see page 293)

**MAKES
ABOUT
8 CUPS**

Melt the butter in a heavy pot over medium-high heat and add the bay leaves and onions. Cook until the onions are translucent and lightly caramelized, about 5 minutes. Add the ginger and garlic and cook until aromatic, about 30 seconds. Add the cinnamon, coriander, and paprika and cook for another 30 seconds. Add the sambal and cook for 2 more minutes. Add the stock, coconut milk, tomatoes with their juices, sugar, and salt; stir to incorporate and lower the heat to a simmer. Cook for about 20 minutes, until the sauce has reduced and thickened a bit. Remove the bay leaves, add the peanuts and coconut powder, and puree using an immersion or standing blender until smooth. Cool and refrigerate for up to 1 week.

THRICE-COOKED POTATOES

IF YOU NEED MORE THAN
4 QUARTS OF WATER TO COVER
THE POTATOES, INCREASE THE
GARLIC, THYME, AND SALT
ACCORDINGLY.

2 pounds Yukon gold
potatoes

1 head garlic, peeled

12 sprigs thyme

¼ cup salt, plus more
to season

Peanut oil, for frying

¼ cup Molho de Aziete,
aka Mojo (page 270),
for serving

**SERVES 4
AS A SIDE
DISH**

Cut each potato lengthwise into 6 relatively equal wedges and put in a heavy pot along with the garlic, thyme, salt. Add 4 quarts of water, making sure the potatoes are covered by the water. Bring to a boil over high heat, then lower to a simmer and cook until a paring knife inserted into a potato can be removed with little resistance. This will happen about 10 minutes after a simmer is reached. Be careful not to overcook the potatoes. Remove the potatoes from the water and lay in a single layer on a rack over a sheet pan to cool.

Heat 2 to 3 inches of the oil in a wok to 375°F. Working in batches so as not to drop the temperature of the oil too drastically, fry the potatoes until golden brown, about 2 to 3 minutes, and transfer to a paper towel-lined plate.

Heat a grill to about medium heat and grill the potatoes for 3 to 5 minutes per side, just until grill marks appear and the skin begins to crisp. Season with salt and serve with a generous dressing of mojo.

GALINHA À AFRICANA MARINADE

1½ teaspoons whole Sichuan pepper (see page 289)

½ cinnamon stick

1 teaspoon coriander seeds

2 teaspoons black peppercorns

3 tablespoons sweet paprika

1 tablespoon extra-hot ground chilli or cayenne pepper

1 bunch cilantro

12 cloves garlic

Juice of 1 lemon

¼ cup fish sauce

3 tablespoons sambal oelek

⅓ cup coconut milk

2 tablespoons hot sauce (Portuguese *piri piri* or your favorite)

MAKES
1 CUP

Grind the Sichuan pepper, cinnamon stick, coriander seeds, and black peppercorns into a fine powder in a spice grinder. Combine with the paprika, cayenne, cilantro, garlic, lemon juice, fish sauce, sambal oelek, coconut milk, and hot sauce in a blender and blend on high speed until smooth. Refrigerate for up to 1 week if not using immediately.

>> continued

MACAU ROAST PIGEON

**SERVES 4
AS AN
APPETIZER**

Roasted squab is a popular Cantonese dish, but it has also found its niche in Macau, where it appears at streetside barbecue stalls, casual eateries, and "soy sauce Western" restaurants (*si-ya`u sai chaan*), a category of restaurant that appeared on the scene in 1950s Hong Kong, and blends Shanghainese-Russian and Cantonese-British foodways. Soy sauce Westerns are relatively fancy, white-tablecloth affairs. Classic dishes include smoked pomfret, borscht, and soufflés the size of your head.

Another thing—this *ain't* really roasted. It's deep-fried! For our version, we marinate the birds in a strong Ceylon tea, star anise, and cinnamon, along with maltose (see page 295) for a lacquer sheen. Look for "New York-dressed" squab at a Chinese grocer or a local butcher; it will just be plucked, with the head still on and the innards intact. It's essential to get the bird in this condition; if it is cleaned and split open, you won't be able to puff air between the flesh and skin to crisp it up.

2 New York-dressed squab

BRINE

8 cups water

1½ tablespoons baking soda

2 tablespoons salt

MARINADE

12 cups water

4 tablespoons loose Ceylon tea

1 (2-inch) piece fresh ginger, sliced ¼ inch thick

2 whole star anise

4 cinnamon sticks

1 tablespoon whole Sichuan pepper (see page 289)

1.1 pounds (1½ cups) maltose

1½ cups tamari

4 quarts peanut oil, for deep-frying

TO SERVE

8 teaspoons salt

4 teaspoons Five-Spice Powder (page 280)

Quartered lemons dipped in Korean chilli flakes

To prepare the squab, using a small knife or scissors, gently make the smallest incision possible to widen the squab's anal opening, just large enough to fit your index finger inside. Slowly and carefully use your finger to remove the bird's innards. Be sure you get everything: the heart, giblet, liver, kidneys, intestinal tract, and anything else you find in there—but be careful not to rupture anything or tear the skin. Gently rinse the bird inside and out, then be sure to get all the water out from inside. Find the incision on the bird's neck from its slaughter, and insert a straw between the skin and flesh along its wishbone until it is securely inside the bird by about 1 inch. Do not pierce the skin with the straw! Securely grasping the straw and bird

around the neck in order to prevent air from coming back out of the neck incision, blow into the straw until you see the skin inflate like a balloon and the legs stretch out in a comical manner. Place in a large, non-reactive container and repeat with the second bird.

To prepare the brine, in a large bowl, mix together the 8 cups water, baking soda, and salt until dissolved. Pour over the squabs to submerge and refrigerate for at least 6 hours, and up to 24 hours. Brining will plump, season, and tenderize your majestic bird.

When you are ready to continue, set a pan on the bottom shelf of your refrigerator and clear out enough room for the squab to hang. Bring a large pot of water to a boil over high heat.

▸▸ continued

Make the marinade in another pot. Combine the 12 cups water, tea, ginger, star anise, cinnamon sticks, Sichuan pepper, maltose, and tamari in a medium pot and bring to a boil over high heat. Remove from the heat and let steep for 10 minutes. Strain and discard the solids, return the liquid to the same pot, and bring the marinade back to a boil.

Remove the birds from the brine and loop a 1-foot piece of twine around each bird's neck. Working with one squab at a time, blanch by dunking them into the boiling marinade mixture for 20 seconds, then remove from the marinade and hang in the refrigerator by tying the loose ends of the twine around the rack above the pan you've set on the shelf. Repeat with the other bird. Brush both birds with some of the remaining marinade, then let hang and dry overnight.

Heat the oil in a large Dutch oven over high heat to 350°F. Working one at a time, deep-fry the squab in oil. If the squab is not fully immersed, use a wok ladle to baste it with the hot oil and use the twine to rotate and flip the bird as needed. When the bird is deeply browned and has an internal temperature along the thigh of 160°F, it is done, 3 to 4 minutes. Transfer to a paper towel–lined plate to drain excess oil, and repeat with other bird. To serve, in a small bowl, combine the salt and five-spice. When both birds are cooked, use a cleaver to swiftly hack the bird into 6 to 8 pieces and serve immediately with the lemons and the mixed five-spice and salt for dipping.

PORTUGUESE CHICKEN

FROM **FAT RICE**

(a cross-section)

chicken thighs
CRUSTED in COCONUT

olives
STRONG and PUNGENT

bread crumbs
CRISPY and DELICATE

potato
GOLDEN and MOUTHWATERING

coconut curry sauce
MILD and FLAVORFUL

spanish chorizo
SPICY and SAVORY

carrots
SWEET and TASTY

PO KOK GAI
("PORTUGESE" CHICKEN CURRY)

This is our take on one of the most famous and recognized restaurant dishes of Macau. As with Galinha à Africana (page 171), the name can be misleading–you'd be hard-pressed to find this dish of chicken thighs braised in coconut milk, turmeric, and preserved lemon back in Portugal, for sure. In traditional Macanese cookery, there are many chicken curries stewed with potatoes, coconut milk, turmeric, and other spices. Some of these recipes include souring agents such as tamarind, tomatoes, or lemon. It's easy to imagine that these dishes were based on the Indian and Goan chicken and potato curries the Portuguese encountered before reaching Macau, which might help explain the name. The curious hallmarks of the modern-day dish–Portuguese chouriço, olives, and hard-boiled eggs–were likely added much later, by clever twentieth-century restaurateurs who either wanted to make the dish more "exotic" for Chinese tourists or more "Portuguese" for visiting Portuguese dignitaries.

Our first exposure to Po Kok Gai came at a *cha chaan teng*, and it was a bad experience: the diner was dirty, the kitchen used evaporated milk and a cheeselike substance instead of coconut milk to cut costs, and they made the dish without chouriço or olives. We knew there was more to the dish, but in the beginning, this was an extremely simple dish for us. We threw some potatoes, chouriço, and olives

▶▶ continued

into our curry, but wanted more mojo out of the dish, so we drew inspiration from restaurants in Macau like Restaurante Litoral and Amagao. Their more developed renditions fulfilled the dish's potential, and we realized that we wanted to make it more of an event. We added Lemon Achar (page 38) because it was a refined way to add the lemon element we found in our Macanese recipe books, included evaporated milk and good cheese in acknowledgment of its history in the *cha chaan teng*, and kept the coconut milk to represent its origins. We heavily caramelized the top, enriching the dish like we found at Litoral and Amagao. And finally, one dark and stormy night, we threw in some hard-boiled tea eggs and croutons fried in chicken fat, adding the final over-the-top textural element that had been missing.

Another important piece of our history with Po Kok Gai is that it brought Sarah Becan, whose lovely illustrations grace the pages of this book, to us. We'd only been open a short time; she came in and ate our Po Kok Gai. Later that night we got an email from her–attached to which was her artist's interpretation of the dish, expressed as a cross-section of the clay pot it comes in. Her talent blew us away, and it was revelatory in that it was one of the first times we realized we were getting through to people with this food. She's been illustrating things for us ever since.

PO KOK GAI

3 tablespoons coconut oil

¼ Spanish onion, julienned

¼ green cabbage, cored and cut into 1-inch squares

½ teaspoon salt

2 tablespoons water, plus more as needed

2 tablespoons extra-virgin olive oil

4 cups "Portuguese" Curry Sauce (page 272)

1 pound Boiled Potatoes (page 184)

5 medium carrots, peeled, diagonally sliced, and poached (see page 25)

Galinha Bafassa (Turmeric Baked Chicken, page 184)

½ Lemon Achar (page 38), julienned

1½ cups shredded semi-firm Portuguese or Dutch cheese (such as São Jorge or young Gouda)

4 Tea Eggs (page 277), halved

½ cup coconut powder (see page 293)

1 cup dried and cured Portuguese chouriço or Spanish chorizo, sliced ¼ inch thick

½ cup good black Portuguese olives (see page 296)

1 cup Chicken Fat Croutons (page 261)

Coconut Rice (page 75), for serving

½ cup parsley and mint leaves dressed with juice of ½ lemon (optional)

Heat the coconut oil in a large, heavy pot over medium-high heat. When melted, add the onions and sauté until translucent, a few minutes. Add the cabbage and salt, stirring to coat the cabbage with the oil. Add the water, reduce the heat to low, cover the pot, stirring as needed to keep the cabbage from sticking to the bottom of the pot, and cook for 15 to 20 minutes. The goal is for the cabbage to soften, but retain a slight crunch. Spread out on a clean sheet pan to cool while preparing the rest of the dish.

Preheat the oven to 375°F. Rub the oil all over the bottom and sides of a 9 by 13-inch baking dish.

Heat the curry sauce in a small saucepan over medium heat until warm. Whisk until smooth and

thin with a splash of water if necessary—you want a béchamel sauce consistency.

Layer the ingredients in the prepared baking dish in the following order: reserved cabbage, potatoes, carrots, chicken, and lemon. Ladle the warmed curry sauce evenly over everything, place the dish, uncovered, in the oven, and bake until heated through, about 30 minutes.

Remove the dish from the oven and sprinkle with the cheese. Nestle in the eggs, yolk-side up, and dust with the coconut powder. Add the chouriço, olives, and croutons. Bake for 15 minutes, until the cheese is melted. Serve hot from the oven with the rice and fresh herb salad.

>> continued

BOILED POTATOES

МAKES
I POUND

**MAKES
I POUND**

1 pound Yukon gold
potatoes, peeled

1 head garlic, cloves
peeled and crushed

6 sprigs thyme

2 tablespoons salt

Put all of the ingredients in a heavy pot and add
8 cups cold water, making sure the potatoes are
covered by the water.

*IF YOU NEED MORE WATER TO COVER THE POTATOES,
INCREASE THE GARLIC, THYME, AND SALT ACCORDINGLY.*

Bring to a simmer over high heat, then lower the heat
to maintain a steady simmer and cook until a paring

knife inserted into the potato can be removed with
little resistance, 10 to 15 minutes after a simmer is
reached. Be sure not to overcook the potatoes—you
want to be able to slice them without much crum-
bling. Remove the potatoes from the water and lay
them on a sheet pan to cool. Store, covered in the
refrigerator, for up to 3 days, or use immediately.
Cut into ½-inch slices when ready to use.

GALINHA BAFASSA
(TURMERIC BAKED CHICKEN)

SERVES 4

1 (1-inch) piece fresh
ginger, peeled and thinly
sliced

4 green onions, white
and green parts, cut
into 1-inch pieces and
flattened with the side of
a knife or cleaver

¾ cup Shaoxing rice wine
(see page 297)

2 teaspoons Malacca
Sweet Curry Powder
(page 280)

1 tablespoon ground
turmeric

1 tablespoon Filipino
cane vinegar

1½ teaspoons salt,
plus more to taste

3 pounds bone-in,
skin-on chicken thighs

Combine the ginger, green onions, Shaoxing wine,
curry powder, turmeric, vinegar, and salt in a bowl
and mix well. Add the chicken and toss to coat,
then transfer to a zip-top bag. Refrigerate for at least
8 hours.

Preheat the oven to 350°F.

Remove the chicken from the marinade, discard
the liquid, and pat the chicken dry with paper
towels. Place the chicken skin-side up in a baking
dish just big enough to hold it all in one even layer.
Add water until the liquid reaches a third of the way
up the side of the chicken; make sure the skin stays
dry. This will ensure that the skin will render some

fat and get crispy. Set in the oven and roast until the
chicken reaches the internal temperature of 150°F,
about 45 minutes. Remove from the oven and let cool
completely.

If you'd like to refine things and debone the
thighs, be sure to remove the small piece of cartilage next to the bone (the bones can be frozen and
added to fresh chicken bones when making stock,
page 282). Strain the juices and refrigerate until the
fat has solidified. Save the fat for Chicken Fat Croutons
(page 261), and save any liquids for "Portuguese"
Curry Sauce (page 272). Keep the thighs refrigerated
for up to 3 days until ready to use.

PATO DE CABIDELA
(DUCK COOKED IN BLOOD)

SERVES 2
AS A MAIN,
4 IN A
MULTI-DISH
MEAL

Cabidela is a preparation known throughout the Portuguese-speaking world in which animals such as suckling pigs, rabbits, chickens, and ducks are stewed in a rich broth of stock, wine, vinegar, garlic, and most importantly, the animal's own blood, which thickens the braising liquid and adds a deep richness to the dish. To keep the blood from coagulating, we mix it with vinegar and add it right at the end of the cooking process, heating it through gently as it thickens the sauce. The version most popular in Macau, and what we serve at Fat Rice, is the duck version (*pato* meaning "duck" in Portuguese). We've added smoked bacon where uncured pork belly is traditionally used and include the familiar Macanese touches that give a bit of the exotic: turmeric, cinnamon, cumin, coriander, and tamarind, and garnish with racy green olives, lemon, and fresh cilantro to balance the dish out. This is commonly a whole animal preparation, but we simplify things by using only duck legs. You could certainly use a whole quartered duck if you like, but the breast and legs cook at different rates; treat accordingly. If you are feeling adventurous and you have access to a live duck, you can drain and reserve its blood for the final preparation; you won't otherwise be able to find duck blood for sale anywhere. More commonly, you can substitute pork or chicken blood; check the Asian markets and see what they've got. This rich, tangy, and savory combination of vinegar and blood dressing the fatty duck meat can also go into a risotto-like dish called Arroz de Cabidela de Pato, where the duck meat is shredded and combined with sauce and cooked rice.

4 whole duck legs

4¹/₂ teaspoons salt, plus more to season

2 cloves garlic, crushed

1 bay leaf

1 sprig thyme

1 (750-ml) bottle dry red wine

3 whole cloves

4 dried red chillies

1 teaspoon cumin seeds

1 tablespoon coriander seeds

1 teaspoon ground turmeric

¹/₂ cinnamon stick

2 teaspoons Filipino cane vinegar

1 small onion, grated

¹/₄ cup lard

¹/₄ pound bacon, cut into lardons

¹/₂ cup Tamarind Extract (page 285)

4 cups Chicken Stock (page 282)

1 tablespoon soy sauce, plus more if needed

5 fingerling potatoes, halved lengthwise and poached (see page 25)

3 medium carrots, peeled and cut into ¹/₂-inch pieces and poached (see page 25)

1 turnip (Japanese, tabletop, or daikon radish), peeled and cut into ¹/₂-inch pieces and poached (see page 25)

Freshly ground black pepper

Small handful green Portuguese olives (see page 296)

1 cup duck blood (or substitute pork or chicken blood)

2 tablespoons unsalted butter

Salt and freshly ground black pepper

TO GARNISH

¹/₄ cup finely chopped fresh cilantro

¹/₂ fresh red chilli, sliced

1 tablespoon thinly sliced Lemon Achar (page 38) or the finely grated zest of 1 lemon

▸▸ continued

Aves

Place the duck in a nonreactive bowl and rub with the salt, garlic, bay leaf, and thyme. Pour in half of the wine, then cover and refrigerate for at least 8 and up to 12 hours.

Remove the duck from the marinade (reserve the marinade) and pat dry with paper towels. Set aside.

Grind together the cloves, dried chillies, cumin, coriander, turmeric, and cinnamon to a fine powder. Transfer to a small bowl and add 1 teaspoon of the cane vinegar to form a paste. Stir in the grated onion and set aside.

Heat the lard in a large Dutch oven over medium heat. When melted and hot, lay the duck legs in the pot skin-side down. Cook for 7 to 10 minutes, letting the skin brown and the fat render out. Flip and brown on the flesh side, another minute or so. Remove the duck and set aside. Add half of the bacon to the pot and cook until brown and starting to crisp, about 5 minutes. Add the spice paste and reduce the heat to medium-low. Stir, cooking until the oil takes on the color of the spices, 5 to 7 minutes. Add the reserved marinade, remaining wine, tamarind, stock, and soy sauce and increase the heat to medium-high. Return the duck to the pot and bring to a boil. Then cover, reduce the heat to a simmer, and cook until the legs are tender, but the meat is not yet falling from the bone, 1¹/₂ to 2 hours.

When the duck is cooked through, remove the legs from the braising liquid and set aside in a warm place, covered with aluminum foil. Discard the garlic, bay leaf, and thyme. Remove the fat from the liquid by skimming with a ladle or using a gravy separator. Bring to a boil over high heat and reduce the liquid by about half.

Meanwhile, put the remaining bacon in a large pan and place over medium heat. Cook until the bacon starts to brown and the fat has rendered out, 4 to 6 minutes. Add the blanched vegetables, season with salt and pepper, stir to coat the vegetables with the fat, and cook until warmed through. Add the olives, remove from the heat, and set aside.

Combine the blood with the remaining 1 teaspoon cane vinegar in a blender and blend well. When the sauce has reduced, add the blood mixture, bring to a gentle simmer, then quickly remove from the heat. (Don't hammer things here, lest the blood coagulate!) Add the butter and whisk into the sauce off the heat until fully incorporated.

To serve, arrange the legs on a platter. Top with the sauce, arrange the vegetables alongside, and serve immediately, garnished with the cilantro, sliced fresh chilli, and Lemon Achar.

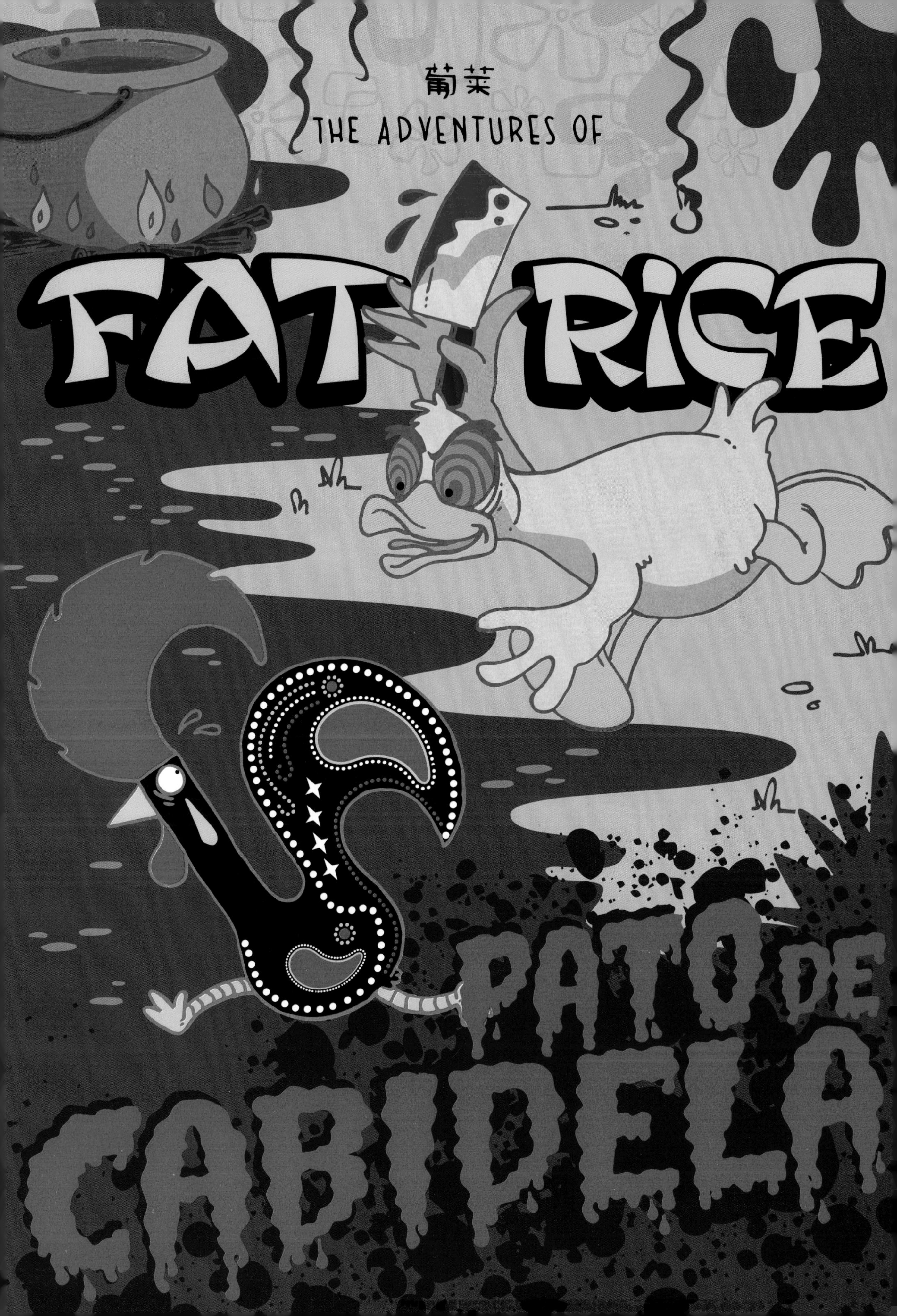
葡菜
THE ADVENTURES OF
FAT RiCE
PATO DE CABIDELA

8

CARNES

MEATS

Long before snout-to-tail was a trend, generations before us knew no other way than to use every piece of the animal. This is still the case all over Asia, and in the "wet markets" of Macau, there are dozens of animal (mostly pig) butchers who source from small farms that sell only one or two animals per day. Both Portuguese and Chinese people worship the pig in all of its gastronomic glory, and don't waste any of it in the kitchen. Under the dim red lamps of the wet markets, each piece of the animal is carefully parsed out and displayed for the customer who is looking for the exact piggy part needed. Some of the popular cuts are feet, ears, shank, belly, shoulder, and ribs.

Beef and veal are next in line in terms of popularity, but these meats are really saved for the most special of occasions since they are quite costly

cuts usually flown in from Australia. Popular cuts are tongue, brisket, tripe, oxtail, and even hooves, which are used to make a special, restorative sweetened port wine-scented gelatin. Lamb and goat are seldom seen—for the most part, the southern Chinese palate finds the flavor too strong. Game meats, however, were abundant in the early days of Macau's settlement, and we have come across a handful of recipes for pheasant, quail, and rabbit. Many Macanese dishes showcase several different types of meat—Diabo (page 221), Arroz Gordo (page 69), and Tacho (page 209), for example. This meaty extravagance and penchant for comingling different animals is one of the main reasons (along with the amazing flavor profiles) we were drawn to this cuisine in the first place.

PORCO BALICHANG TAMARINDO

(PORK BRAISED WITH TAMARIND AND BALICHÃO)

For us, learning about the history and cultures behind food is one of the most important parts of cooking. Porco Balichang Tamarindo is an example of this; not only do the roots of its family tree run deeply through many regions, but it also shares an ancestor with the common pickling method of *escabeche*. Well before the Portuguese set out on their voyages, a dish called *al-sikbaj* (from the Middle Persian word *sik*, meaning "vinegar") was brought to the Iberian Peninsula during the Moorish conquests. This dish preserved cooked meat or fish in a highly acidic, sweet, and flavorful liquid. Ultimately, this dish would morph into two separate things: *escabache*, the name of the technique as it has come to be known in Portugal today, and Carne de Vinha d'Alhos (Meat with Wine and Garlic). Carne de Vinha d'Alhos has spawned many dishes of pork braised in acidic ingredients throughout the Portuguese provinces (and elsewhere). In Goa, the tellingly named Vindaloo (surely an adaptation of Vinha d'Alhos) stews meat with vinegar in place of wine and adds chillies. Malaysia's Babi Assam replaces the vinegar with tamarind and is deepened by the *belachan* (shrimp paste). Though spread far geographically, these interpretations of the original Carne de Vinha d'Alhos always maintain the crucial essence of a familiarly indulgent pork braise, balanced with sour and savory flavors.

Porco balichang tamarindo is the sweet-and-sour dish of Macau, well rounded with succulent pork belly

braised in a mixture of sour tamarind, deeply sweet jaggery, and funky, fragrant balichão. This was the first family-meal dish we prepared and served each other during Fat Rice's infancy. We were amazed that such potent ingredients created such a simple and well-rounded dish, and we knew we had to put it on the menu. From there, it evolved during travels in Portugal; we found ourselves perched atop the highest point in Lisbon in a tiny, humble restaurant whose chef was of Portuguese, Goan, and Mozambican descent. We ordered his version, Balchão de Porco (similar to balichang, with dried, salted shrimp–*balchão*–used as a flavoring agent), and found all of the familiar components: sweet and porky, backed up with that unmistakable shrimp funk. However, he incorporated warm nuances of spices such as cinnamon, cumin, and clove and included a blast of capsicum (chilli) heat, giving more depth of flavor and taking the dish in a different direction than we'd ever tasted before. This was a whole new world. In the same spirit of curiosity and expansion, these ingredients have found their way into our version.

You can use a high-quality Malaysian shrimp paste in place of the balichão if you are short on time and don't have the three months necessary to age it, but it is so worth it to make the *chão* (check out "Balichão: An Odyssey" page 257). As with most braises, this is great the next day, as the mojo just keeps on building.

>> continued

PORCO BALICHANG TAMARINDO

SERVES 2
AS A MAIN,
4 IN A
MULTI-DISH
MEAL

2 tablespoons lard
or peanut oil

¼ cup Balichão
(page 260)

4 cloves garlic, minced

1 (1-inch) piece fresh
ginger, peeled and
minced

2 tablespoons Balichang
Masala (recipe follows)

4 cups Pork Stock
(page 283) or water

¾ cup Tamarind Extract
(page 285)

6 ounces palm sugar or
jaggery (see pages 296 or
295 respectively), grated
(about 1 cup)

2 pounds Salt-Cured
Pork Belly (page 195)

GARNISHES

¼ pineapple, peeled and
cut into bite-size pieces

Small handful of fresh
cilantro, coarsely
chopped

1 fresh red chilli,
thinly sliced

2 whole shallots,
cut into eighths

4 Arroz Carregado Frito
(page 195)

Put the lard and Balichão in a medium-size Dutch oven over medium heat. Continuously stir with a wooden spoon; as the pot heats, the Balichão will start spattering and popping, turning from a grayish-purple color to a more golden hue, about 1 to 2 minutes. At this point, add the garlic, ginger, and masala and stir constantly as they become aromatic, about 1 minute. Be careful here—it is crucial that it does not burn, so have your stock or water ready and close at hand. Once the spices are fragrant, add the stock and stir. Be sure to scrape anything on the bottom of the pot up into the liquid before proceeding.

Add the tarmarind and palm sugar and bring to a simmer, stirring until the sugar dissolves. Add the pork belly and bring back to a simmer. Cover the pot, lower the heat to low—just enough to maintain a simmer—and braise until the pork is tender, about 2 hours. Alternatively, you can place the covered Dutch oven into a 300°F oven and cook for roughly the same amount of time. The most important thing here is that the pork and its skin become tender and easily pierced with a chopstick. Remove from the heat and let cool slightly. Garnish with the pineapple, cilantro, chilli, and shallots and serve the Arroz Carregado Frito on the side.

BALICHANG MASALA

MAKES
ABOUT
¼ CUP

Masala is a South Asian word for a spice blend that we use in several places in this book. This is our list of spices for Porco Balichang Tamarindo as developed after our trip to Lisbon.

5 dried red chillies

2 teaspoons cumin seeds

1 tablespoon coriander
seeds

2 whole cloves

½ cinnamon stick, broken
into small pieces

1 tablespoon
black peppercorns

1 teaspoon ground
turmeric

Grind all of the ingredients to a fine powder in a spice grinder or mortar and pestle. Use immediately or store tightly covered at room temperature for up to 3 months.

SALT-CURED PORK BELLY

THE AMOUNT OF SALT USED DEPENDS ON THE WEIGHT OF THE PORK BELLY. WE USE 1.25 PERCENT OF THE PORK BELLY WEIGHT. THIS RECIPE IS WRITTEN FOR 2 POUNDS OF PORK, SO IF YOU USE MORE OR LESS, ADJUST THE SALT ACCORDINGLY. AROMATICS AREN'T AS EXACT— BULK UP AS DESIRED.

0.4 ounce (2¼ teaspoons) salt

1 sprig thyme, leaves stripped and stem discarded

5 cloves garlic, lightly crushed with the side of a cleaver

1 small yellow onion, diced

2 pounds pork belly, skin on, cut into 1½-inch cubes

MAKES ABOUT 2 POUNDS

Combine the salt with the thyme leaves, garlic, and onion. Rub all over the pork belly. Store in a sealable plastic bag, refrigerated, overnight or up to 3 days.

Remove the pork from the bag and discard all other ingredients and any liquid. Rinse and dry the pork and use as directed in the recipe.

ARROZ CARREGADO FRITO (FRIED RICE CAKE)

Arroz Carregado is the traditional accompaniment to Porco Balichang Tamarindo, wherein glutinous (sticky) rice is pressed into a dense cake with green onions and lard and served at room temperature. For our version, we take fragrant coconut jasmine rice, press it, deep-fry it, and top it with green onion for a crispy accompaniment to the soft and tender braise. You can use whatever mold you want to shape these—just be sure to keep things even in size! We use a vacuum sealer for maximum pressure, so at home, be sure to use five or six heavy bricks or a small child to press the rice.

MAKES 4 RICE CAKES

4 cups Coconut Rice (page 75), still warm

Peanut oil, for deep-frying

Salt

4 green onions, white and green parts, fisheye-cut (see page 27)

Line an 8 by 4-inch loaf pan with plastic wrap and fill with the warm rice. Cover with a layer of plastic wrap, then place a similarly sized container on top of the plastic. Weight down with something heavy and refrigerate overnight.

Heat 2 to 3 inches of oil in a heavy pot to 400°F. Remove the rice cake from the pan and cut into

4 equal-size pieces, approximately 4 by 2 inches in size. Cooking them one at a time, gently slide a cake into the oil and fry until golden brown, about 2 minutes. Transfer to a paper towel-lined plate, season with salt, and keep in a warm spot while cooking the rest. When all the cakes have been fried, transfer to a serving dish, top with the green onions, and serve.

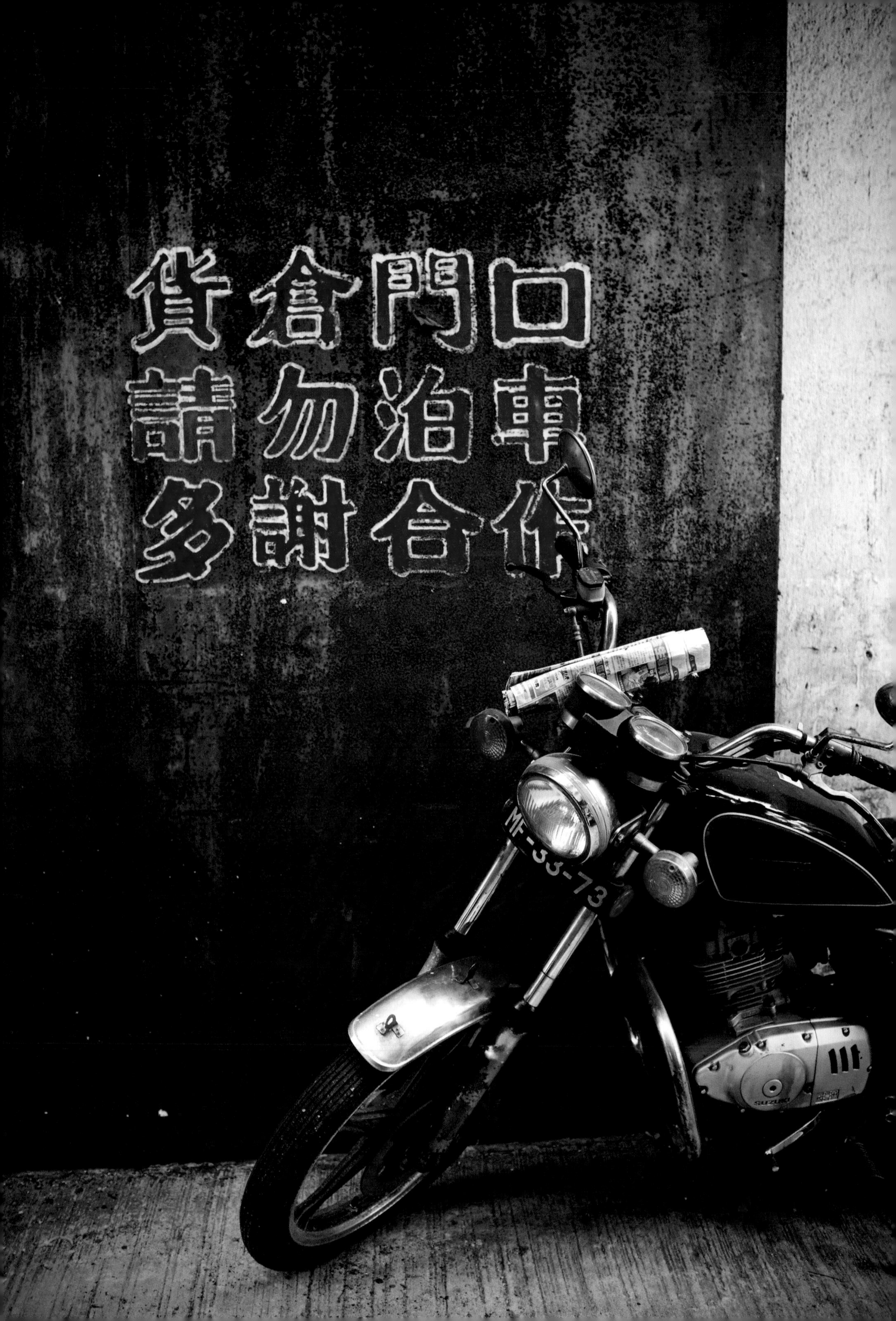
貨倉門口
請勿泊車
多謝合作
MF-33-73

PORCO BAFASSA (SMOTHERED AND ROASTED TURMERIC PORK SHOULDER)

Bafassa is a super-tender pork roast with a tinge of acidity balancing its high fat content. The Portuguese words *abafar* ("smothered") and *assar* ("to roast") combine to create the word *bafassa*, a combination term from Lingu Maquista, the Macanese creole Patuá, a seldom-heard (even in Macau) and endangered language that combines Portuguese, Chinese, and Malay dialects. Rather than the usual sear-then-braise method, our bafassa is braised first and seared just before serving, creating a nice crust. A Macanese lady who came to the restaurant told us that she actually has served Bafassa as an accompaniment to Arroz Gordo (page 69)!

SERVES 6 TO 8 IN A MULTI-DISH MEAL

2 tablespoons Filipino cane vinegar

4 teaspoons ground turmeric

4 tablespoons lard

15 cloves garlic, minced

2 green onions, white parts only, fisheye-cut (see page 27)

¼ cup dry Portuguese white wine

¼ cup Chinese glutinous cooking wine (see page 295)

Juice of ½ lemon

2 tablespoons salt

3 tablespoons sugar

2 bay leaves

5 to 6 pounds boneless, fatty pork shoulder, skin on

2 Spanish onions, one julienned and one halved pole to pole and sliced ¼ inch thick with a mandoline

6 cups Pork Stock (page 283)

6 cups Chicken Stock (page 282)

1 pound fingerling potatoes, sliced ¼ inch thick with a mandoline and covered in water

Salt and freshly ground black pepper

1 pound small carrots, unpeeled, scrubbed clean, and sliced ⅛ inch thick with a mandoline

4 ounces purslane or watercress

Mix the cane vinegar and turmeric together to form a paste and set aside. Melt 2 tablespoons of the lard in a saucepan over medium-high heat, add the garlic and green onions, and cook until fragrant, about 60 seconds. Add the turmeric paste and cook until the turmeric is fragrant, another 60 seconds. Add the wines, lemon juice, salt, sugar, and bay leaves; stir once and remove from the heat. Let cool fully, then rub all over the pork. Seal in a bag and refrigerate for 24 hours.

Preheat the oven to 350°F.

Melt the remaining 2 tablespoons lard in a large Dutch oven over high heat. When the lard starts to smoke, add the julienned onion and sauté until softened and just beginning to caramelize. Add 3 cups of each of the stocks and bring to a boil. Put the marinated pork in the pot, then add enough of the remaining stock to leave about ¼ inch of the pork uncovered. Bring back to a boil, then cover and place in the oven to braise until the pork is tender but not falling apart when poked with a chopstick, about 2½ hours. If more time is required, check the pork every 30 minutes or so until done. When done, remove the pan from the oven and cool to room temperature, cooking liquid and all. When cool, cover with parchment paper and a pan or other pot that fits in the pot on top of the pork. Weight this down with a couple of heavy items such as cans and refrigerate overnight.

▶▶ continued

The next day, remove the pork from the liquid and remove its skin using a sharp knife. Slice the pork in half lengthwise, then cut it into rough ³/₄-inch-thick slices and set aside.

Preheat the oven to 375°F. Remove any fat from the pork's cooking liquid and set aside. Puree the liquid with all of the solids left in the pan, strain through a fine-mesh strainer into a saucepan, and bring to a simmer over medium-low heat. Drain the potatoes, pat dry, and set aside.

Heat a wide, lidded sauté pan over medium-high heat. When hot, add a couple tablespoons of the reserved pork fat. Working in batches, sear the sliced pork until brown on both sides and transfer to a rectangular baking dish, shingling the pork on both sides

of the dish. When all of the pork is seared, pour three-quarters of the sauce over the pork and place in the oven to heat through. Meanwhile, give the sauté pan a quick wipe, place over medium-high heat, and add a couple more tablespoons of the reserved pork fat. When the fat has melted, carefully add the potatoes to the pan in one layer, then add the remaining sauce. Season with salt and pepper to taste and give the pan a swirl. Bring to a simmer, add the remaining sliced onion, cover the pan, and cook for about 3 minutes. Add the carrots and purslane to the pan and cover for 1 minute to cook through. Remove the baking dish from the oven and neatly arrange the vegetables in among the pork. Serve immediately.

CAPELA (MACANESE MEAT LOAF)

SERVES 12
IN A
MULTI-DISH
MEAL

The word *capela* has a couple of interpretations, both referring to its circular shape. One is the literal translation of "chapel" from Portuguese. Going further back, though, the root of the word can mean "crown," referring to the round shape of the loaf. Either way, this is the meat loaf to end all meat loaves, loaded with the usual suspects of pork, beef, bread, and bacon, joined by fragrant olives, almonds or pili nuts, and cheese on top. Come on now, you need this in your life.

We used to make it with briny green olives, but after experiencing it in the home of our friend Marina Senna Fernandes in Macau, we realized that the ripe black olives in her version add a lovely sweet fragrance that permeates the whole meat loaf. As for the cheese, in Macau the grassy Azorean cheese São Jorge would be used, but don't sweat it too much: just find a semi-firm cheese that can be grated easily, such as Edam, young Gouda, or mozzarella. We tweak tradition by adding wood ear mushrooms for their snappy texture; the move was inspired by our chef de cuisine at Fat Rice, Eric Sjaaheim, who after an extended trip to Vietnam made us a Vietnamese pork pâté that included wood ears.

When folks talk about Capela in Macau, it always comes back to "Was it dry?" (in the same way we talk about the Thanksgiving turkey here in the States). A moist end product is key, but don't get lured into using super-fatty ground meat to achieve this; leaner meat will result in a more consistent texture. The moisture is provided by the milk-soaked bread, so don't skip that.

At the end of the day, Capela is that classic dish that works all the scenes–great as a party dish, as a home-style family meal dish, or leftovers as a sandwich, pan-fried and topped with an egg. Serve your Capela hot from the oven with something like Stir-Fried Greens with Green Papaya, Mushroom, and Mackerel Pickle (page 110) and Coconut Rice (page 75), and even top it with Portuguese-Style Tomato Sauce (page 271) if you like.

8 ounces good day-old bread, sliced and crust removed

1½ cups milk

⅓ cup olive oil

1 pound yellow onions (about 2), finely diced

2 pounds ground pork (the leaner the better)

2 pounds ground beef (the leaner the better)

6 ounces chouriço or linguiça, minced

½ cup pitted and chopped black olives

1½ cups grated semi-firm cheese

Finely grated zest and juice of 1 lemon

4 eggs, beaten (beat 3 in one bowl and 1 in a separate bowl)

½ ounce wood ear mushrooms, soaked and julienned

2 teaspoons salt

1 tablespoon freshly ground black pepper

¼ cup pine nuts, toasted

¼ cup almonds or pili nuts, toasted and coarsely chopped

6 slices bacon, halved crosswise

➤➤ continued

Preheat the oven to 350°F.

Combine the bread and milk in a bowl and soak for 20 minutes. Remove the bread from the bowl and squeeze to remove excess milk. (Discard the milk.) Tear the bread into rough 1-inch pieces and set aside.

Meanwhile, heat the olive oil in a pan over medium-high heat. Add the onions and cook until they just start to caramelize, 3 to 5 minutes. Set aside.

Combine the pork, beef, and chouriço in a large bowl and mix together well with your hands. Add the olives, 1 cup of the cheese, lemon zest and juice, 3 of the eggs, the mushrooms, salt, pepper, nuts, reserved bread pieces, and cooked onions. Mix well with your hands until thoroughly incorporated. Form the meat into a ball and place in the center of a 10-inch cast-iron pan. Use your hands to push the meat into a ring shape, making sure the top of the meat is even with the rim of the pan and leaving about a 4-inch hole in the center.

Brush the top of the Capela with half of the remaining egg, sprinkle with the remaining ½ cup cheese, and brush again with the last bit of egg. Place the bacon slices center to edge like the hands of a clock evenly around the Capela, then place an oven-safe 4-inch bowl in the hole in the center of the loaf, making sure it's under the peak of the meat so that it catches excess fat that runs off. Put on a parchment paper-lined sheet pan, place in the oven, and bake until an internal temperature of 150°F is reached, about 1 hour and 20 minutes.

Let cool for about 20 minutes, then carefully remove the bowl and discard the collected fat. Slice the Capela into 12 pieces and serve. Wrap any leftovers tightly and store in the refrigerator for up to 1 week.

CHAR SIU
(CANTONESE BARBECUED PORK)

MAKES
ABOUT
3 POUNDS

Char siu means "fork roast" because it was often cooked on skewers. You can find jars labeled "Chinese barbecue sauce" in most markets, but don't buy any of them, because they won't come near approximating the flavors you get when you make it from scratch. The rose wine brings a floral element (note that this is *not* the summertime-and-the-livin'-is-easy *rosé* wine you are thinking of–rather, it is a fragrant, sorghum-based spirit flavored with petals from actual rose flowers), while the fermented bean curd and red yeast rice add a depth of flavor as well as the traditional red color, naturally avoiding red dye no. 5. Maltose gives a sticky texture (if you're having trouble getting the maltose out of the container, throw it in the microwave for 30 seconds or so, until it's nice and free-flowing). Look for a fatty cut of pork shoulder for a more tender end product. We find recipes using oyster sauce or Balichão, but since we use Balichão in so many other places on our menu, we leave it out here. But hey–it's your kitchen, so feel free to funk it up if you're into that.

4 pounds fatty boneless pork shoulder (skin off)

4 teaspoons salt

½ teaspoon pink salt (see page 296)

1¼ cups Char Siu Glaze (page 206), plus more for brushing

Cut the pork into strips approximately 1 by 2 by 6 inches in size and set inside a gallon-size zip-top bag.

In a small bowl, combine the salts, then whisk in the glaze. Pour over the pork in the bag, making sure the marinade is evenly distributed over the pork and getting in there with your hands if necessary. Wash your hands well and seal the bag, squeezing as much air out of it as possible. Refrigerate for at least 24 hours and up to 48 hours.

▸▸ continued

Prepare a charcoal grill to medium heat. Remove the pork from the bag and place directly on the grill. Cook, turning every few minutes, until the pork is charred and has an internal temperature of 145°F. Depending on your grill, this should take about 25 minutes. Brush with extra glaze and let rest for a few minutes, then slice against the grain and serve. Wrap leftovers tightly and refrigerate for up to 1 week.

CHAR SIU GLAZE

**MAKES
2 CUPS**

¹/₂ cup dry white wine

¹/₂ cup rose wine
(see page 297)

¹/₂ cup water

¹/₂ teaspoon freshly
ground white pepper

1 tablespoon fermented
bean curd (see page 293)

2 tablespoons fermented
bean curd juice

1 tablespoon red yeast
rice (see page 296)

¹/₄ cup soy sauce

1¹/₂ teaspoons sweet
paprika

1 teaspoon ground
cinnamon

3 cloves garlic, minced

1¹/₄ cups maltose
(see page 295) or honey

3 tablespoons cornstarch
mixed with 3 tablespoons
water

Pour the wines into a small saucepan and set over high heat. Use caution–the wine can possibly flambé. Reduce the wine to half of its original volume. Add the water, white pepper, fermented bean curd, fermented bean curd juice, red yeast rice, soy sauce, paprika, cinnamon, garlic, and maltose and stir well. Bring to a boil, then lower the heat and simmer for 5 minutes.

Remove from the heat and strain through a fine-mesh strainer. Pour back into the pot, bring to a boil over high heat, then whisk in the cornstarch slurry. Return to a boil, whisking constantly. Remove from the heat and let cool completely before use. Store tightly covered in the refrigerator for up to 1 month.

TACHO
(MACANESE BOILED DINNER)

If we had to choose one recipe that embodies the "East meets West" influences of Macanese cooking, this would be it. It combines the northern Portuguese *cozido*–a boiled meat and *enchido* (sausage) dinner with cabbage, potatoes, and root vegetables–with southern China's cured meats, along with Macanese balíchão. Not dissimilar to France's famed Pot au Feu, Tacho falls in with the hot pot dishes beloved by both the wealthy and the humble, the white collar and the blue; the bourgeois *and* the rebel.

We were taught this quintessential wintertime dish (whose name simply means "pot" in Portuguese) in Macau by our friend Marina Senna Fernandes. It's a hearty braise consisting of chicken, pig trotters, beef, *lap cheong* (Chinese fermented sausage), *lap yuk* (Chinese bacon), and *lap ap* (Chinese cured "waxy" duck), along with Ibérico or Jinhua ham from Yunnan province, all flavored with Balichão (page 260), cumin, coriander, and white pepper. Winter vegetables like cabbage, daikon, and sweet potatoes become mashably soft and supple, and Chinese broccoli or snap peas are added last minute to bring a much welcome freshness to the dish. Our procedure and presentation have been adapted from Marina's; we remove the bones from the duck, make a roulade with the trotters, and the way we prepare the beef differs.

>> continued

She poached lean beef at the end of cooking; we add a seared piece of steak to lend another form of cooked meat texture and visual presentation.

Tacho is also known as Chau-Chau Pele, in which *pele* refers to what we see as the most important part of this multi-component dish: the braised puffed pig skin, which absorbs all the meaty, umami-laced flavors and has a silky almost noodlelike texture that holds all of the cooking broth, releasing it upon first bite. The dried, puffed pig skins are different than chicharrón found in a Mexican grocery; there is no meat or fat on them and they have a bubbly, cobweblike puff from the baking process; look for them in Asian grocers at butcher counters, usually prepackaged in bags. If there is any English on them, they will be labeled "dried puffed pork skins"–but just look at what is inside the package. They must be soaked in water overnight, then blanched in water seasoned with a little bit of salt and vinegar to remove the musty funk that they may have developed.

We've written this recipe as a three-day process, and it's important to follow each step. The blanching and long braise of the *pele* create a soft, deliciously gelatinous texture that allows for maximum absorption. Sometimes noodles are even added to the bottom of the dish to absorb all that delicious liquid.

TACHO

SERVES 6 TO 8

DAY 1: SOAKING

4 hind pig trotters

2 tablespoons salt

6 ounces dried puffed pig skin

DAY 2: BLANCHING AND BUILDING THE BROTH

1 tablespoon coriander seeds

2 teaspoons cumin seeds

1 teaspoon white peppercorns

8 ounces boneless pork shoulder, cut into cubes about 1½ inches square

½ *lap ap* (Chinese salted duck)

4 ounces *lap yuk* (Chinese bacon), skin on

½ green cabbage, 8 whole leaves reserved, remaining cored and cut into 1-inch squares

2 bay leaves

1 large carrot, scrubbed

2 tablespoons Filipino cane vinegar

1 (1-inch) fresh unpeeled piece ginger, sliced

4 green onions, green and white parts, cut into pieces

½ Spanish onion

2 tablespoons salt

DAY 3: TACHO

8 ounces *lap cheong* (Chinese fermented sausage)

6 tablespoons olive oil

2 tablespoons Balichão (page 260)

2 tablespoons julienned Lemon Achar (page 38)

Juice of ½ lemon

½ Spanish onion

2 pounds root vegetables (carrot, sweet potato, turnip, daikon, taro, and so on), peeled, cut into bite-size pieces

1 thick (3-ounce) slice Ibérico, Jinhua, or Smithfield ham

6 Galinha Bafassa (Turmeric Baked Chicken, page 184), halved

2 cups assorted mushrooms cut into bite-size pieces

½ ounce wood ear mushrooms, rehydrated and hard bits removed

6-ounce boneless sirloin or rib-eye steak, about 1 inch thick

Salt

2 tablespoons peanut oil

2 cups Chinese broccoli or snap peas cut into bite-size pieces

4 green onions, green parts only, horse-ear cut (see page 27)

DAY 1 Place the trotters in a nonreactive container. Add cold water to cover and sprinkle the salt over the water. Cover and refrigerate overnight.

Place the puffed pig skin in a nonreactive container. Add cold water to cover, weight down with a plate, and refrigerate overnight.

DAY 2 Make a cheesecloth sachet with the coriander, cumin, and peppercorns. Set aside.

Preheat the oven to 350°F. Bring 6 quarts of water to a boil in an 8-quart pot over high heat and prepare an ice bath of similar size. Meanwhile, remove the trotters from their soaking liquid and discard the liquid. Using a kitchen torch, carefully singe off any hair left on them. Be sure to do this gently so as not to cause the skin to seize up, which will

inhibit proper cooking. Scrape with a small knife or rub with a kitchen towel to remove any burnt hairs, dirt, and so on. Set aside.

Remove the pig skin from its soaking water. Discard the water and squeeze any residual water from the skins. Blanch in boiling water for 2 minutes. Shock in cold water and squeeze out again. Place in a colander to drain excess water. Cut into 2 by 2-inch squares.

Bring the water back to a boil and blanch the trotters for 2 minutes. Transfer the trotters to a colander to drain excess water.

Bring the water back to a boil. Blanch the pork shoulder for 1 minute and transfer to a colander. Pat dry and refrigerate.

Bring the water back to a boil and blanch the *ap ap* (duck) for 1 minute. Transfer to the colander.

Bring the water back to a boil and blanch the *ap yuk* (bacon) for 1 minute. Transfer to the colander. Discard the blanching liquid, rinse the pot, and fill with 3 quarts fresh water. Bring to a boil over high heat.

When cool enough to handle, use a sharp knife to remove the skin from the bacon and reserve. Cut the bacon into ¼-inch slices, pat dry, and refrigerate.

Blanch the cabbage leaves in the fresh boiling water for 30 seconds, then shock in the ice bath and drain well.

Arrange the trotters in a large Dutch oven, making sure they don't overlap. Add fresh water just until the trotters are submerged, then add the bacon skin, bay leaves, carrot, 1 tablespoon of the cane vinegar, ginger, green onions, onion, 1 tablespoon of the salt, and spice sachet. Bring to a boil over high heat, then cover and transfer to the oven.

> continued

Braise for 3 hours, until the skin is soft and bones are poking out.

Remove from the oven and let the trotters cool in the liquid at room temperature until cool enough to handle. Wearing gloves (it's going to get messy here– you don't *have* to wear the gloves, but you might be glad if you do), delicately transfer the trotters to a baking sheet, and remove the bones from the trotters, being careful to keep the skin intact. Reserve the bones and cooking liquid.

To shape the trotter roulade, prepare a new ice bath. Cut a piece of plastic wrap that measures 18 by 12 inches and set on a work surface. Lay the blanched cabbage leaves down in a shingled pattern on the plastic wrap. Carefully lay the deboned trotters skin-side down on the cabbage. Season evenly with the remaining 1 tablespoon salt and 1 tablespoon cane vinegar. Carefully pull the top of the plastic over the trotters and roll to form a log (as in the Minchi Croquettes, page 53) about 1½ inches in diameter.

on the roulade away from you until all the plastic is used, keeping the roulade as tight as possible. Pinch the plastic on both ends of the roulade and roll it away from you. This will twist the ends of the plastic, seal the meat in, and tighten the roulade up. Poke holes with a sterilized safety pin anywhere there are air gaps. Wrap in another sheet of plastic, repeat the process, and cool in an ice bath to solidify. Once cold, remove from the ice bath, keeping the roulade wrapped, and refrigerate overnight.

Return the bones from the trotters to the trotter cooking liquid and add water to cover the bones by 2 inches. Bring to a boil and reduce to a simmer. Add the *lap ap* (duck), return to a boil, then reduce to a simmer and cook for 15 minutes. Remove the duck from the liquid. When cool enough to handle, remove the duck from the bones and slice the meat from the breast, leg and thigh into 1/4-inch slices. Pull any meat from the bones and refrigerate. Return the duck bones to the broth with the trotter bones and bring to a simmer over low heat. Cover and cook for 2 more hours. Strain, discarding the bones, cool to room temperature, and refrigerate overnight.

DAY 3 Pour the reserved broth into a large Dutch oven, bring to a boil over high heat, and reduce to a simmer. Add the *lap cheong* (sausage) and simmer for 10 minutes. Remove the sausage from the liquid, cut diagonally into 2-inch pieces, and refrigerate.

Add the blanched puffed skins to the liquid in the Dutch oven and bring to a boil over high heat. Cover, transfer to the oven, and braise for about 2 hours. Remove from the oven and add the blanched pork shoulder and braise for 1 more hour, until the puffed skins are soft and easily pierced with a knife and the pork shoulder is tender but not falling apart. Remove from the oven and set aside.

Heat 3 tablespoons of the olive oil in a small saucepan over medium-high heat. Add 1 tablespoon of the Balichão and stir, blooming until fragrant and beginning to brown, about 2 minutes. Remove from the heat and let cool. Place in a small serving bowl and top with the achar and lemon juice. Set aside.

Slice the cabbage wrapped trotter roulade into 1/2-inch slices and set aside. Cut off the top and tail of the onion half, peel it, and cut it into 6 pieces from top to bottom. Separate the petals and set aside.

In a separate large Dutch oven, combine the remaining 3 tablespoons olive oil and the remaining 1 tablespoon Balichão. Bloom until the Balichão starts to brown, about 2 minutes. Add the onion petals and cook until soft, about 3 minutes. Add 2 cups of the braising liquid and remove from the heat.

Begin your assembly. Start by placing the root vegetables in an even layer on the bottom of the Dutch oven with the onions and broth. In an even layer, distribute the green cabbage squares on top of the root vegetables. Using a spider, the remove the pork shoulder and braised puffed pig skin from the broth and evenly distribute on top of the vegetables. Place the ham slice on top of the skins. Lay in the chicken thighs on top in a pinwheel pattern. Add the mushrooms in the same pinwheel pattern. Continuing this pinwheel motif, add the *lap cheong* (sausage), *lap ap* (duck) and *lap yuk* (bacon) with the smallest pieces on top. Top with the remaining broth–it should come just to the bottom of the cured meats. Bring to a simmer over medium-low heat and cook, covered, for 45 minutes. (If you feel you have too much liquid, reduce over high heat. It's only going to get better the more water you remove.)

Heat a cast-iron pan or grill over high heat. Season the steak with salt. Add the peanut oil to the pan and sear the steak until rare or medium rare, 2 to 3 minutes per side. Set aside and let rest for 3 to 5 minutes, then slice thinly.

Add the Chinese broccoli to the Tacho, cover, and steam for about 45 seconds, until the stem is tender and vibrant green.

Turn off the heat. Remove the lid, add the sliced trotter roulade, and cover to warm through, only about 20 seconds.

Remove the lid again and garnish with the sliced steak and green onions.

You made it! Serve immediately and enjoy! . . . or go to bed and have Tacho for breakfast.

ZHU PA BAO (MACAU'S FAMOUS PORK CHOP BUN)

The pork chop bun known in China as Zhu Pa Bao is one of Macau's most recognizable Macanese snacks. It's found in many cafés and bakeries around the city and is an assembly of all things simple, unadorned, and beautifully delicious: juicy, tender pork, good bread for soaking up those juices, and finally, a nice bit of bone to gnaw on. What's that? A *bone* in a *sandwich*? Well, in Chicago, we have an expressway-side place called Jim's Original that sells a decent griddled bone-in pork chop sandwich, so the idea of a bone-in sandwich wasn't that crazy to us. In the Zhu Pa Bao, the Portuguese influence is clear—in Portugal's *tascas* (bars) you get beer, Caldo Verde (a traditional Portuguese soup), and a similar sandwich of thinly sliced pork called a Bifana. There, as in Macau, and here in Chicago, you eat it straight-up Earl of Sandwich-style: slap that meat between the bread, shove it in your face, and get on with things! For a special Chicago touch, we add sinus-clearing mustard.

2 cups peanut oil

2 cups lard

1 tablespoon unsalted butter, at room temperature

2 Papos Seco (page 264), split in half horizontally

2 Pork Chops in Brine (page 262)

Sweet and Spicy Mustard (recipe follows), for serving

Heat the oil and lard in a wok over high heat to 375°F. Meanwhile, spread the butter on the inside of the bread and toast.

Remove the pork chops from the brine and pat dry with paper towels. Carefully add the pork chops to the oil and fry for approximately 90 seconds, until golden brown and cooked through. Remove from the oil, shaking off excess oil, and place each pork chop in a roll. If desired, spread the top half of the roll with some mustard or simply serve the mustard on the side. Serve immediately.

SWEET AND SPICY MUSTARD

1/4 cup mustard powder

3 tablespoons cold water

4 teaspoons Filipino cane vinegar

1 tablespoon toasted sesame oil

2 tablespoons soy sauce

4 teaspoons sugar or honey

Whisk the mustard powder with the water in a bowl and let sit at room temperature for at least 30 minutes. Whisk the cane vinegar, sesame oil, soy sauce, and sugar together in a separate bowl until the sugar dissolves. Stir the mustard mixture into the vinegar mixture, taste, and adjust the seasoning as desired. Use immediately or store in an airtight container in the refrigerator for up to 1 month.

SALADA DE ORELHOS DE PORCO (PIG EAR SALAD)

SERVES 3 OR 4

Thinly sliced pig ears served as a salad of sorts is popular in many of Macau's restaurants, from the fancy and straightforward Portuguese restaurants to the home-style spots like the community center APOMAC (Associação dos Aposentados, Reformados e Pensionistas de Macau), to the hole-in-the-wall Burmese restaurants in the street market-rich Three Lamps District. Ours is clean and bright, with a bracing vinaigrette containing chillies, garlic, and Balichão (page 260). The flavors of the vinaigrette and garnish can be changed to your liking but always follow this method for cleaning and cooking the ears; the singeing, soaking, blanching, and braising are key to removing their barnyard funk and achieving the snappy texture.

7 tablespoons salt

2½ pounds pig ears

4 cloves garlic, whole

3 green onions, whole

4 bay leaves

1 teaspoon black peppercorns

1 (2-inch) piece fresh ginger, peeled and sliced ¼ inch thick

1 tablespoon Filipino cane vinegar

GARNISHES

1 carrot, peeled and finely diced

1 stalk celery, finely diced

½ small onion, finely diced

Pig Ear Salad Vinaigrette (page 218)

Small handful of fresh cilantro leaves

Mix 1 gallon of water with 6 tablespoons of the salt in a 2-gallon container and set aside. Using a torch, singe any hair off the pig ears, then rinse well and add to the salted water. Refrigerate for 24 hours–this step removes any residual blood from the ears.

Bring a pot of water to a boil over high heat. Remove the ears from the soaking solution and discard the solution. Blanch the ears in the boiling water for 3 minutes, then strain through a colander, discarding

>> continued

the water. Repeat this process one more time to remove gaminess from the ears.

Put the ears in a stockpot and cover with 6 cups of water and add the garlic, green onions, bay leaves, peppercorns, ginger, cane vinegar, and remaining 1 tablespoon salt. Cover the stockpot with a tight-fitting lid. Bring to a boil over high heat, reduce to a simmer, and braise for at least 1 and up to 2½ hours, checking for doneness by piercing the thickest part of an ear with a small knife. The knife should easily pierce the skin and cartilage–if there is strong resistance, cover the pan, cook for an additional 30 minutes, and check again, repeating this process until the ears are done. Let cool briefly, then strain the liquid through a colander, reserving all braising liquid. Discard all of the solids other than the ears and layer the ears in a loaf pan.

Cover with the braising liquid and wrap the loaf pan in plastic. Place another loaf pan on top of the ears, and weight this pan down with a couple of cans of tomatoes or the like. Refrigerate for 24 hours.

To remove the terrine from the pan, gently heat the bottom of the pan with a blowtorch or over a gas burner, then flip out onto a cutting board. If not using immediately, wrap tightly and keep refrigerated for up to 1 week.

To serve, slice the terrine as thinly as possible, using long strokes with your longest, sharpest knife or an electric slicer if you have one. Serving about 8 slices per person, arrange attractively on individual plates or a larger serving platter if sharing. Combine the carrot, celery, onion, and about 2 tablespoons vinaigrette in a small bowl, and drizzle over and around the slices. Drizzle with more vinaigrette as desired, and finish with the cilantro leaves. Serve immediately.

PIG EAR SALAD VINAIGRETTE

MAKES 1 CUP

1 tablespoon peanut oil (optional, if using Balichão)

1 teaspoon Balichão (page 260, optional)

²/₃ cup Filipino cane vinegar

¹/₃ cup sherry vinegar

2 cloves garlic, minced

1 tablespoon sugar

1 teaspoon sambal oelek

2 teaspoons Chilli Oil (page 274)

¹/₄ teaspoon salt

Pinch of ground white pepper

Heat the peanut oil in a wok over high heat until smoking, add the Balichão, and cook while stirring until light brown in color, about 2 minutes. Let cool, then whisk all of the ingredients together. Store tightly covered and refrigerated for up to 1 week. Whisk before using.

PORCO PO BOLACHO (POWDERED BISCUIT PORK CHOP)

SERVES
2 TO 4

Po bolacho means "powdered biscuit," and refers to a breading for coating thin pork chops and steaks. In some cases (definitely ours), that biscuit is Maria cookies. (If you're gonna deep-fry a pork chop, why not coat it with crushed-up cookies?!) Our Porco Po Bolacho is elemental in Baked Pork Chop Rice (page 82) and the crowning glory of Diabo (page 221), and illustrates the richness and over-the-top-ness of much of Macanese cuisine. Sometimes, Porco Po Bolacho is coated in mashed potatoes, *then* breaded, *then* deep-fried–it's like a state fair in one dish!

Peanut oil, for deep-frying

2 Pork Chops in Brine (page 262), boned and each cut into 8 equal pieces

1¹/₂ cups Po Bolacho Breading (recipe follows)

Heat 2 inches of oil for deep-frying in a wok to 375°F.

Press the pork in the breading, shake off any excess, and fry until golden brown, crisp, and cooked through, about 45 seconds, turning from time to time.

Remove to a paper towel-lined plate and set aside. Slice and use to top Tacho (page 209), Pork Chop Rice (page 82), or just eat it straight up.

PO BOLACHO BREADING

MAKES
2 CUPS

1³/₄ ounces (¹/₄ sleeve) Maria cookies (see page 295)

1 cup panko bread crumbs

Place the cookies and bread crumbs in a food processor and process until fine. Store in an airtight container at room temperature for up to 1 week.

Carnes

DIABO

(DEVIL'S CURRY)

The devil goes by many names and has many faces, and Diabo is an ever-changing enigma that can never be pinned down or exactly replicated. This dish is tricky, as most devils are, but once you master the sauce and technique, you will turn to Diabo time and time again to breathe new life into your leftovers. Diabo arose from the servant kitchens of wealthy Europeans (Portuguese, Dutch, and English) in South and Southeast Asia. After lavish dinner parties held on holidays or special occasions, a variety of roast meats, braises, and curries would be left over. The resourceful cooks, in order to use every last bit of meat and juice, would make Diabo for their families, and it became a Boxing Day tradition.

Versions vary across the Eurasian communities of India, Malaysia, Singapore, and Macau, but a few things remain constant. As a general rule, Diabo is a complex curry with chillies (dry and/or fresh), mustard (seeds, powder, or prepared), vinegar, Worcestershire sauce, and piquant pickled vegetables (such as cucumber, cabbage, ginger, and shallots).

Our first introduction to Diabo was in Cecília Jorge's book *Macanese Cooking*. Her version combines a multitude of leftovers–which could include roast meats (beef, pork, chicken, turkey, or duck), chicken and beef curries, Cantonese *char sui* pork, breaded pork chops (in the Macanese version, considered essential)– with prepared mustard, ginger, chilli, soy, and chopped cucumber pickles. We built our first recipes on her version. However, the dish was relatively mild in our first iterations. Delicious, but not so devilish.

We knew that we would have to travel to find the roots of Diabo. As you will see, the devil is in the details, and the more you dig, the closer to hell you get. We visited Quentin's Eurasian Restaurant in Singapore, where the dish "Curry Dabel" (a cousin of sorts)

▶▶ continued

contained a modest array of meats (chicken, oxtail, pork ribs, frankfurters), and was sour and slightly sweet with big chilli heat. At Mary Gomes's Mary's Kafe, also in Singapore, she presents a more cosmopolitan, milder, less sweet, pork-free curry. Delicious indeed. The Devil's tail gets longer.

In Malacca, our friend Big Ben (see page 139) is down with the devil too, but is strongly against using anything but chicken in his Curry Devil: *"Pork rib? Pork rib?! You don't put no fucking pork rib in Diabo Kari!"* His chicken-based version is very intense with chilli heat, mustard seed, and vinegar; concentrated and dry; with a *red* sauce and oil that splits at the edges, like the oily shores of a molten lake.

Our experiences and research have led us to this hearty, spicy, and chunky version. The flavors of Malaysia and Singapore dominate: lemongrass, candlenut, palm sugar, chillies, vinegar, and whole mustard seed. We garnish with a chunky pickle that acts more like vegetable, and honor the Macanese tradition of meaty abundancy by including braised beef, Porco Po Bolacho (page 219), Char Siu (page 205), Galinha Bafassa (page 184), and turkey, but use whatever meats you like. (Next time you cook a feast, cook a bit extra and save the leftovers and drippings.)

The last thing to know is that the devil likes to get down and dirty and feel the burn, so cook your Diabo for as long as you like; it will intensify and concentrate the meaty flavors, spices, heat, and acidity. With careful eye, a trusty wooden spoon, and a bit of extra oil, you can make this as saucy or concentrated as you like (although note that after a point, the oil will split and begin to sizzle). Make that devil fry! Despite the name, this is a very forgiving dish and an important tradition that varies among people and across regions. Diabo is not just a recipe; it is a ritual and practice.

DIABO (DEVIL'S CURRY)

8 cups Chicken Stock
(page 282), Pork Stock
(page 283), or juices from
the meats you're using,
or a combination thereof

6 tablespoons Filipino
cane vinegar

1 pinch of saffron

1 tablespoon Chinese
mustard powder

5 tablespoons water

¹/₂ cup dried red chillies

4 cloves garlic, minced

1 (¹/₂-inch) piece fresh
turmeric, peeled and
minced

1 (¹/₂-inch) piece fresh
ginger, peeled and
minced

1 Asian shallot, minced

1 stalk lemongrass, rough
outer layers removed
and tender inner layers
minced

1 tablespoon sambal
oelek

¹/₄ cup candlenuts
(see page 192), toasted
(macademia nuts,
cashews, or almonds
may be substituted)

¹/₂ cup coconut oil

1 tablespoon black
mustard seeds

1 tablespoon yellow
mustard seeds

4 tablespoons
grated palm sugar
(see page 296)

2 tablespoons soy sauce

2 tablespoons
Worcestershire sauce

2 to 3 pounds of various
meats cut into rough
1-inch cubes, including
leftover Galinha Bafassa
(Turmeric Baked Chicken,
page 184), Curried Beef
and Tendon with Turnip
(page 229), Rabo de Boi
Estufada (page 233), Char
Siu (page 205), cooked
turkey, roast beef, pork
roast, duck, or any
other meats you want,
including their juices

1 pound Boiled Potatoes
(page 184)

¹/₂ cucumber, peeled,
seeded, and cut into
bite-size pieces

Blistered Onion Petals
(page 227)

¹/₂ cup Diabo Pickle
(page 40)

¹/₄ cup Ginger Achar
(page 41)

1 breaded and fried pork
chop, as prepared in
Baked Pork Chop Rice
(page 82)

2 Tea Eggs (page 277)
yolks grated and whites
thinly sliced

Handful of fresh cilantro

➜➜ continued

ROAST BEEF OR
BEEF CURRY

CHICKEN CURRY

ROAST
TURKEY LEG

BARBECUE PORK
(CHAR SIU)

POTATOES

ONIONS

BREADED
PORK CHOP
(PO BOLACHO)

SHALLOTS

MUSTARD
POWDER

VINEGAR

WORCESTERSHIRE
SAUCE

FRESH
TURMERIC

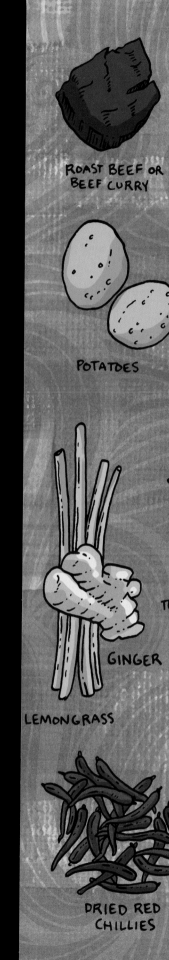
GINGER

PALM SUGAR

LEMONGRASS

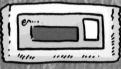
PICKLED
GINGER ACHAR

SINGAPORE
SOUR CABBAGE
WITH MUSTARD SEEDS

PICKLED GREEN
TOMATOES

ASSORTED PICKLED
CHILLIES + SHALLOTS

DRIED RED
CHILLIES

TEA EGGS

FRESH CUCUMBER

Combine the stocks and juices in a heavy pot over high heat and reduce by half, skimming any scum that rises to the top as necessary. Remove from the heat and set aside.

Meanwhile, combine 2 tablespoons of the cane vinegar and the saffron in a small bowl and set aside. Mix the mustard powder with 1 tablespoon of the water to form a thick paste and set aside.

To make the curry paste, put the chillies in a bowl. Bring the remaining 4 tablespoons cane vinegar and remaining 4 tablespoons water to a boil, pour over the chillies, and let soak for 1 hour. Combine in a blender the garlic, turmeric, ginger, shallot, lemongrass, sambal oelek, and candlenuts. Blend until very smooth, adding water if necessary to thin the paste into something the machine can work with. Set aside.

Heat the coconut oil in a large, wide pot over medium heat. When melted and shimmering—but not smoking—add the mustard seeds. They will start to pop pretty quickly—be careful not to let them burn by stirring with a wooden spoon for 30 to 45 seconds. Gently add all of the curry paste, stirring as the paste fries and blooms and the oil begins to separate from the solids. You are reducing the water content of the curry paste and allowing the oil-soluble aromatics to develop flavor and color, so give it time (about 10 to 15 minutes) and let that happen. When bright red and broken looking, add the reduced stocks, vinegar and saffron mixture, prepared mustard mixture, palm sugar, soy sauce, and Worcestershire sauce and mix well. Bring to a simmer, stirring often because the sauce will get thick and can burn on the bottom of the pot easily. When the sugar is dissolved and the other ingredients are well incorporated, remove from the heat. This curry should have the quadruple threat of sour, spicy, sweet, and *big-time* aromatics.

At this point, add the various meats and juices to the curry and slowly simmer for about 15 minutes. Add the potatoes and continue simmering for 15 minutes.

Remove from the heat and add the cucumber, onions, pickle, and achar. Top with the pork chop, eggs, and cilantro. Serve immediately or reheat when ready to serve.

BLISTERED ONION PETALS

1 large Spanish onion

2 teaspoons peanut oil

MAKES
1 ONION

Cut off the top and tail of the onion, peel it, and cut it into 6 pieces from top to bottom. Separate the petals and set aside.

Heat a wok over high heat until it begins to smoke, add the onions, and let sit for a minute, shaking the pan to spread out the onions. Drizzle the oil around the pan, stir-fry quickly for 30 seconds, and remove from the heat. Set aside and use as directed above.

CURRIED BEEF AND TENDON WITH TURNIP

In Macau "turnip" usually means daikon, or another large radish, so technically, there's no turnip in the original version of this dish. At Fat Rice, we mostly follow tradition, but run with the turnip thing and garnish with crunchy raw turnips, radishes, and their greens. Don't be scared to work with the tendons–they do require long cooking, but add great texture.

Try grilling the rubbed beef; it adds a great smoky dimension.

SERVES 10 IN A MULTI-DISH MEAL

6 tablespoons salt, plus more for seasoning

1½ pounds beef tendon (2 or 3 pieces)

6 tablespoons Filipino cane vinegar

3 Spanish onions, sliced

15 cloves garlic, sliced

1 (3-inch) piece unpeeled fresh ginger, sliced

4 tablespoons Macau Hot Curry Powder (page 279)

4 pounds beef chuck roast

2 tablespoons peanut oil

3 quarts Chicken Stock (page 282)

1 large daikon radish, peeled, quartered lengthwise, cut into 1-inch pieces, blanched and poached (see page 25)

Papo Seco (page 264) or Coconut Rice (page 75), for serving

GARNISHES

Variety of radishes and baby turnips of varying colors and shapes, thinly sliced

Shredded green onions (see page 27), white and green parts

Radish sprouts

Mix 8 cups water and 3 tablespoons of the salt in a large container until the salt dissolves. Add the tendons and soak for 12 hours. Drain, discarding the water and setting the tendons aside.

Bring a large pot of water to a boil over high heat. Blanch the tendons for 5 minutes, then drain, discarding the water. Return the tendons to the pot along with 1 tablespoon of the salt, 1 tablespoon of the cane vinegar, and a third each of the onions, garlic, and ginger. Cover with fresh water. Bring to a boil over high heat, then lower the heat to maintain a simmer and cook, covered, for 2 hours. Drain and set the tendons aside.

Preheat the oven to 375°F. Mix the remaining 2 tablespoons salt, 2 tablespoons of the cane vinegar, and 2 tablespoons of the curry powder and rub all over the chuck roast.

Heat the oil in a large Dutch oven over medium-high heat. Add the beef and sear until golden brown on each side, about 5 minutes per side. Remove the beef from the pan and add the remaining onions, garlic, and ginger and cook until the vegetables start

to caramelize, about 5 minutes. Mix the remaining 2 tablespoons curry powder with 2 tablespoons of the cane vinegar, add to the pan, and stir until fragrant, about 1 minute. Add the stock and stir well. Nestle the beef and tendons back into the pot and bring to a boil. Cover the pot, transfer to the preheated oven, and braise until tender when pierced with a chopstick, about 2½ hours. When done, remove from the oven and let cool for at least 3 hours, or overnight.

When cooled, remove the beef and tendons and set aside. Remove the solidified fat and ginger slices and discard. Puree the sauce with an immersion blender until smooth. Cut the beef into rough 2-inch pieces and cut the tendon crosswise into ¼-inch slices. Return, evenly dispersed, to the pot, along with the daikon.

Bring to a simmer over medium-high heat. Cook until the meat is heated through and the sauce has a nice unctuous texture, about 5 to 10 minutes. Season to taste with salt and the remaining 1 tablespoon cane vinegar, remove from the heat, and generously top with the garnishes.

MINCHI
(MACANESE MINCED MEAT HASH)

SERVES 4

This humble minced meat preparation is one of the most Macanese dishes there is. The term "minchi" most likely came from the English word *mince*, but there is a bit of debate over its origins. Did it come from the English enclave of Hong Kong, or did it originate in Goa, India, a cousin of a dish of minced meat *keema*? Either way, making Minchi has become a sort of ritual in Macau; every family has their own version, and every family thinks theirs is best. Luckily for us, our pork and beef version has gotten many nods of approval from our guests, both Macanese and non-.

We follow the lesson of our friend Florita Alves and use three types of soy sauce: sweet soy (*kecap manis*) for its molasses tones, dark soy for depth and color, and light soy for salinity. We add a bit of baking soda to the marinade to help hold in moisture and keep the Minchi tender during the cooking process.

Minchi can be eaten for any meal of the day, be it the main event, incorporated as an ingredient in pastries (rolled in mashed potatoes to make Minchi Croquettes, page 53), put in between a bun to make a loose meat sandwich, spooned over noodles, or simply served it as we do at Fat Rice with crispy diced potatoes, a sunny-side-up egg, and some green vegetable.

MARINADE

¹/₂ teaspoon baking soda

1 tablespoon Shaoxing rice wine (see page 297)

2 tablespoons light soy sauce

2 tablespoons dark soy sauce

2 tablespoons sweet soy sauce

3 tablespoons Worchestershire sauce

2 tablespoons preserved mustard greens (suimi ya cai, see page 296)

1 teaspoon brown sugar

¹/₂ teaspoon salt

¹/₂ teaspoon white pepper

¹/₄ teaspoon ground cinnamon

1 tablespoon curry powder

1 teaspoon crushed red chillies

MINCHI

1 pound ground pork

1 pound ground beef

3 tablespoons olive oil

3 bay leaves

1 onion, finely chopped

1 Asian shallot, finely chopped

4 cloves garlic, crushed and chopped

1 tablespoon tapioca starch mixed with 2 tablespoons cold water

ACCOMPANIMENTS AND GARNISHES

Potato Croutons (page 232)

Green onions, fisheye-cut (see page 27)

1 egg, cooked sunny-side up (optional)

Pickled chillies (optional)

Coconut Rice (optional, page 75)

Steamed green vegetables (optional)

>> continued

To make the marinade, combine the ingredients, then mix with the pork and beef. Refrigerate for at least 4 hours, but no longer than 12 hours.

To make the minchi, heat the olive oil in a wok or large skillet over medium-high heat. Add the bay leaves and stir until fragrant, about 30 seconds. Add the onion and cook until softened and lightly browned, about 5 minutes. Add the shallot and garlic and cook until the garlic is fragrant, a couple of minutes or so.

Add the marinated meat to the pan and stir constantly, breaking the meat up until fine and uniform. Continue cooking until most of the liquid has evaporated and the meat is browned, about 10 minutes. Stir in the tapioca starch slurry and continue to cook until the sauce has thickened. Transfer to a serving plate and garnish with the Potato Croutons, green onions, and any other accompaniments.

POTATO CROUTONS

**MAKES
2 TO 3 CUPS**

2 pounds (about 3) potatoes, preferably Kennebec, peeled

Peanut oil, for deep-frying
Salt

Cut the rounded sides from the potatoes until they are as square as possible–you're going for a block of potato. Proceed to cut into medium dice. Put into a container and run under cold water until the water runs clear. Drain thoroughly.

Heat 2 inches of oil in a wok to 350°F and add the potatoes. Fry for 10 to 15 minutes, stirring occasionally, until the potatoes are golden brown and crisp. Transfer to a paper towel-lined plate and season liberally with salt.

RABO DE BOI ESTUFADO (STEWED OXTAIL WITH TOMATOES AND PORTUGUESE WINES)

This sticky braise is another example of the sort of dish that can be found at any level of eatery in Macau, from humble cafeterias to fancy white-tablecloth restaurants. This is a perfect East-meets-West dish that combines dry red wine, sweet fortified wine, soy sauce, and tomatoes, with the *rabo de boi* (oxtail) breaking down to enrich the deeply flavored sauce. If by chance you have leftovers, you can pick the meat from the bones for an easy reheat, and use the bones to make a broth (which goes great, *cha chaan teng*-style, over boiled macaroni, wilted cabbage, and poached carrots).

SERVES 2 AS A MAIN, 4 IN A MULTI-DISH MEAL

3 bay leaves

1 bunch green onions, white and green parts, cut into 1-inch pieces

1 (2-inch) piece fresh ginger, peeled and sliced

6 cloves garlic, minced

2 teaspoons turmeric powder

1/4 cup soy sauce

1 whole oxtail (about 2 pounds), cut into 2 to 3-inch pieces along the joints

7 dried red chillies

4 whole star anise

1 1/2 teaspoons whole Sichuan pepper (see page 289)

3 whole cloves

2 tablespoons sherry vinegar

1/4 cup peanut oil

1 Spanish onion, grated

1 large carrot, cut into 1/2-inch pieces

1/2 cup port wine

1/2 cup Madeira

1 cup Portuguese red wine

3 tablespoons grated palm sugar (see page 296)

2 cups Chicken Stock (page 282), vegetable stock (page 283), or water

1 1/2 cups tomato puree

GARNISHES

Poached carrots (see page 25)

Poached potatoes (see page 25)

Blistered Onion Petals (page 227)

Blanched green vegetable, such as bok choy or yu choy (see page 25)

Small handful cilantro leaves

Combine the bay leaves and half each of the green onions, ginger, garlic, turmeric, and soy sauce in a bowl and mix well. Add the oxtail, toss, and marinate, refrigerated, for 12 hours.

Make a masala by combining the remaining turmeric, dry chillies, star anise, Sichuan pepper, and cloves in a spice grinder and grind to a fine powder. Transfer to a small bowl, add the sherry vinegar, and stir to combine. Set the masala aside.

Remove the oxtail from the marinade and pat dry. Heat the oil in a Dutch oven over medium-high heat. Working in batches, if necessary, carefully add the oxtail and brown on each side, about 4 minutes per side. Transfer to a plate. Add the onion to the Dutch oven and sweat until some of the moisture cooks out, about 4 minutes. Add the carrot and the remaining ginger and garlic and cook until the onion starts to brown, another 3 to 5 minutes. Reduce the heat to medium and add the masala to the pot and bloom, stirring occasionally, until quite fragrant, about 10 minutes. Add the remaining soy sauce to the pan along with the port, Madeira, red wine, palm sugar, stock, and tomato puree and stir, scraping any browned bits off of the bottom of the pot. Return the oxtail to the Dutch oven. Bring to a boil, then reduce the heat to a simmer and cover. Simmer for 3 to 4 hours, until the meat is tender and just starting to fall from the bone. Add the poached carrots and potatoes to the pot to heat through, and spread the blistered onions and green vegetable around the pot. Garnish with the cilantro and the remaining green onions and serve immediately.

9

DOCES E SOMBREMESAS

SWEETS AND DESSERTS

The Macanese love their sweets, and we do too. In fact, a majority of the Macanese recipes we've found are for sweets and desserts: Macanese cooking relies on a strong oral tradition, and, for the most part, any adept Macanese cook can wing it through a Tacho or an Arroz Gordo. But the recipes for Macanese cakes, puddings, and complicated egg-based confections are hard to memorize, so we are thankful to those who have documented them.

One surprise we encountered when collecting older Macanese recipes was the fact that they were often used as shopping lists—meaning, the ingredient quantities were often listed by cost rather than, say, cups or tablespoons. This has been one of the many challenges of recreating these old recipes. For this book, we decided to present a few new takes on some classic desserts: Batatada (page 247); Almond Gelee (page 252); Hong Kong-Style French Toast (page 242); and a newcomer from our own kitchen in Chicago, the Macau Rice Crisp (page 239). Some require a certain technical proficiency, but at the end of the day, these are humble sweets that can be dressed up as much or as little as you like.

MACAU RICE CRISP

A Fat Rice classic! The idea for this tasty treat came from the Yat Heng Tong Bakery on the island of Taipa during our first trip to Macau. There we found a Taiwanese baker making crisp puffed rice balls coated with all kinds of things, but the one that stood out for us was the one with nori and rousong (pork floss)—a weirdly delicious, fluffy, MSG-laden porcine treat. The balls had the texture similar to Rice Krispies Treats, with a super-addictive, slightly oceanic, and savory taste. Back home, we added sesame and chilli flakes, and the dynamic texture of not-melted-all-the-way marshmallows for a strangely delicious taste combination of sweet and salty, with a bonus porky flavor putting it over the top. Making this dessert is a rite of passage at Fat Rice that all new cooks need to master, and it is always interesting to watch how someone not from the United States (and therefore, who has never made or even experienced Rice Krispies Treats before) interprets the recipe.

MAKES 24 FUN-SIZE PORTIONS

10 nori sheets, about 7 by 8 inches

1 cup rousong (see page 297)

9 ounces (about 11 cups) puffed rice cereal

1 tablespoon sesame seeds, toasted

1 tablespoon Korean chilli flakes

4 tablespoons unsalted butter, plus a bit to grease hands

1/2 teaspoon salt

1 tablespoon toasted sesame oil

1 (28-ounce) bag marshmallows

Finely julienne the nori sheets into strips about 1 inch long—you'll need a good, sharp knife and some serious elbow grease, or take the nori into your office after everyone else is gone and use the boss's paper cutter.

On the bottom of a dry 9 by 13-inch baking dish, first sprinkle half of the rousong, *then* half of the nori on top of the pork and set aside. You want the pork floss to be on the outside of both sides of the rice crisps or the seaweed will not adhere.

Toss the cereal, sesame seeds, and Korean chilli flakes in a bowl and set aside.

Melt the butter with the salt and sesame oil in the biggest and widest pot you've got. Add the marshmallows and stir to slightly melt, taking care not to melt them more than about halfway, just a few minutes. Remove from the heat and immediately add the cereal mixture, stirring well to combine. With buttered hands, press the cereal mixture firmly and evenly onto the floss and seaweed in the baking dish, pressing into an even layer. Top with the remaining seaweed, followed by the remaining pork floss. Top with parchment paper and weight down with another baking dish or something similar. Allow to cool for 1 hour, weighted, then remove from the pan and cut into serving-size portions. Serve immediately. Store any leftovers tightly wrapped at room temperature for up to 5 days.

SERRADURA
(MACAU'S FAMOUS SAWDUST PUDDING)

SERVES 6

The exotic-sounding name belies the accessibility of this dessert. Found on many street corners and dessert shops in Macau, this relatively modern dessert is simply sweetened cream, either topped or layered with cookie crumbs. The cookie crumbs are the reason for the dish's name: *serradura* is the Portuguese word for "sawdust." We've built from these humble beginnings by making a pastry cream to fold into the whipped cream/condensed milk combo, bolstered by the addition of cream cheese and contrasted by a tangy and floral guava sauce.

2½ cups heavy cream

4 ounces cream cheese, at room temperature

½ cup Pastry Cream (page 241)

½ (14-ounce) can sweetened condensed milk

5 ounces guava paste

¼ cup water

7 ounces (1 sleeve) Maria cookies (see page 295)

3 ounces palm sugar (see page 296), grated (about ⅓ cup)

Chill the bowl of a standing mixer and whisk attachment in the refrigerator for at least an hour.

Pour the heavy cream into the chilled bowl. Whip on medium speed until firm peaks form. Be careful to not overwhip. If cream gets overwhipped, it will start to turn into chunks of butter. (If this happens, congratulations, now you have homemade butter–but you're going to have to start the Serradura over.) Transfer to a different bowl and reserve in the refrigerator.

Clean the mixer bowl and attach the paddle to the mixer. Beat the cream cheese on high speed until very smooth, scraping down the bowl with a rubber spatula as needed. Add the Pastry Cream and continue to mix on medium speed until incorporated and very smooth, again scraping down as needed. Add the sweetened condensed milk and continue to mix on medium speed until very smooth, again scraping down as needed. The name of the game here is smooth and it's essential that the mixture be lump free.

Fold half of the reserved whipped cream into the cream cheese mixture. When fully incorporated, fold the other half in. When the pudding is nice and smooth, set aside in the refrigerator.

Puree the guava paste and water in a blender until smooth and set aside.

Put the cookies in a food processer and pulse until slightly broken down. Add the palm sugar and process until you have a uniform, sandy texture with no large chunks. Set aside.

To serve, fill 6 small bowls or teacups with the pudding, then top each with a couple spoonfuls of guava sauce and a hearty sprinkling of cookie crumbs. Serve immediately, and save any leftover ingredients separately in clean, odorless, airtight containers.

PASTRY CREAM

1¹/₂ cups milk

¹/₃ cup sugar

4 egg yolks

2 teaspoons high-quality
vanilla extract

Pinch of salt

4 teaspoons cornstarch

MAKES
2 CUPS

Combine the milk and half of the sugar in a heavy pot over medium heat and warm gradually, stirring gently, until you see steam rising from the surface of the milk; remove from the heat.

In a bowl, whisk together the egg yolks, remaining half of sugar, vanilla, salt, and cornstarch until smooth and lighter in color. Temper the yolks by slowly drizzling the hot milk mixture into the egg mixture while whisking. When you've added at least half of the milk mixture to the eggs, pour everything back into the pot and place over medium heat.

Gently stir with a rubber spatula, scraping the sides and bottom of the pot from time to time to make sure nothing is sticking. When the mixture comes to a full boil and thickens, transfer to a heatproof container and lay plastic directly on the surface of the pastry cream to prevent a skin from forming. Cover and refrigerate until fully cooled. Store refrigerated and tightly wrapped for up to 3 days.

HONG KONG-STYLE FRENCH TOAST

**SERVES
1 OR 2**

This is our take on the deliciously gluttonous "French toast" that one finds in Hong Kong and Macau. At its most basic, it's a peanut butter sandwich dipped in egg, deep-fried, and topped with a massive slab of butter and imitation maple syrup; sometimes it gets a dose of sweetened condensed milk on top as well. Here we've added banana to the mix, as well as some tropical flavors to lighten things up a bit–as if that were possible–but feel free to garnish as you like. Try it Elvis-style with crispy bacon and maple syrup–we call that Honka-Honka Hong Kong-Style!

2 slices thick-cut white bread (Texas Toast)

2 tablespoons peanut butter

1/2 banana, sliced into 3/8-inch-thick rounds

Peanut oil, for deep-frying

4 large eggs, beaten with 2 tablespoons water

Salt

GARNISHES (TRY ONE, TRY 'EM ALL!)

Granulated sugar

Papaya Jam (page 243)

Canned young coconut, drained and sliced 1/4 inch thick

Toasted cashews

Lime zest

Coconut Cream (page 243)

Fresh mint leaves

Make a peanut butter and banana sandwich, making sure there is peanut butter on each slice of bread, leaving about 1/4 inch uncovered around the edges.

Preheat the oven to 200°F.

Heat 3 inches of peanut oil in a wok over high heat to 350°F. With a clean hand, dip the sandwich into the egg batter, being sure to cover all sides well. Drain lightly over the bowl and carefully slip into the hot oil. Cook until golden brown on the bottom, about 1 minute, then flip and cook the other side. Use a large spider to transfer the sandwich to a paper towel-lined plate and place in the oven.

Bring the oil back up to 300°F and drizzle the remaining egg batter through your fingers while waving your hand above the oil to separate the eggs into

threads. Cook the egg threads for about 1 minute, until lightly browned and crispy. Remove with the spider to a new paper towel-lined plate, season with salt, cover with more paper towels, and press lightly to remove excess oil.

To serve, place the French toast in the center of a plate (or cut it in half and serve on 2 plates) and cover with the crispy egg threads. Top with a sprinkling of granulated sugar and spoon a few mounds of the jam around the plate. Top the jam with the coconut and toasted cashews. Zest the lime over the plate and pour the cream all over. Finish with a few fresh mint leaves. Have a cardiologist on speed dial and serve immediately.

LOOK IN THE CANNED SECTION OF YOUR LOCAL ASIAN GROCERY TO FIND CANNED YOUNG COCONUT.

COCONUT CREAM

| 1 (13.5-ounce) can coconut milk | ¹/₂ (14-ounce) can sweetened condensed milk | Pinch of salt | **MAKES 2 CUPS** |

Blend all the ingredients in a blender thoroughly. Store refrigerated for up to 1 week.

PAPAYA JAM

| Juice and finely grated zest of 1 lemon ¹/₃ cup white vinegar | 8 ounces sugar 1 ripe Mexican papaya, peeled, seeded, and cut into 1-inch chunks | 2 teaspoons ground cinnamon | **MAKES 2 CUPS** |

Combine all the ingredients in a small pot and bring to a simmer over medium-high heat. Reduce the heat to low and simmer, stirring occasionally, for about 1 hour, until the papaya has broken down and the jam has a thick consistency. Leave chunky or puree with an immersion blender if a smoother consistency is desired. Store refrigerated for up to 1 week.

>> continued

MAKE A PEANUT BUTTER AND BANANA SANDWICH. MAKE SURE THERE IS PEANUT BUTTER ON EACH SLICE OF BREAD, LEAVING ABOUT 1/4" AROUND THE EDGES.

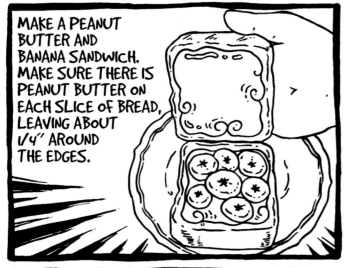

IN A WOK, HEAT 3" OF PEANUT OIL TO 350°F OVER HIGH HEAT.

WITH A CLEAN HAND, DIP SANDWICH INTO EGG BATTER, BEING SURE TO COVER ALL SIDES WELL.

DRAIN LIGHTLY OVER BOWL.

CAREFULLY LAY IT INTO THE HOT OIL.

COOK UNTIL GOLDEN BROWN ON THE BOTTOM — ONLY ABOUT 1 MINUTE.

1 minute

THEN FLIP, AND COOK THE OTHER SIDE.

245

USE A LARGE SPIDER TO REMOVE THE SANDWICH AND REST IT ON A PAPER TOWEL-LINED PLATE IN A 200°F OVEN.

BRING THE OIL BACK TO 300°F.

DRIZZLE THE REMAINING EGG BATTER INTO THE OIL, MOVING THROUGH FINGERS OR CHOPSTICKS TO SEPARATE IT INTO THREADS

COOK THREADS FOR ABOUT A MINUTE, UNTIL LIGHTLY BROWNED AND CRISPY.

REMOVE WITH THE SPIDER TO A NEW PAPER TOWEL-LINED PLATE.

COVER WITH MORE PAPER TOWELS, AND PRESS LIGHTLY TO REMOVE EXCESS OIL. SEASON WITH SALT.

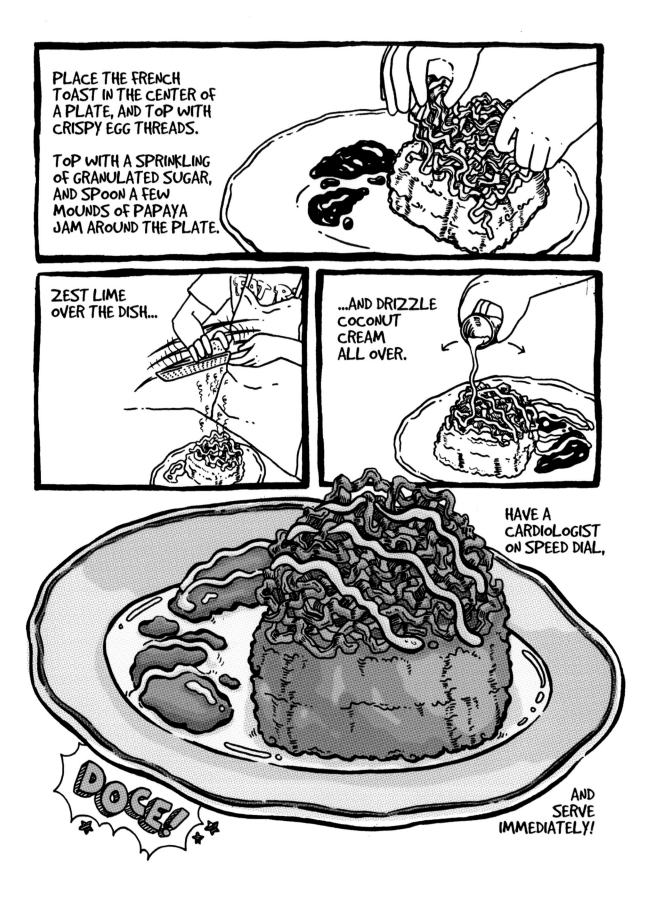

PLACE THE FRENCH TOAST IN THE CENTER OF A PLATE, AND TOP WITH CRISPY EGG THREADS.

TOP WITH A SPRINKLING OF GRANULATED SUGAR, AND SPOON A FEW MOUNDS OF PAPAYA JAM AROUND THE PLATE.

ZEST LIME OVER THE DISH...

...AND DRIZZLE COCONUT CREAM ALL OVER.

HAVE A CARDIOLOGIST ON SPEED DIAL,

AND SERVE IMMEDIATELY!

DOCE!

BATATADA (MACANESE POTATO CAKE)

SERVES 8

The Macanese have two types of Batatada: one with white potatoes and one with sweet potatoes. In both cases, Batatada is so moist from the potatoes that it is typically served unadorned, enjoyed as a dessert or a teatime snack. In the following pages we have included our recipes for both. Here is a *very* modernized interpretation of the white potato Batatada served to us at Dona Aida de Jesus's Riquexó. The texture of Dona Aida's Batatada was reminiscent of a dense cheesecake, so we ran with that and incorporated coconut yogurt for a little zing and seasonal fruit for garnish. We are probably going to authenticity hell for this, but we even added salted potato chips for crunch. Sorry, Aida . . . it's delicious! That being said, it is great enjoyed on its own with tea, as the Macanese do. Or treat this as a blank canvas for in-season fruits: we shot this book in the fall and used cape gooseberries, fresh figs, and pomegranate.

6 tablespoons unsalted butter, cut into small cubes, plus 1 tablespoon for the pan

1½ pounds Yukon gold potatoes, peeled and cut into rough 2-inch pieces

1 cup plain coconut yogurt

1 cup evaporated milk

2 cups sugar

½ cup potato starch

2 teaspoons vanilla extract

Finely grated zest of ½ lemon

9 egg yolks plus 2 whole eggs

Fruit garnishes of your choice

Prepare a loaf pan by coating it with 1 tablespoon butter, then line with a piece of parchment paper. Set aside.

Place the potatoes in a pot and cover with cold water by 1 inch. Bring to a boil over high heat. Once boiling, lower the heat to a simmer and cook until the potatoes are soft, about 15 minutes, then drain. Allow to cool slightly, then transfer the potatoes to a food processor and puree until smooth. Set aside.

Preheat the oven to 375°F.

Combine the coconut yogurt and evaporated milk in a small saucepan and place over medium heat. Cook, stirring from time to time, just until you see wisps of steam rising from the surface. Add the mixture to the potato puree in the food processor,

along with the sugar, potato starch, vanilla, remaining 6 tablespoons butter, and lemon zest. Puree until smooth. With the machine running, add the egg yolks and whole eggs one at a time, pureeing until smooth after each addition.

Pour the batter into the prepared pan. Place the loaf pan in a 9 by 13-inch baking dish and fill the baking dish halfway with water. Place in the oven and bake until set, browned on top, and a chopstick inserted into the center of the cake comes out clean, 45 to 60 minutes.

Fully cool before cutting. Slice into 8 even pieces, and serve with any desired fruit garnishes. To store, wrap the cooled cake tightly in plastic wrap and keep at room temperature for up to 3 days.

SWEET POTATO BATATADA

The beauty of this Sweet Potato Batatada is in its home-style humility; this is the cake you eat with your beloved grandmother, adorned with nothing but a sprinkle of confectioners' sugar and served alongside a hot cup of tea. Rich with coconut milk, butter, and eggs, with a deep, yet not cloying flavor from the sweet potatoes, it's like a pound cake crossed with a pumpkin pie. Unlike our white potato Batatada (page 247), we keep it pretty traditional here, save for a dash of ground coriander for a bit of brightness. Serve gently warmed, sprinkled with confectioners' sugar.

1 pound sweet potatoes, peeled and cut into rough 1-inch cubes

1 teaspoon coconut oil or unsalted butter

1 cup plus 1 tablespoon granulated sugar

2½ cups coconut powder (see page 297)

⅓ cup coconut milk

¾ cup cake flour

1 teaspoon baking powder

¾ teaspoon salt

1 tablespoon ground coriander

6 eggs

1 cup (2 sticks) unsalted butter, at room temperature

Confectioners' sugar, to serve

Put the sweet potatoes in a pot and cover with cold water by 1 inch. Bring to a boil over high heat. Reduce to a simmer and cook until the sweet potatoes are soft, about 15 minutes, then drain. Allow to cool slightly, then transfer the sweet potatoes to a food processor and puree until smooth, adding a touch of water if necessary. Set aside.

Preheat the oven to 375°F. Coat the inside of an 8-inch cast-iron skillet with the coconut oil, then add 1 tablespoon of the granulated sugar and swirl around the pan until coated.

In a small bowl, stir the coconut powder with the coconut milk until fully absorbed.

In a large bowl, sift together the cake flour, baking powder, salt, and coriander. Whisk together and set aside.

Separate the eggs, reserving the egg yolks. In the bowl of a stand mixer fitted with the whisk attachment, or by hand with a whisk, whip the egg whites to firm peaks, about 2 minutes on medium-high speed. Set aside at room temperature.

In the bowl of a stand mixer fitted with the paddle attachment, or by hand with a wooden spoon, cream together the butter and remaining 1 cup granulated sugar until light and fluffy and the sugar has partially dissolved. Stop the machine, add one egg yolk, and mix on medium speed until fully incorporated. Repeat this process, adding one yolk at a time, until all the yolks have been incorporated.

Add the sweet potato puree and coconut mixture and mix on medium speed. Fold the egg whites into the sweet potato mixture until just combined, then gently stir in the dry ingredients until combined. Be careful not to overmix at this stage.

Pour the batter into the prepared cast-iron skillet and bake until a chopstick inserted into the center of the cake comes out clean, about 1 hour and 15 minutes. Note that the cake will be quite dark when done. Also, take note that there is a difference between quite dark and burnt! When done, cool slightly, then dust with confectioners' sugar and serve. Wrap any remaining cake tightly and store refrigerated for up to a week.

ALMOND GELEE

SERVES 4 TO 6

This recipe was inspired by the almond gelatin dessert with canned mandarins and grapes that Adrienne grew up eating. Adapting a recipe found in a Chinese cookbook, her mother Alison swapped out the snappy seaweed-based agar-agar with gelatin, which was more pleasing to a Midwestern palate. We have kept the practice of using a combination of fresh and canned fruit but have elevated things by using more exotic fruit, such as longan, dragon fruit, Asian pear, and lemon simple syrup–soaked basil seeds and white "cloud" fungus (the crunchy texture of which is found in many syrup-based Chinese desserts). You can make this using small, individual molds, but keep an eye out for large, old-fashioned gelatin molds in the thrift store to make it more interactive, shareable, and elegant. We make suggestions for the garnish, but let your creativity run wild to top the snow-white gelee like a blank canvas.

3¹/₂ teaspoons (11 grams) powdered plain gelatin

2¹/₂ cups cold water

7 tablespoons sugar

6 tablespoons evaporated milk

¹/₂ teaspoon almond extract

OPTIONAL GARNISHES

Various canned fruits, such as young coconut, lychees, or longans

Fresh fruits such as dragon fruit, Asian pears, or apples, cut into cubes or balled with a melon baller

White cloud fungus, soaked in cool water for 1 hour, then in lemon simple syrup for 1 hour (see note)

Basil seeds, soaked in cool water for 1 hour, then in lemon simple syrup for 1 hour (see note)

Put the gelatin in a bowl and mix in ¹/₂ cup of the cold water. Let bloom for 5 minutes. Meanwhile, bring the remaining 2 cups water and sugar to a simmer over high heat, stirring until the sugar dissolves. Pour in the bloomed gelatin, stirring until the gelatin dissolves. Add the evaporated milk and almond extract and stir gently, taking care not to create bubbles. Pour into a mold of your choosing, cover tightly, and refrigerate overnight, until set.

When ready to unmold, gently loosen the gelee from the sides of its container, fill a bowl larger than the mold with warm water, then dip the mold in the water for about 5 seconds. Place an inverted plate on top of the mold and carefully flip the mold and plate over. Set everything down, and gently slip the mold off of the gelee. Garnish as desired and serve immediately.

To MAKE LEMON SIMPLE SYRUP, BOIL 1 CUP OF WATER WITH 1 CUP OF SUGAR UNTIL DISSOLVED. COOL, THEN ADD THE JUICE AND ZEST OF 1 LEMON.

COCOA-NUT GELEE

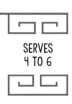

SERVES
4 TO 6

A nice break in the day when exploring Macau is ducking into Manuela Ferreira's Restaurante Litoral to enjoy an espresso and a refreshing snack of chocolate and coconut pudding. Manuela serves hers in separate coupe glasses without garnish, and we like to combine them on our spoons to get both flavors in one bite. Amazing. Back in Chicago, we also make separate puddings, but combine them on one plate and garnish them with ingredients that complement both the chocolate and the coconut, tying the two together. (It's worth noting that in China, "pudding" is a loose term to describe many different gelled desserts; to avoid confusion, we call ours "gelee." Fancy, right?)

As with Manuela's, our gelling agent is agar-agar. Derived from seaweed, agar agar brings a remarkably snappy and juicy texture that carries the purity of the main flavors. Use a high-quality cocoa powder for the cocoa gelee; since there is no cream or fat present, you will be able to taste every nuance of the cocoa. Take it to the next level by caramelizing your banana to give a pleasant temperature contrast to the cool gelee cubes.

COCOA GELEE

1½ cups water

1 tablespoon agar-agar powder

7 tablespoons sugar

1 cup coconut milk

⅓ cup unsweetened cocoa powder

COCONUT GELEE

1½ cups water

1 tablespoon agar-agar powder

7 tablespoons sugar

1 cup coconut milk

GARNISHES

2 ripe bananas, cut into 1-inch wedges

½ cup roasted and salted Spanish peanuts

½ cup young coconut, cut into 1-inch strips

¼ cup grated palm sugar (see page 296)

Large-flake sea salt

To make the cocoa gelee, combine the water, agar-agar, and sugar in a small saucepan and bring to a boil over high heat. Boil for 3 minutes, then remove from the heat and set aside.

Pour the coconut milk into a separate small saucepan and bring to a boil over high heat. Add the cocoa powder and whisk well to combine. Pour into the agar-agar mixture, stir well, and return to a boil over high heat. Remove from the heat and pour into a loaf pan. Let cool on a countertop for about 30 minutes, then wrap in plastic wrap and chill in the refrigerator overnight.

To make the coconut gelee, combine the water, agar-agar, and sugar in a small saucepan and bring to a boil over high heat. Boil for 3 minutes, then remove from the heat and set aside.

Pour the coconut milk into a separate small saucepan and bring to a boil over high heat. Pour into the agar-agar mixture, stir well, and return to a boil over high heat. Remove from the heat and pour into a loaf pan. Let cool on a countertop for about 30 minutes, then wrap in plastic wrap and chill in the refrigerator overnight.

Once both gelees are set, cut them into 1-inch cubes. Arrange the cubed gelees on individual dishes in varying patterns. Garnish attractively with the remaining ingredients, and serve immediately.

10

BUILDING BLOCKS

BALICHÃO: AN ODYSSEY

All across Southeast Asia, salted and fermented shrimp products are used as a source of protein and as the umami flavor-booster for just about anything: cooked fish and meat dishes; soups, stews, and curries; even fresh fruit and vegetables. In Goa, dried shrimp pastes show up in pickles, chutneys, and stews; in Malaysia, Sri Lanka, and Indonesia, they are essential to many sambals.

You may be thinking, "Fermented shrimp? Gross!" But look a bit closer–fermentation and bacteria are our friends. It seems to us that human civilization has always had a penchant for consuming things of–to be blunt–a foul or rotten nature. In the Western world, think of the rich and complex flavor of an aged, smelly cheese, jamón Ibérico hanging for a year or two to develop its intricate spectrum of flavors, the sour snap

of a naturally fermented pickle. Even Worcestershire sauce, first created in England in the early 1800s from a recipe brought from India, was only palatable after being mistakenly aged for a couple of years; it is essentially a doctored-up fish sauce.

Who can be sure how this affinity began? Necessity in rough times, experiments gone bad, or perhaps just an aloof caveman king who screwed up a wooly mammoth rump roast and used fermented pterodactyl eggs to make his people think it was actually really tasty? For whatever reason, we humans are *really* down with the funk. Thus, it was only a matter of time before the Portuguese and their descendants in South and Southeast Asia became enamored of these salted and fermented shrimp pastes. But were they really new to them?

When the Romans ruled the Iberian Peninsula, giving it the name Hispania (218 BC to AD 400), a hot commodity was *garum*—a fish sauce made by salting and fermenting fish in the sun. *Garum* was added to dishes, diluted with wine for drinking, and even included in Roman first-aid kits. Variants of *garum*, including *allec* and *liquamen*, were traded throughout the Roman Empire, but the best-quality *garum* was said to come from Hispania—modern-day Spain and Portugal.

Unfortunately, once the Roman Empire fell, taxes on salt increased drastically, greatly limiting the production of *garum, allec,* and *liquamen*, essentially eliminating them from the cuisines of the region. So when the Portuguese encountered deliciously stinky shrimp pastes in Southeast Asia during the Age of Exploration in the fifteenth century, it was possibly more of a rediscovery. Maybe someone muttered the word *allec* (a thick by-product of *garum* used by the Romans), and another misheard it and added a "b" sound in the front? And then that guy told his crew what he thought he heard, and they set out to many different ports carrying this incorrect name? Did *ballec* become the generic, one-size-fits-all term of commerce for these fermented seafood products? And did this lead to a lot of very similar names throughout Asia, such as *belacan* in Malaysia, *balchao* in Goa, *balachaung* in Burma, *balachiam* in Cochinchina, or *balichão* in Macau? Or, as one of our Macanese friends suggested, perhaps it is a combination of the words *bali*, meaning "whale," and *chão*, meaning "floor" (of the ocean), where said whales would feast on these tiny shrimp. Who knows? This is a lot of conjecture by us amateur historians, but it's a fun rabbit hole to get lost down.

In Porco Balichang Tamarindo (page 193), the word *balichang* simply indicates the use of fermented shrimp paste, or balichão. We like to say that "you must use *chão* to *chang*." The main difference between most traditional Southeast Asian fermented shrimp and our beloved Macanese balichão is the addition of European ingredients: for example, brandy (reminding us of the Romans, who added *garum* to wine for drinking), bay leaves, lemons, chillies, peppercorns, and cloves.

Sadly, balichão is increasingly difficult to find even in Macau. In the small fishing village on Coloane known for selling every kind of dried and fermented seafood product under the sun, all we found when we asked after balichão were quizzical looks. Discouraged, we turned to the next best thing: big, beautiful blocks of ground shrimp paste in the window of a shop run by Burmese merchants, which was, oddly enough, located in a more touristy corridor of Taipa. This is where we started our balichão quest and developed our first recipes, and after trips back to Macau and exposure to more traditional versions, our recipe progressed to using jars of whole salted tiny shrimp (found in Korean groceries, where you can also get a kimchi crock to age the balichão in).

THE CHILLI LEMON

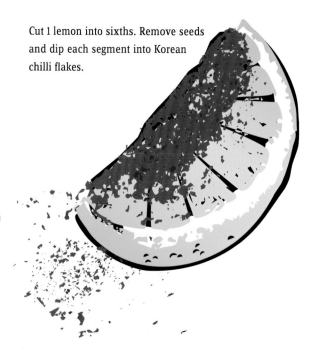

Cut 1 lemon into sixths. Remove seeds and dip each segment into Korean chilli flakes.

THE CHILLI LEMON & FAT RICE
Together at Last

BALICHÃO
(MACANESE SHRIMP PASTE)

**MAKES
4 CUPS**

If we had to pick one defining element of Macanese cuisine, it would surely be Balichão, a rarely-seen concoction tasted by few and made by even fewer. Those who do still make their own, like Manuela Ferreira and Florita Alves, each have their own special touches. Here we present our (as traditional as possible) recipe from the restaurant. When Balichão is called for in this book, yes, you can substitute regular old shrimp paste–but it won't be the same as this uniquely Macanese condiment. Over time, Balichão will ripen (like a nice cheese); try to take it as far as your nose can handle (up to a year!), and your taste buds will thank you.

1 kg (about 4 cups) whole salted tiny shrimp

1/2 lemon, seeds removed

2 fresh red chillies

2 teaspoons black peppercorns

5 bay leaves

3 whole cloves

1/4 cup Shaoxing rice wine (see page 297)

3 tablespoons Portuguese brandy or aguardente (such as Adega Velha)

1/2 cup water

1/4 cup olive oil

Put the shrimp in a bowl. Cover with water to rinse of excess salt, mix gently with your hands, and drain, discarding the water. Set aside.

Combine the lemon (peel and all) and chillies in a food processor and process until finely minced. Add to the shrimp.

Grind the peppercorns, bay leaves, and cloves in a spice grinder until fine and add to the shrimp. Add the Shaoxing wine, brandy, and water to the bowl and gently but thoroughly mix all of the ingredients with a wooden spoon. Pour into a 2-quart mason jar, top

with the olive oil, cover with cheesecloth, and screw the mason jar's ring on. Note that you're only using the ring here and not the lid–the mixture will ferment, and the gasses produced as a by-product of fermentation need somewhere to go, lest you blow up the mason jar! The cheesecloth will keep undesirables out and the oil will minimize mold. Leave at room temperature to ferment and age for at least 3 months. If any mold forms during aging, scrape it off and discard. When the desired ripeness is achieved, store in the refrigerator indefinitely, tightly covered.

WE RECOMMEND BUYING THE WHOLE SALTED TINY SHRIMP AT YOUR LOCAL KOREAN STORE, WHERE THEY ALSO SELL THE JAR IN WHICH YOU CAN AGE IT.

CHICKEN FAT CROUTONS

Melted rendered chicken fat from Galinha Bafassa (Turmeric Baked Chicken, page 184), plus additional olive oil to make a total of $1/2$ cup fat

2 cups cubed day-old Papo Seco (page 264) or baguette ($1/2$-inch cubes)

Salt

MAKES 2 CUPS

Preheat the oven to 350°F. Toss all of the ingredients together in a bowl, making sure to thoroughly coat the bread cubes with fat. Transfer to a baking sheet and bake for 10 to 15 minutes, until crisp and golden brown. If not using immediately, cool completely, then store in an airtight container for up to 3 days.

FRIED RICE RICE

In this process, we are simply removing moisture from the cooked rice so that it can fry well. The absence of excess moisture decreases the chance of the rice sticking to itself and the pan, promoting individual grains and increasing your chance for achieving the coveted wok *hei* discussed in the wok technique section (see page 24). Basic Fried Rice (page 77), Crazy Squid Rice (page 132), and Baked Pork Chop Rice (page 82) all use this rice. Scale the recipe up or down depending on how much rice you need.

MAKES 1$1/2$ CUPS

$1/2$ cups Coconut Rice (page 75)

Cook the Coconut Rice as directed. While the rice is still warm, spread it out in a flat, roughly $1/2$-inch-thick layer on a sheet pan. Let cool outside of the refrigerator for about 30 minutes (lest you steam out the fridge and create a rainforest in there), then transfer the sheet pan, uncovered, to the refrigerator for 12 to 24 hours.

Remove the rice from the refrigerator and gently separate the grains, using your fingertips, into a small bowl. Take care not to crush or break the individual grains of rice—just separate them. If you feel it's too sticky and you are not getting individually free-running grains, dry the rice for a few more hours in the fridge and try again. The rice is now ready to be used in fried rice recipes. If not using immediately, cover and keep in the refrigerator for up to 3 days.

PORK CHOPS IN BRINE

**MAKES
2 PORK CHOPS**

People always ask: "How is the pork chop in the Zhu Pa Bao (Macau's Famous Pork Chop Bun, page 215) so damn tender?" Our answer until this moment: ancient Chinese secret! But now, the big reveal of the enigma the Far East has been employing forever to tenderize meat: it's baking soda!

When meat is cooked, the protein it's made of contracts and firms up. Think of holding a raw strip steak by one end. Kinda floppy, right? Now think of it after it comes off of the grill—much firmer. Sodium bicarbonate's magic touch creates an alkaline environment in which meat's protein has difficulty contracting. The result is a perfectly cooked piece of meat with less contracting and firming, leaving things more tender than ever.

As for the flavor in this brine, we use the bay leaf and garlic ubiquitous in the pork chop buns of Macau; they usually use soy sauce as well, but we prefer the depth of flavor that fish sauce brings to the party.

2 (7-ounce) bone-in pork chops, cut ¹/₂-inch thick

³/₄ cup cold water

2 teaspoons sugar

1¹/₂ tablespoons fish sauce

¹/₂ teaspoon baking soda

3 cloves garlic, crushed

1 bay leaf

Prepare the pork chops as shown on page 263 and place in a zip-top bag. Whisk together the cold water, sugar, fish sauce, baking soda, garlic, and bay leaf in a bowl and pour over the pork chops in the bag. Remove as much air as possible from the bag, seal it, then place in a bowl and refrigerate for at least 4 hours, or up to 12 hours.

PREPARING THE PORK CHOP

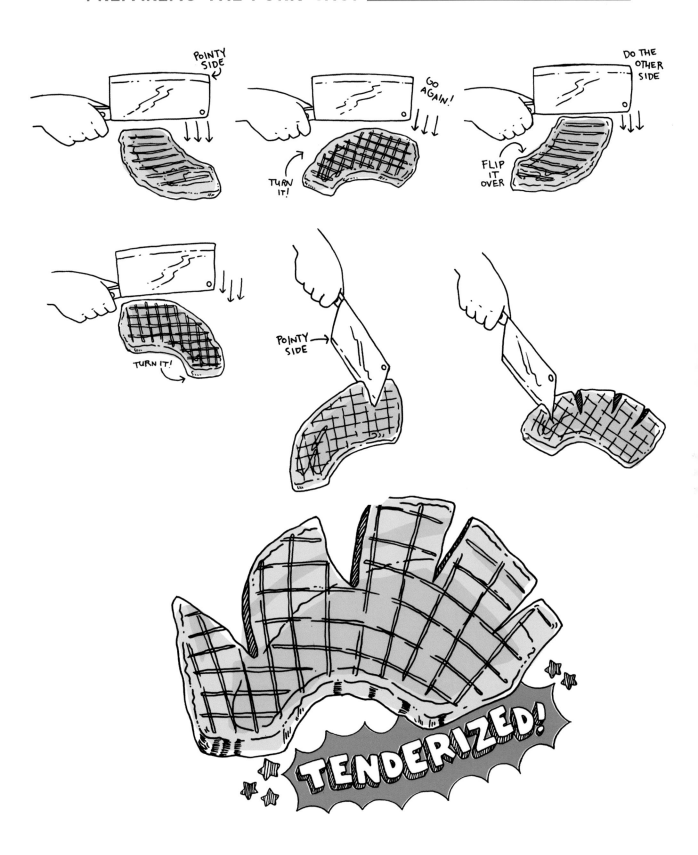

PAPO SECO (PORTUGUESE BREAD ROLLS)

MAKES 8 ROLLS

Bread is one of Portugal's legacies in the East: Western-style leavened breads are everywhere the Portuguese have been, even in places it seems unusual, including Macau. We serve these small, tender yet crispy-crusted rolls alongside Bacalhau de Vóvó (page 141), stuff them with fried pork chops for Zhu Pa Bao (page 215), turn leftovers into Chicken Fat Croutons (page 261); and use it to sop up any number of curries.

SPONGE

1¼ teaspoons active dry yeast

½ cup water, just warm to the touch

2½ ounces (½ cup) bread flour

DOUGH

1¼ teaspoons active dry yeast

7 tablespoons water, plus more if needed

16 ounces (3¼ cups) bread flour, plus more if needed

2 teaspoons lard or olive oil

1¾ teaspoons salt

2½ teaspoons sugar

Cornmeal, for dusting

To make the sponge, whisk all of the sponge ingredients together in a bowl and leave at room temperature for 1 hour. It should become nice and foamy.

To make the dough, scrape the sponge into the bowl of a stand mixer fitted with a dough hook. Add the yeast, water, bread flour, lard, salt, and sugar. Mix on the lowest speed for about 2 minutes, until the dough comes together, then increase to medium speed and mix for about 5 minutes, until the dough pulls away from the sides of the bowl. Keep an eye on the dough and adjust as necessary, adding a small amount of flour if the dough seems too wet or a splash of water if it seems too dry.

Grease a bowl with a thin coating of olive oil. Shape the dough into a tight ball and rub top-side down in the bowl to coat with oil, then cover the bowl with plastic wrap and let the dough rise in a warm place until doubled in size, an hour or so.

Prepare a sheet pan (or multiple pans, if needed) by lining with parchment paper. Spray with nonstick cooking spray and lightly dust with cornmeal.

On an unfloured work surface, use a metal bench scraper to portion the dough into 8 (3-ounce) pieces. Using a cupped hand, shape each portion into a smooth-topped ball. Cover the balls of dough on the work surface with a lightweight towel or a piece of plastic wrap and let rest for 20 minutes.

When rested, shape each portion of dough into a football-shaped loaf by rolling forward and outward with cupped palms. Place on the prepared baking sheet(s), allowing a couple of inches around each loaf for expansion, and dust with flour. Cover with a lightweight towel and let rise for about 45 minutes, until the dough doubles in size.

Preheat the oven to 500°F (450°F if using a convection oven) with a cast-iron pan on the bottom rack. When the final rise is done, score the dough from end to end with a razor blade. Using a spray bottle, spritz the dough with water and have a small handful of ice cubes at the ready. Place the baking sheet(s) in the oven and toss the ice cubes into the hot cast-iron pan. Close the door immediately.

This step creates steam, which keeps the surface of the dough moist, allowing for a better rise.

Bake for 5 minutes, rotate the baking sheets, and bake for 5 more minutes. The rolls are done when they're golden brown and sound hollow when tapped. Let cool slightly, then serve. If not using immediately, let cool fully, then store in an airtight container for up to 2 days.

A GREAT SPOT TO LET YOUR DOUGH RISE IS IN AN OVEN WITH ONLY A PILOT LIGHT GOING.

SHAPING PAPO SECO

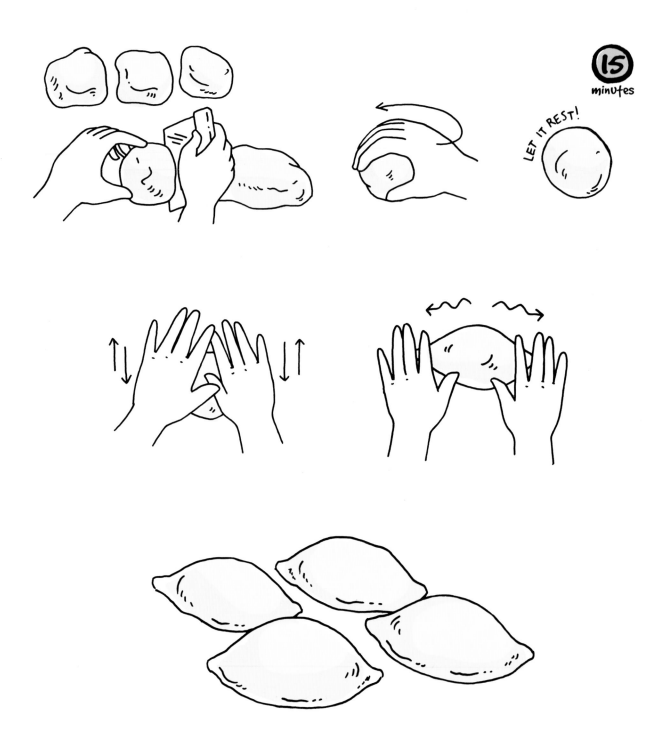

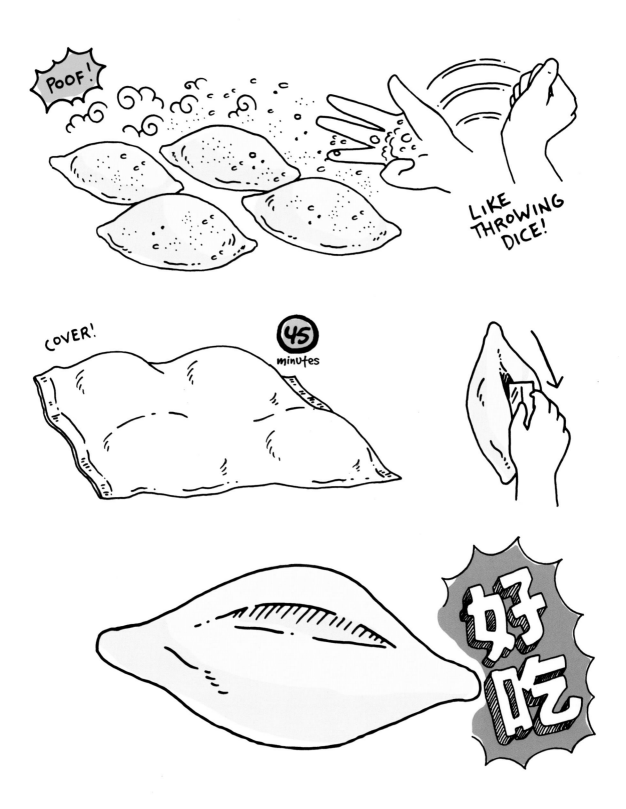

XO SAUCE

**MAKES
1 QUART**

XO Sauce as we know it today is a relatively new creation, invented in Hong Kong in the 1980s. Its origins are probably much older; we believe it is a derivative of *sha cha jiang*, also known as *sa-te* sauce, a pungent condiment of chilli, garlic, dried fish, and shrimp. XO Sauce is all about sourcing quality product and cooking it carefully: the highest-quality dried seafood and ham, and just enough heat to coax out the delicate flavors. This equals expensive, especially for the dried scallops–like upwards of a hundred bucks a pound expensive–which is one of the reasons why the name XO is used. XO is based on the Cognac designation XO ("extra old"), indicative of a carefully aged, luxurious product. (Cognac isn't an ingredient in the sauce, though we've considered adding it!)

Part of the XO adventure is the exploration of your local Chinatown food markets. Most have a dried seafood section, however, there's a better–if more expensive– option. Look for an old-style Chinese pharmacy, which will be stocked with jars of dried mushrooms, herbs, and roots. The Chinese have been drying nature's bounty for centuries, making tonics and infusions to treat everything from indigestion to male virility issues. If you thought your Xanax prescription was expensive, give the dried abalone or cordyceps a look–a brisk $500 per ounce!

Get the best dried scallops you can afford, anywhere between the size of a dime and a nickel, golden brown, and with the rich smell of a nicely seared scallop, with sweet and saline oceanside notes. Avoid scallops with white dust.

For the dried shrimp, you'll need to stick to the food markets (rather than the pharmacy). Check the refrigerated section of your Chinese grocer and look at the label, man! No artificial color! Each shrimp should also be the size of a dime, and when squeezed they should offer slight resistance.

Finally, read through the recipe in its entirety before beginning the cooking process–and use a thermometer. After all the time and money you spent on your adventure to Chinatown, it'd be a shame to burn this stuff! You're making a lot here, but like Cognac, it does get better with age–and there are a ton of uses: Fat Noodles with XO Sauce (page 97) and Bebinca de Rabano (page 122); atop Coconut Rice (page 75), green vegetables, and eggs; or go all out and use it on grilled oysters or a prawn stir-fry.

3 ounces (about ½ cup) dried scallops (see page 293)

1½ ounces (about ¼ cup) dried shrimp (see page 293)

2 cups Chilli Oil (page 274)

5 ounces (about 1 cup) good-quality cured ham (such as Ibérico, Jinhua, or Smithfield ham), finely diced, fat included, no skin

3 shallots, minced

1 (2-inch) piece fresh ginger, peeled and minced

9 cloves garlic, minced

¼ cup Chinese black olives (see page 296), pitted and finely chopped into a paste

1½ teaspoons sherry vinegar

1½ teaspoons fish sauce

1½ teaspoons sugar

1½ teaspoons sweet paprika

1 teaspoon extra-hot ground chilli or cayenne pepper

Soak the dried scallops and dried shrimp in cold water in separate small metal bowls overnight.

Fill a wok half full of water, place a steamer basket insert with a lid in the wok, and bring the water to a boil. Water should not enter the steamer basket. Place the bowl of scallops and their soaking liquid inside the steamer basket and steam until plump and easily shredded, about 20 minutes. Repeat the process with the shrimp, steaming until plump and tender, about 20 minutes. Carefully drain the shrimp and scallops, reserving the liquid. Finely chop the shrimp and shred the scallops by hand into small strips.

Combine all of the soaking liquid in a small saucepan and reduce to ¼ cup over medium heat. Don't burn it! This is shellfish gold! Set aside.

Prepare two small pots: one equipped with a candy thermometer and one equipped with a wire mesh strainer over it. In the pot with the candy thermometer, heat the oil with the diced ham to 180°F over low heat. Adjust the flame to hold at this temperature for 20 minutes, stirring gently from time to time. You aren't frying the ham here–you are simply dehydrating it a bit and infusing the oil with its flavor.

Pour the oil and ham directly into the strainer/pot setup. Reserve the ham and return the oil to the heat. Transfer the candy thermometer to this pot and return the oil to 180°F. Add the shrimp and hold at 180°F for 10 minutes. Strain the shrimp and reserve with the ham. Return the oil to 180°F. Add the scallops to the oil, sprinkling the pieces in to prevent clumping, and hold at 180°F for 15 minutes, stirring often until the scallops develop a glassy, translucent appearance. Strain the oil and reserve the scallops with the ham and shrimp.

Heat the oil to 200°F. Add the shallots, stirring for a couple of minutes until translucent, then add the ginger and garlic and cook until fragrant, about 60 seconds. Add the olives and cook, stirring, for another 2 minutes.

Carefully add the sherry vinegar, fish sauce, and reserved shellfish gold to the oil. Stir for a couple of minutes–things will get bubbly–then stir in the sugar, paprika, and cayenne. Return the ham, scallops, and shrimp to the oil and gently stir until thoroughly combined.

Remove from the heat and let cool fully, then store tightly sealed in a glass jar in the refrigerator for up to 3 months.

MOLHO DE AZIETE, AKA MOJO (OIL AND GARLIC SAUCE)

**MAKES
I CUP**

By now you know that you've gotta have a lotta mojo to cook from this book, but we're not talking about this sauce! This sauce is garlicky, citrusy, and oily, great on roasted pork and potatoes and really, wherever else you want to put it!

$^1/_3$ cup minced garlic

1 fresh red chilli, seeded and minced (more or less to taste)

$^3/_4$ cup olive oil

Finely grated zest and juice of 1 lemon

1 tablespoon sherry vinegar

1 teaspoon salt

Combine the garlic, chilli, and olive oil in a small heavy pot over low heat. Slowly cook until the garlic becomes very fragrant, about 5 minutes. Remove from the heat and add the lemon zest, lemon juice, sherry vinegar, and salt. Stir well and let cool. Store tightly covered in the refrigerator for up to 3 months.

PORTUGUESE-STYLE TOMATO SAUCE

The *cha chaan teng* tea restaurants in Macau and Hong Kong always seem to have three European-ish sauces floating around to top various rice and meat dishes: a yellow curry-based sauce, a creamy béchamel-like white sauce, and a tomato paste- or possibly ketchup-based red sauce. Our version of this red sauce can be used on the Baked Pork Chop Rice (page 82) and Capela (page 203), and we like to smooth it out by adding evaporated milk. Why not just regular milk from a cow instead of a can? It is a tribute to the fact that the *cha chaan teng* dishes are usually made out of convenient, highly shelf-stable ingredients, not unlike cream of mushroom soup here in the States.

1 tablespoon olive oil

1 yellow onion, minced

Salt

4 cloves garlic, minced

1 red bell pepper, stemmed, seeded, and pureed in a food processor

1 tablespoon tomato paste

2 tablespoons red wine

1/2 (14-ounce) can whole peeled tomatoes

1/2 teaspoon extra-hot ground chillies

3/4 cup evaporated milk

1 tablespoon sherry vinegar

1 teaspoon sugar

Heat a heavy Dutch oven over medium-high heat. Add the oil, then the onions. Season with salt and cook until soft and lightly caramelized, about 5 minutes. Add the garlic and cook until fragrant, about 1 minute. Add the red bell pepper puree, season with salt, and cook for an additional 5 minutes, until the flavors have melded. Add the tomato paste and stir, cooking for about 2 more minutes. Deglaze with the red wine, scraping the bottom of the pot with a wooden spoon until the wine has cooked down a bit, about 1 minute. Add the tomatoes with their juices, lower the heat to medium, and stir well, using your spoon to break up the tomatoes as they cook, about 5 minutes. Add the ground chillies, evaporated milk, sherry vinegar, and sugar; stir well and cook for an additional 5 minutes, adjusting the heat to maintain a low simmer. Once the desired consistency is reached (go for a typical tomato sauce consistency here), remove from the heat and season to taste.

If not using immediately, let cool and store in the refrigerator for up to 5 days.

"PORTUGUESE" CURRY SAUCE

MAKES ABOUT 6 CUPS

We put quotes in the title of this sauce because you'd never find it in Portugal! It's famous in Macau though, most likely finding its way there via the rich, mildly spiced, coconut milk–based curries brought to Macau by the Portguese and their Malay companions in the mid-sixteenth century. At one time, saffron may have been probably involved, but as travelers sailed away from the Iberian Peninsula, North Africa, and Persia (where saffron is typically grown), the vibrant yellow was probably produced by turmeric root instead. We're fancy and use both turmeric *and* saffron. We use this sauce on the Baked Pork Chop Rice (page 82), Curry Crab (page 162), and Po Kok Gai ("Portuguese" Chicken Curry, page 181).

¼ cup unsalted butter

1 Spanish onion, coarsely chopped

Pinch of salt

1 (2-inch) piece fresh ginger, peeled and minced

1 tablespoon Malacca Sweet Curry Powder (page 280)

2 tablespoons ground turmeric

1 teaspoon freshly ground black pepper

1 bay leaf

2 whole star anise

4 cups Chicken Stock (page 282)

2 (13.5-ounce) cans coconut milk

1 cup evaporated milk

¾ teaspoon saffron threads

¾ teaspoon extra-hot ground chilli or cayenne pepper

¼ cup cornstarch mixed with ½ cup cold water

Freshly squeezed lemon juice, for seasoning

ACID IS JUST AS IMPORTANT AS SALT WHEN SEASONING. IN THIS CASE, THE FRESH BRIGHTNESS OF ABOUT HALF A LEMON'S JUICE WILL BRIGHTEN AND OPEN THE FLAVORS IN THE SAUCE. IN OTHER CIRCUMSTANCES, VINEGAR WORKS AS WELL. JUST AS YOU WOULD USE SALT TO SEASON THINGS WITHOUT MAKING A DISH SALTY, USE ACID TO SEASON WITHOUT MAKING THINGS SOUR.

Heat the butter in a large, heavy pot over medium-high heat. Add the onion and a hearty pinch of salt and cook until the onions are soft and translucent, about 5 minutes. Add the ginger and sauté until aromatic, another minute or two. Add the curry powder, turmeric, black pepper, bay leaf, and star anise and cook until aromatic, another 30 to 60 seconds. Stir in the stock, and when the initial sizzling and bubbling subsides, add the coconut milk, evaporated milk, saffron, and cayenne. Adjusting the heat as necessary and stirring occasionally, simmer to meld the flavors and slightly reduce the sauce, approximately 20 minutes.

Stir the cornstarch slurry well, then stir half of it into the sauce and return to a simmer. You want a thick, béchamel-like consistency; adjust using more slurry to thicken or a bit of water to thin out. Taste and adjust the seasoning using lemon juice and salt.

If not using immediately, let cool and store in the refrigerator for up to 3 days.

STARCH-BASED THICKENING AGENTS ONLY REACH THEIR FULL POTENTIAL WHEN THEY'VE BEEN BROUGHT TO THE BOILING POINT—SO BE SURE THIS HAS HAPPENED, LEST YOU PREMATURELY ADD MORE STARCH AND FIND YOURSELF WITH A CEMENTLIKE SAUCE!

REFOGADO (PORTUGESE SOFFRITTO)

Most Arroz Gordo recipes have tomato, garlic, and onions—but we like to use this condiment instead, bringing a deep level of flavor due to its long, slow cooking time, which ups the flavor quotient in any dish it is used in. Called *soffritto* in Italy, *sofrito* in Spain, and *refogado* in Portuguese-speaking provinces, this recipe works on so many levels—as the base for a rice dish or stir-fry, an addition to scrambled eggs, even a dipping sauce for Papo Seco (page 264). This looks like a large amount of ingredients, but it cooks down quite a bit. The process takes a long time, so be sure to keep an eye on it and don't let it burn!

MAKES ABOUT 1 QUART

1/2 cup olive oil

3 pounds Spanish onions, julienned

4 pounds red bell peppers, seeded and julienned

3 tablespoons salt

2 tablespoons tomato paste

1/2 cup minced garlic

2 teaspoons smoked paprika

2 tablespoons sherry vinegar

1 1/2 teaspoons freshly ground black pepper

Heat the olive oil in a heavy pot over medium-high heat. Add the onions, bell peppers, and 1 1/2 tablespoons of the salt, stir well, and cover the pot. Decrease the heat to low and cook slowly until the peppers and onions are very soft, about 20 minutes, stirring every 5 minutes or so. Remove the lid and continue to cook until the vegetables start to caramelize as water evaporates from the pan, another 20 to 30 minutes, stirring every 5 minutes or so. When the vegetables are lightly caramelized, add the tomato paste, garlic, and smoked paprika and stir well.

Continue to cook over low heat, stirring occasionally, until all of the liquid has evaporated and the oil has separated from the vegetables, at least 1 hour. Deglaze the pan with the sherry vinegar and adjust the seasoning with the remaining 1 1/2 tablespoons salt and the pepper. The flavors should be richly caramelized and intensely seasoned.

Remove from the heat and let cool completely. Store tightly covered in the refrigerator for up to 1 month.

We occasionally use this hot, flavorful oil to quickly cook things we want to give heat to, but mainly we use it as our go-to seasoning and dressing, which is why we add some olive oil to give it a robust and fruity flavor–and to nod to Portuguese heritage. Use a thermometer to make sure that the spices don't burn!

1¹/₃ cups peanut oil

²/₃ cup olive oil

5 whole star anise

3 cinnamon sticks

1 (2-inch) piece fresh ginger, sliced ¹/₄ inch thick

10 cloves garlic, crushed with the side of a knife

¹/₂ cup dried red chillies, ground in a spice grinder

2 teaspoons whole Sichuan pepper (see page 289)

1 teaspoon sweet paprika

Combine the oils, star anise, cinnamon, and ginger in a small heavy pot fitted with a candy thermometer. Set over medium heat and bring to 140°F. Add the garlic and bring to 180°F. Remove from the heat, cool to 160°F, and add the ground chillies, Sichuan pepper, and paprika.

Transfer to a storage container and let steep for 24 hours at room temperature, then strain through a cheesecloth-lined fine-mesh strainer. Discard the solids and store the oil, tightly sealed, in the refrigerator for up to 1 month.

SAMBAL TUMIS
(SPICY SWEET-AND-SOUR SAMBAL)

In the Malay language, *sambal* connotes a sauce based on dried or fresh chillies, and *tumis* means to slowly fry. Sambal Tumis is spicy, slightly sweet and sour, and has a red oil slick from its long cooking process. We omit the traditional shrimp paste so that our vegetarian guests can enjoy this, too; however, if that's not a concern and if you've got some Balichão (page 260) lying around, you can add a teaspoon or so with the garlic to give the tumis a little extra oomph.

**MAKES
2 CUPS**

2 tablespoons peanut oil

1 large red onion, julienned

2 cloves garlic, minced

¹⁄₃ cup sambal oelek or minced fresh red chillies

2 tablespoons grated palm sugar (see page 296)

¹⁄₃ cup Tamarind Extract (page 285)

¹⁄₂ cup coconut milk

Heat a heavy pot over medium-high heat. Add the oil, then add the onion and cook for about 5 minutes, until the onion softens and starts to caramelize. Add the garlic and cook until fragrant, about 30 seconds, then add the sambal and cook until nearly dry, about 5 to 10 minutes more. Add the palm sugar and tamarind and cook for 3 more minutes to combine the flavors.

Add the coconut milk, decrease the heat to medium-low, and simmer, stirring constantly, until the coconut milk breaks and the sambal begins to fry in the coconut oil, 10 to 15 minutes.

Remove from the heat and let cool completely. Store tightly covered in the refrigerator for up to 1 month.

PEIXINHOS FRITOS (TINY FRIED FISH)

Peixinhos fritos is Portuguese for "little fried fish"–a made-up name we gave these guys since "fried whitebait" isn't all that appealing, plus, they've got the cutest little eyes! One finds these tiny dried fish in Chinese stores–they're pretty expensive and usually used in luxurious preparations. We use them in the Dry-Fried Asparagus (page 107) and Fat Noodles with XO Sauce (page 97) dishes, but feel free to sprinkle them wherever you might like a bit of extra flavor and a crisp, almost baconlike crunch.

Peanut oil, for frying

1 cup dried whitebait
(yin yú, see page 299)

Salt

Heat 2 to 3 inches of oil in a wok to 350°F over high heat. Add the dried whitebait and quickly fry until golden and crisp, about 45 seconds. Transfer to a paper towel-lined plate and season with salt. Let cool, then store in an airtight container lined with a paper towel for up to 7 days.

TEA EGGS

While in Sichuan province, everywhere we went, we saw huge jars filled with eggs, their shells soaking up the dark liquid they were submerged in. The sizes were wildly different: from hen eggs to quail eggs to duck eggs, all with a lovely spiderweb pattern. Back in the restaurant, we tried to make them the traditional way, partially cracking boiled eggs with a spoon to create the spiderweb pattern, then staining them, but ultimately we decided to skip this time-consuming process and go for the solid-colored and still delicious eggs we serve today.

2 cups water

1/2 ounce pu-erh tea leaves (about 1/2 cup) (see page 296)

1/2 teaspoon whole Sichuan pepper (see page 289)

2 cinnamon sticks

1 (2-inch) piece fresh ginger, peeled and julienned

3 whole star anise

1 cup soy sauce

6 eggs

To make the marinade, bring the water to a boil in a small pot over high heat. Add the tea, Sichuan pepper, cinnamon sticks, ginger, and star anise. Reduce the heat to low and maintain a simmer for 10 minutes. Remove from the heat, stir in the soy sauce, and strain the mixture into a 1-quart heatproof container. Discard the solids. Let cool to room temperature.

Rinse the same pot and fill with 2 quarts water. Bring to a boil over high heat. Carefully add the eggs using a spider and cook for 12 minutes. Meanwhile, prepare an ice bath for the eggs. When the eggs are done, transfer them to the ice bath to cool.

When the eggs are completely cooled, peel them and put in the marinade. Refrigerate for 1 hour. Remove the eggs from the marinade and store tightly sealed in the refrigerator for up to 3 days.

VITOR'S CURRY PASTE

MAKES ABOUT 2 CUPS

We met our friend and well-known Macanese cuisine authority Florita Alves on our second trip to Macau, in 2015, when she generously brought us into her home to cook a feast. Her husband, Vitor, inspired this spicy curry paste for Shrimp Curry with Okra and Tomato (page 166), and like many Macanese, understandably guarded the recipe a bit. So, back home, we re-created it to the best of our abilities. We start with a small amount of oil to fry the onions in, then add quite a bit more in which to carefully bloom the spicy curry powder. It may seem like a lot of oil—just remember that the oil gives the spice its vehicle to deliver the goods.

5 tablespoons Macau Hot Curry Powder (page 279)

2 tablespoons Korean chilli flakes

3 tablespoons Filipino cane vinegar

¾ cup peanut oil

1 large onion, diced

2 cloves garlic, minced

1 (1-inch) piece fresh ginger, peeled and minced

In a small bowl, mix the curry powder, chili flakes, and vinegar and set aside. Heat ¼ cup of the oil in a saucepan over medium-high heat. Add the onion and cook until it starts to caramelize, about 5 minutes. Add the garlic and ginger and cook until fragrant, 60 to 90 seconds. Add the remaining ½ cup oil and the curry mixture and allow the spices to bloom into the oil until fragrant and copper in color, about 60 seconds, then remove from the heat. Let cool fully, then puree in a blender until smooth. Store tightly covered in a cool place (cellar temperature is ideal, but the refrigerator will do). The curry paste will be usable immediately, but at its peak after 1 month. After 1 month, store in the refrigerator for up to 6 months.

MACAU HOT CURRY POWDER

MAKES
ABOUT
1 CUP

Curry powder is ubiquitous in Macau's shops, markets, and kitchens. We recreated this chilli-forward curry powder based on a few of our favorites in Macau. It is a building block of Vitor's Curry Paste (page 278), and also adds a flavorful slow burn to our Curried Vegetable Chamuças with Fragrant Tamarind Chutney (page 49) and Curried Beef and Tendon with Turnip (page 229). We recommend you "bloom" the powder before using it by adding a bit of cane vinegar to the powder to make a paste.

4 tablespoons ground turmeric

5 tablespoons extra-hot ground chilli or cayenne pepper

1 tablespoon ground ginger

2 tablespoons coriander seeds

1 tablespoon white pepper

2 whole star anise

1 whole cinnamon stick

2 teaspoons fennel seed

3 whole green cardamom pods

1 teaspoon whole Sichuan pepper (see page 289)

10 whole cloves

Finely grind all the spices together in a spice grinder. Store tightly covered for up to 3 months.

MALACCA SWEET CURRY POWDER

MAKES ABOUT 1 CUP

This is a mild blend based on a curry powder we encountered in Malaysia. It is heavy on the coriander, with a mellow aroma from fenugreek and fennel. We generally use this curry powder in conjunction with coconut milk.

5 tablespoons coriander seeds

1/2 cup dried red chillies

2 teaspoons ground turmeric

2 teaspoons fenugreek seeds

2 1/2 teaspoons fennel seeds

2 teaspoons cumin seeds

Grind all of the ingredients into a fine powder in a spice grinder. Keep tightly sealed at room temperature for up to 3 months.

FIVE-SPICE POWDER

MAKES ABOUT 1/2 CUP

This warming, vibrant blend is essential to regional Chinese and Chinese-influenced cuisines.

8 teaspoons whole Sichuan pepper (see page 289)

8 teaspoons fennel seeds

15 whole star anise

6 cinnamon sticks

8 whole cloves

5 teaspoons ground ginger

Preheat the oven to 300°F. Spread the Sichuan pepper, fennel seeds, star anise, cinnamon sticks, and cloves onto a sheet pan and toast in the oven until fragrant, about 3 to 5 minutes. Cool and grind into a fine powder and mix with the ginger. Store in a tightly sealed container for up to 3 months.

VEGETABLE STOCK

This is a neutral stock that we use in a lot of different dishes, which is why we avoid overpowering flavors like peppers, cabbages, and the like.

MAKES
4 QUARTS

5 quarts water

1 Spanish onion, diced large

1/2 bunch celery, diced large

2 large carrots, peeled and diced large

1/2 bunch green onions, white and green parts, trimmed and cut into 1-inch segments

1 (1-inch) piece fresh ginger, unpeeled and sliced 1/4 inch thick

1 1/2 teaspoons whole Sichuan pepper (see page 289)

1 cup fresh mushrooms (your choice; this is a great place to use any trimmings you may have)

Combine all the ingredients in a stockpot and bring to a boil over high heat. Reduce the heat to a simmer and cook for 10 minutes. Remove from the heat and let steep for 30 minutes. Strain, discarding all the solids, and cool.

Keep refrigerated until ready to use, up to 3 days, or freeze for up to 6 months.

CHICKEN STOCK

MAKES 8 QUARTS

For best results, a combination of necks, backs, and feet are great, but use whatever you can get your hands on!

4 pounds raw chicken bones (preferably necks, backs, and feet)

10 quarts water

1 large Spanish onion, diced large

1/2 bunch celery, diced large

3 large carrots, peeled and diced large

1 bunch green onions, trimmed and cut into 1-inch segments and flattened with the side of a knife or cleaver

1 (1-inch) piece fresh ginger, unpeeled, sliced 1/4 inch thick, and flattened with the side of a cleaver

1 tablespoon whole Sichuan pepper (see page 289)

1 cup fresh mushrooms (your choice; this is a great place to use any trimmings you may have)

Combine the chicken bones and water in a large pot and bring to a boil over high heat. As it comes to a boil, stir with a spoon to separate the bones. Reduce the heat to the lowest simmer possible, skim off any scum that has risen to the top, and cook for 3 hours. Add the onion, celery, carrots, green onions, ginger, Sichuan pepper, and mushrooms and simmer for an additional 45 minutes. Remove from the heat and strain, discarding all the solids, and cool.

Keep refrigerated until ready to use, up to 3 days, or freeze for up to 6 months.

PORK STOCK

This recipe is not very involved, but long on flavor; the Chinese-style blanching technique removes blood and impurities. Hit up your trustworthy local butcher to get the bones and trotter, then freeze the unused stock for a rainy day.

MAKES
ABOUT
3 QUARTS

4 pounds pork bones

1 pig trotter

1 (2-inch) piece fresh ginger, unpeeled and thinly sliced

6 green onions, white and green parts, crushed with the side of a knife or cleaver

1 tablespoon Sichuan pepper (see page 289)

4 quarts water, or more as needed

Put the bones and trotter in a large stockpot and cover with cold water. Bring to a boil over high heat and cook for 10 minutes, then skim off any scum that floats to the top of the pot. Drain the bones and trotter and discard all the liquid. Rinse the bones and trotter and return to the pot with the ginger, green onions, Sichuan pepper, and water. Bring to a simmer over high heat, then lower the heat, and simmer very gently for at least 4 hours, skimming off any scum that forms on top.

Let the stock cool a bit at room temperature, then strain and refrigerate. When fully cooled, remove and discard the fat that has solidified on top of the stock. The stock is ready to be used at this point. Freeze it if not using within 5 days.

VEGETARIAN WOK SAUCE

MAKES ABOUT 2½ CUPS

This sauce brings a nice vegetarian bolt of flavor to stir-fries and other wok preparations.

2 cups Vegetable Stock (page 281)

¼ cup glutinous rice cooking wine (see page 295)

1 tablespoon soy sauce

1½ teaspoons Filipino cane vinegar

1 tablespoon sugar

⅛ teaspoon freshly ground black pepper

1½ teaspoons tapioca starch mixed with 1 tablespoon cold water

Combine the stock, wine, soy sauce, cane vinegar, sugar, and pepper in a pot and bring to a boil over high heat. Stir in the tapioca slurry and return to a boil while stirring. Taste, adjust the seasoning, and cool. Store in an airtight container in the refrigerator for up to 1 week.

PORK WOK SAUCE

MAKES ABOUT 2½ CUPS

This mild sauce is a great way to add moisture to pretty much any wok stir-fry.

1 cup Chicken Stock (page 282)

1 cup Pork Stock (page 283)

¼ cup glutinous rice cooking wine (see page 295)

1 tablespoon soy sauce

1½ teaspoons Filipino cane vinegar

1 tablespoon sugar

1½ teaspoons tapioca starch mixed with 1 tablespoon cold water

Combine the stocks, wine, soy sauce, cane vinegar, and sugar in a pot and bring to a boil over high heat. Stir in the tapioca slurry and return to a boil while stirring constantly. Taste, adjust the seasoning, and remove from the heat. Let cool completely. Store in an airtight container in the refrigerator for up to 1 week.

UMAMI JUICE

MAKES
ABOUT 5 CUPS
OF STRAINED
JUICE

Double your pleasure with this condiment: it's a nice stir-fry sauce *and* flavorful marinated mushrooms, all in one! Use the mushrooms in any dish that calls for rehydrated mushrooms, such as the Tchai de Bonzo (page 119).

2 ounces dried shiitake mushrooms

6 cups water

2 tablespoons *tian mian jian* (sweet bean paste, see page 298)

2 tablespoon soy sauce

4 teaspoons sugar

Soak the mushrooms in the water overnight. Combine the mushrooms and soaking liquid with the sweet bean paste, soy sauce, and sugar in a medium saucepan and bring to a simmer over high heat. Lower the heat to a gentle simmer and cook for 10 minutes. Remove from the heat and let cool. Pour everything (mushrooms and liquid) into a container and store in the refrigerator for up to 2 weeks.

TAMARIND EXTRACT

MAKES
1 QUART

Tamarind is native to Africa, and it brings an earthy acidity to the cooking of India, Southeast Asia, and Macau. The pods harvested from the trees can be used, but a simpler, more consistent product comes in the form of a block of tamarind pulp (we prefer seedless). It is imperative that only 100 percent tamarind be used.

14 ounces tamarind pulp

4 cups water

Combine the tamarind pulp and water in a heavy pot, completely breaking up the tamarind with your hands. Bring to a boil over high heat and cook for about 10 minutes, continuously mashing the pulp to a thin applesauce-like consistency. Let cool slightly, place in a colander, and use your hands or a plastic spatula to push the extract through, making sure to remove all seeds and shell particicles. Let cool completely and store tightly covered in the refrigerator for up to a month.

IT'S SUPER IMPORTANT TO BREAK UP THE PULP AS MUCH AS POSSIBLE WITH YOUR HANDS BEFORE BRINGING THE MIXTURE TO A BOIL. THIS WILL ENSURE THAT AS MUCH OF THE TAMARIND GETS EXTRACTED INTO THE WATER AS POSSIBLE. FAILURE TO DO THIS WILL ALTER THE CONSISTENCY, TEXTURE, FLAVOR, AND ULTIMATE SUCCESS OF THE FINAL PRODUCT!

INGREDIENTS GLOSSARY

It's no exaggeration to say that spices have had a greater impact on the world than any other foodstuff. For millennia, the quest for spices has established trade routes the world over, the search taking travelers through continents on foot and sailing across seas as trade built between Europe and points in Africa and Asia. During the Middle Ages, this trade made the seats of power in Europe quite rich—and when these mostly land-based trade routes were blocked by the Ottoman Turks in the mid-1400s, new sea-based trade routes had to be explored and opened. This gave birth to the Age of Exploration; the Spanish sailed west for the most part, the Portuguese sailed east. Unknown lands were discovered and new trade routes were opened, and the foundations of new cuisines were born as new spices, flavors, and techniques incubated along the new routes.

THE SPICE CABINET

Buying and Storing Spices

Spices sold throughout Asia are generally available loose at spice markets and are—due to high turnover—extremely fresh and pungent. In the same spirit, you should look for spices in markets where they are briskly sold—usually the ethnic markets as opposed to the big box superstores. It's also important to buy *whole* spices whenever possible—their volatile aromas do the heavy lifting in cooking; however, once the spices are ground, those aromas are released, so you want to grind them yourself as much as possible right before using. When using whole spices, give them a once-over for dirt or small stones before grinding or throwing them in a pot.

Store spices away from heat and direct sunlight in glass (we use mason jars) because plastic containers permit the volatile oils to escape, making your whole spice cabinet and its content smell like the same curry powder.

Spices

BAY LEAVES The plump, oval-shaped leaves from the ancient Mediterranean laurel tree (*Laurus nobilis*) are one of the most widely used culinary herbs in Europe and North America. Bay leaves are most frequently used in stews such as our Tacho (page 209), and in sauces like the Galinha à Africana (page 171), and are so essential in making Balichão (page 260) that Cantonese-speaking locals in Macau refer to bay leaves as *ham ha ip*, literally translated as "salt shrimp leaf."

CARDAMOM Native to India, cardamom comes from the seeds of several plants in the Zingiberaceae family. There are two types: green and black.

- Green cardamom (*Elettaria cardamomum*), known as *true* cardamom, is one of the most expensive spices by weight, surpassed only by vanilla and saffron. This richly fragrant spice consists of oval pods that are sun-dried until pale green. Generally, the pods are ground before adding to curries, or left whole for rice dishes. This spice's flavor blends well with dairy and is commonly used in Indian milk-based desserts.

- Black cardamom (*Amomum cardamomum*) is also known as brown, greater, longer, or Nepal cardamom. These pods are much larger than the green variety and have a distinctly smoky flavor and aroma derived from traditional methods of drying over open flames, which lends black cardamom well to savory and hearty meat stews.

CEYLON CINNAMON Also known as *true* cinnamon (*Cinnamomum verum*), this is the dried inner bark of a tree native to Sri Lanka. What is mostly available on the market–and labeled "cinnamon"–is actually *not* true cinnamon, but rather, *Cinnamomum cassia* (a much cheaper and more assertive relative). In the early sixteenth century, the Portuguese sought *true* cinnamon in Sri Lanka, where they controlled all cinnamon trade for over a century. Since this time, cinnamon has been revered by the Portuguese and is integral in many of their sweets, as well as in savory dishes.

CLOVE This strong, pungent spice (*Syzygium aromaticum*), which has been in use for thousands of years, is indigenous to the Moluccas (the Spice Islands) in Indonesia. Clove was once the most precious and sought-after spice in the world, so much so that control over distribution spurred many expeditions and conflict. The popularity of cloves in Europe prompted the Portuguese to find a direct route to the Spice Islands in the early sixteenth century. By the late eighteenth century, cloves were being grown in Africa, including Zanzibar, Madagascar, and Mauritius, making them more common and less valuable. The buds of the evergreen clove tree are picked before flowering and are sun-dried. Cloves add a distinct dark, warm sweetness to our various spice blends and preparations.

CORIANDER The small round seeds from the cilantro plant (*Coriandrum sativum*) have a mild citrus fragrance, which is maximized when slightly toasted before grinding. It is one of the most used spices in Macanese cooking, along with white pepper, cumin, and bay leaf. Coriander seeds, whether whole or ground, are present in almost all of our spice blends.

Cilantro is native to regions spanning from southern Europe to North Africa and Southwest Asia and is said to be the world's most commonly used herb. All parts of this aromatic plant, from the seeds to the leaves, stems, and root, can be eaten.

CUMIN Native to Egypt, cumin (*Cuminum cyminum*) has been cultivated in the Middle East, India, and Asia for millennia, and was brought to the New World by both the Portuguese and the Spanish. Cumin seed is used for its distinctive earthy flavor and aroma in Portuguese and Indian cuisines as well as many Macanese preparations including Tacho (page 209) and Esmargal (page 33).

FENNEL SEED Fennel (*Foeniculum vulgare*) is a flowering plant and part of the carrot family, indigenous to the shores of the Mediterranean. The green elongated seeds of the fennel plant are used as a spice in Asian cooking, while the plant itself is used as an herb and a vegetable in Europe. The seeds add a sweet, vegetal anise fragrance to many of our spice blends and curries.

FENUGREEK The fresh green bitter leaves of the fenugreek plant (*Trigonella foenum-graecum*) are used as an herb in parts of India, but most common are the dried yellow or amber seeds, which are used as a spice. Available both whole and powdered, fenugreek is used in pickles (*achars*) as well as Indian masalas.

FIVE-SPICE POWDER Five-spice powder is essential to regional Chinese and Chinese-influenced cuisines. This versatile blend is vibrant and complex, and adds a warming, sweet dimension. Five-spice powder contains cinnamon, clove, fennel, Sichuan peppercorn, star anise, and sometimes ginger or other spices. See our recipe for Five-Spice Powder on page 280.

MUSTARD SEEDS AND MUSTARD POWDER
The English word *mustard* is derived from the Latin *mustum*, meaning "must" or "young wine," and *ardens*, meaning "hot" or "flaming." Mustard seeds are the small round seeds of various mustard plants native to Europe. Their flavors range from the most pungent, black variety to a much milder flavor with the yellow variety. Mustard seeds have a rather bitter taste on their own when raw, but become nutty after being bloomed in hot oil, as in Singapore Sour Cabbage (page 39).

- Black mustard seed is a hard round seed that varies in color from dark brown to black. It is smaller and much more pungent than the yellow.

- Brown mustard seeds are similar in size to the black variety and vary in color from light to dark brown and are more pungent than the yellow, but less than the black. Brown mustard seeds are used for pickling and as a seasoning and are the main ingredient in European and hot Chinese mustards.

- Yellow mustard seeds are hard, round, beige or straw-colored seeds and are much larger than the brown variety, but a lot less pungent. With its milder flavor, yellow mustard seed is most commonly used in ballpark mustard and is great for pickling. Yellow and brown seeds are blended to make English mustard.

- Mustard powder is simply mustard seed that has been finely ground. At Fat Rice we use hot Chinese mustard powder mixed with vinegar, honey, soy, and sesame to produce a pungent condiment for our Pork Chop Bun (page 215).

PAPRIKA Paprika is a spice made from dried peppers (*Capsicum annuum*). Spanish paprika (pimentón) has a distinct smoky flavor and aroma from drying the peppers over smoldering oak wood. Pimentón is available sweet (pimentón dulce), moderately spicy (pimentón agridulce), or very spicy (pimentón picante). At the restaurant, we use both smoked paprika and sweet (unsmoked) paprika. Look for smoked and sweet paprika at a local spice shop or at a grocer specializing in European products.

PEPPERCORNS Pepper was once such a valuable spice that it was often referred to as "black gold" and used as a form of collateral or even currency. Peppercorns are the dried berries of a flowering vine native to the Malabar coast of southwest India, where nearly all of the black pepper found in Europe, the Middle East, and North Africa came from until the late fourteenth century. The pepper vine, now grown in much of tropical Asia, particularly in East Malaysia, produces, depending on the stage of maturity, black, white, and green peppercorns; however, for our purposes, we generally use black and white pepper.

- Black peppercorns are whole berries that were picked unripe and sun-dried until shriveled. Before the arrival of chillies from the New World in the sixteenth century, black peppercorns were the main source of heat in Indian and Asian cuisines.

- White peppercorns are ripe berries with the pink skins removed before being bleached white by drying in the sun. With a slightly hot and earthy flavor, white peppercorns are common in Chinese cuisine.

SAFFRON Among the world's costliest spices by weight, saffron is cultivated from the threadlike stigmas of the saffron crocus flower (*Crocus sativus*). Saffron threads are usually soaked in a little warm water before use to release the color. Both the threads and the liquid are added to the dish to give it a distinct pigment and aroma. Many Macanese recipes call for *açafão*; however, this refers most always to turmeric, which is far more affordable and imparts a similar pigment and fragrance.

SICHUAN PEPPERCORN This spice is not a true peppercorn, but rather the dried berry of the prickly ash tree (*Zanthoxylum piperitum*). The unique flavor and aroma of Sichuan peppercorn is not hot or pungent like black, white, or chilli peppers. Instead, it has a piney and lemony spice that brings a numbing

tingle to the palate, which is why in Sichuan cuisine they are paired with chillies: to ease the painful burn. After removing the black seed inside, the red husk can be used whole, or finely ground. Finding good-quality Sichuan peppercorns can be difficult in the United States. Look in Chinese markets for peppercorns with a deep red color and an open "four clover" shape. Avoid Sichuan peppercorns that are dirty, dull in color, closed, or have a lot of the black seeds still inside the husks. Be sure to clean peppercorns well by picking out thorns, twigs, and any black seeds.

STAR ANISE Star anise is the dried flower head of a small evergreen tree native to China *(Illicium verum)*. These star-shaped seedpods have a distinctive and powerful licoricelike flavor, and are often simmered whole for a lengthy period of time, like in Charlie's Peanuts (page 37) or Tea Eggs (page 277).

PANTRY

A well-stocked pantry is key to any kitchen, but can be difficult to achieve. Many of the items that follow aren't going to be in your megamart grocery store; you'll need to get out to Asian markets (or at least online) to find a lot of these ingredients. However, many of the harder-to-find ingredients are used in several recipes, and many more are (relatively) nonperishable. It's completely worth the effort to source these ingredients; once your pantry is stocked, your cooking options will open up greatly. At Fat Rice, we have an extensive pantry, and have done a lot of research and testing on many varieties of products and brands—specific brands that work best with our recipes are listed in the following section.

CANDLENUTS A native of Malaysia and Indonesia, candlenuts are related to the macadamia nut. These hard, waxy, cream-colored nuts are always used cooked, never raw, and common in sambals and curries. Macadamia nuts are sometimes substituted for candlenuts, as they have a similarly high

oil content and texture. The flavor, however, is different, as the candlenut is slightly bitter. Candlenuts are found as a thickener in our Diabo (page 221). Store candlenuts tightly sealed in the freezer. Look for raw candlenuts in vacuum-sealed packages at Southeast Asian markets.

CHINESE BLACK OLIVES IN BRINE These come from a species of trees (genus *Canarium*) that grows in the subtropics of Asia. The fruits of the tree are known as Chinese black olives, or *lam* to the Macanese. These olives are completely different from the Mediterranean olive. They are sold packed in brine, and have an elongated shape, pointed ends, and a hard seed inside. We use these "olives" in our XO Sauce (page 268). These are not the easiest things to find–and unfortunately, although they come from the same genus, salted preserved olives are not a substitute. Look for the bright orange canned "Best Quality" brand from Thailand, as they are free of preservatives.

CHINESE BLACK VINEGAR This rich woody and smoky black vinegar comes from the Zhenjiang Jiangsu province in China, and is made from fermented black glutinous rice. Look for the yellow label of the "Chinkiang" brand, which is the most common and always available in Asian grocers.

CHINESE COOKING WINES There are many different Chinese cooking wines out there, and they are not all created equal. Some aren't even what we think of traditionally as wine. At Fat Rice we generally use two different types of "wines" for specific purposes. *Huangjiu* cooking wines have a low alchohol by volume (ABV), ranging from 12 to 20 percent. *Baijiu* have a higher ABV, more like 40 to 55 percent. See Glutinous Rice Cooking Wine (*Mijiu*), page 295, Rice Cooking Wine (*Shaoxing*), page 297, and Rose Wine (*Mei Kuei Lu Chiew*), page 297.

COCONUT CREAM Coconut cream is made from simmering four parts shredded coconut with one part water. At Fat Rice we are devout users of the "D'Best" brand of frozen coconut cream. It is a product of the Philippines and has absolutely no additives, just good old coconut. Look for it in the freezer section of Southeast Asian markets. Be sure not to confuse coconut cream with cream of coconut, which is sweetened and common in many Western grocers.

COCONUT MILK Coconut milk is extracted from the grated pulp of mature coconuts and then blended with water. Fresh-pressed coconut milk is readily available in Southeast Asia and parts of Macau; however, it can be rather difficult to find in the United States, so canned or boxed is your best bet. Be sure to buy the unsweetened coconut milk. We like to use Chaokoh brand, which comes in a brown can and is available at Southeast Asian stores.

COCONUT OIL Look for organic brands at many common grocers, as they are cold-pressed and never chemically treated during production. Coconut oil is a great alternative to butter and we like to use it in a lot of our vegetable dishes as it has great flavor and aroma and keeps things vegan.

COCONUT POWDER Coconut powder is made from the grated, dried meat of a mature coconut. It adds a wonderful texture to both sweet and savory dishes, and is easily found in Southeast Asian as well as Indian markets. Be sure to avoid the sweetened shredded coconut that is commonly found at big grocery stores.

CURRY POWDERS There are various types of curry powders ranging from mild to hot, light to dark, bitter to sweet. Curry powders, especially those containing turmeric, should be mixed with a little vinegar before using. At Fat Rice we have recreated a few different curry powder blends we tasted around Macau: Macau Hot Curry Powder (page 279) and Malacca Sweet Curry Powder (page 280).

DRIED SCALLOP This is a pungent ingredient with a highly concentrated flavor of the ocean, and as such, we use it sparingly. It is also quite expensive, and can range anywhere from $30 to $300 per pound. When choosing dried scallops, trust your nose: they should have a rich, sweet, and saline aroma, be golden brown in color, and in whole pieces between the size of a dime and a nickel. They are going to be an investment, but will last at least a year if kept in an airtight container in a cool dry place.

DRIED SHIITAKE MUSHROOM The word shiitake comes from the Japanese *shii*, the name of the tree that provides the dead logs on which the mushroom is typically cultivated (*take* is Japanese for "mushroom"). Sun-drying the mushrooms results in a rich umami flavor, and dried shiitake mushrooms should be soaked in water before using. Look for dried shiitakes in Asian markets.

DRIED SHRIMP Drying intensifies the shrimp flavor, so just a couple of tiny shrimp can go a long way in recipes such as stir-fries and soups. Look for whole dried shrimp that are bright pink (no artificial color!), dime-size, and give little resistance when squeezed. They'll be in the refrigerated section of your Chinese or Southeast Asian grocer. Store dried shrimp in an airtight container in the refrigerator.

DUMPLING WRAPPERS We prefer round, wheat-based potsticker wrappers, which are found in the frozen section of Asian markets.

FERMENTED BEAN CURD Also known as fermented tofu, wet bean curd, or even bean curd "cheese," this has a soft and spreadable texture and a salty, savory quality reminiscent of certain cheeses. There are many different types of fermented bean curd, but for our purposes we are always referring to red fermented tofu. The tofu is inoculated with mold spores, then marinated in a mixture of *baijiu*, salt, red yeast rice, and spices. Both the tofu and the liquid are used in small amounts as a flavoring in dishes such as Char Siu (page 205) and Tchai de Bonzo (page 119).

FERMENTED BEAN PASTE (*PIXIAN*) *Pixian* in Sichuan province is famous for making a type of *doubanjiang* (also known as fermented bean paste, Sichuan chilli bean paste, or chilli broad bean paste) from fresh red chilli peppers and dried broad beans fermented in terra-cotta crocks. High-quality *pixian*s are aged for up to eight years and are individually hand-stirred every day. On good-weather days, the lid is removed and the paste is left open to soak up the Sichuan sun and dew that contribute to its incomparable flavor. Look for *pixian* wrapped in brown paper and tied with twine at Chinese markets,

and avoid products from Taiwan or Hong Kong. *Pixian* brings that chilli heat and funk to our Sweet Plum Sauce (page 56).

FERMENTED BLACK SOYBEANS Also called salted black beans, salty black beans, or just black beans, these brined, boiled, and fermented beans bring a funky salinity to our version of Macau Chilli Prawns (page 136). These beans do not need to be rinsed, but remember a little bit goes a long way. Look for the canned and brined Temple brand at Southeast Asian stores. If you can't find them, you can substitute dried salted black beans, but be sure to soak those before using. Also, don't get confused: the dry or canned black turtle beans found in Western stores won't work as a substitute!

FILIPINO CANE VINEGAR We like to use the Filipino Datu Puti brand, which is found in Southeast Asian markets and is often labeled *sukang maasim* (which in Tagalog means "sour vinegar"). Cane vinegar is low in in acidity compared to other vinegars, and has a smooth and mellow flavor that makes it great for pickling and marinating.

FINE SEA SALT Whenever a recipe calls for "salt," we recommend you use fine sea salt because it dissolves easily and seasons evenly.

FISH SAUCE This is the liquid essence extracted when salted, barrel-fermented, anchovy-like fish are slowly pressed. When there's a delicious *je ne sais quoi* element in one of our dishes, you can often thank fish sauce. We use it as a marinade and flavoring agent for poultry, pork, and seafood. There are many brands available at Asian markets. Be sure to look for one without preservatives, sugars, or MSG; we like Squid brand.

GLUTINOUS RICE COOKING WINE (*MIJIU*) Used to give sweetness and round texture to sauces such as our Pork Wok Sauce (page 284).

JAGGERY Also known as *jagra*, this brown, minimally processed sugarcane product is an indispensible sweetener in the Macanese pantry. Sold in flat slabs in packs of five or so, jaggery can be found at most well-stocked Asian grocers. It is a key ingredient in our Porco Balichang Tamarindo (page 193).

JASMINE RICE Rice is the starchy mainstay of the Macanese table, although it just barely surpassing potatoes and bread. Usually eaten alongside curries, meats, and stews, rice plays a supporting role—this is in contrast to Chinese and other Asian cuisines, where rice is the focal point. We mainly use jasmine rice, a long-grain variety produced in Thailand, which we like for its sweet, aromatic fragrance.

LILY BUDS The air-dried bud of the tiger lily (*Hemerocallis fulva*) is one of the most notable edible flowers in Chinese cuisine, and has been used as both a food and a medicine for more than two thousand years. Lily buds need to be rehydrated in water before using. Look for amber, unsulfured specimens sold in vacuum-sealed plastic bags. With a delicate, earthy, and sweet flavor, dried lily buds are used in Tchai de Bonzo (page 119).

LONGAN A tropical fruit native to South and Southeast Asia, longan (*lóngyan* in Chinese) literally means "dragon eye." When fully ripened, the shell is thin and firm; the fruit inside is sweet, juicy, and very similar to a lychee fruit. Longans can be found canned in Asian markets at any time of year, but if you can get them in July or August when they are in season, the fresh fruit are incomparable! We use them in our Almond Gelee (page 252).

MALTOSE (MALT SUGAR SYRUP) Most commonly used in Peking duck, Char Siu (page 205), and some confections, maltose gives meat a shiny, lacquered finish. There really isn't a substitute for maltose, but luckily it is easy to find in Asian stores (look for small white containers with an orange lid). Honey can be used in a pinch.

MARIA COOKIES The original name *Maria* was derived from Russia's grand duchess, Maria Alexandrovna, who married the Duke of Edinburgh. Their wedding was the inspiration for the cookie, which became very popular throughout Europe, especially in Spain. This cookie is the basis of our Serradura dessert (page 240), a dish that is known all over Macau and was one of Fat Rice's original menu items.

NORI Roasted and dried seaweed is frequently found in Taiwanese and Chinese bakeries on various buns and pastries. Nori adds a slight ocean flavor to our sweet and savory Macau Rice Crisp (page 239).

OLIVES Many of our recipes call for good-quality Portuguese olives. When we say "good-quality," we mean firm olives with pits such as Galega, Cordovil, or Verdeal, but finding good olives, not to mention Portuguese varietals, can be a bit of a challenge. Look online or in small specialty shops, which should have some decent Spanish olives (Arbequina, Manzanilla, and Gordal are perfectly fine substitutes for Portuguese varietals).

OLIVE OIL We like to use extra-virgin Portuguese or Spanish brands; olives from the Iberian Peninsula have a fruity spicinesss that we love.

OYSTER SAUCE A rich, salty-sweet, dark brown condiment, oyster sauce is traditionally made by slowly simmering oysters in water until they caramelize into a viscous, intensely flavorful sauce. It is difficult to find oyster sauce made this way, as it is rather costly to produce; many modern versions have additives like wheat, cornstarch, and MSG. Seek out the best additive-free oyster sauce you can; we like Lee Kumkee Panda Brand.

PALM SUGAR Palm sugar is produced by boiling the sweet sap of the sugar palm tree, then pouring the dark rich syrup into bamboo tubes to solidify into cylindrical blocks. Not to be confused with coconut sugar (produced from the coconut palm), palm sugar is darker, fragrantly smoky, and more complex than coconut sugar. Due to the fact that palm sugar is not highly processed like brown sugar, the color, consistency, flavor, and level of sweetness can vary from batch to batch, even within the same brand. Although palm sugar is used primarily for making sweets and desserts, its creamy, caramelly sweetness also enhances the flavor of curries and rich sauces for savory dishes as well. Palm sugar is tough to cut through, so we recommend using a cheese grater to grate it. You can find palm sugar from Indonesia (*gula jawa*) in Southeast Asian markets.

PEANUT OIL This mild-tasting oil has a high smoke point relative to many other cooking oils, so it is great for frying and wok cooking. We also like to use peanut oil because it is a non-GMO crop.

PILI NUT Known as *pinhão* (pine nut) to the Portuguese-speaking Macanese, the pili nut is not a pine nut at all, but rather comes from a tropical tree in the same genus as the Chinese olive (*Canarium*) native to maritime Southeast Asia. Pili nuts are difficult to find—the Philippines is the only country that produces and processes the pili nut commercially—so they can be substituted with pine nuts in dishes such as in Empada de Peixe (page 126) or Capela (page 203).

PINK SALT Also known as "curing salt," pink salt is made from a mixture of table salt (sodium chloride) and sodium nitrate. It is used in food preparation to inhibit the growth of bacteria and fungi and also helps preserve the red color of cured meats. Curing salts are most commonly used in meat and sausage preparations in small very quantities.

PRESERVED DUCK LEGS Look for these at Chinese grocery stores, either vacuum-packed in the refrigerated section or hanging behind the butcher counter.

PRESERVED MUSTARD GREEN STEMS (*YA CAI*) Most famously used in *dan dan* noodles and dry-fried green beans, *ya cai* are a pickle made in Yibin, a city in southern Sichuan province, along the Yangtze River. *Ya cai* comes either whole or chopped (*suimi*). We use *suimi ya cai* for ease and recommend Sichuan Famous brand, which is found in 100-gram foil packages in Chinese stores. *Ya cai* contributes a deep, vegetal umami note to our Fat Noodles with XO Sauce (page 97) and fried rice dishes.

PU-ERH TEA LEAVES Pu-erh is a dark fermented *máochá* (an unoxidized green tea) produced in the mountains of Yunnan province, China. Pu-erh can be aged from a few months up to several years, and becomes more valuable the older it is. We use it for our Tea Eggs (page 277) as it gives an earthy flavor to the marinade. Young pu-erh teas can be found loose in cans at Asian markets.

RED YEAST RICE Commonly used in the cuisine of the Fujian region of China, red yeast rice is used to color and flavor a wide variety of foods, including fermented tofu, red rice vinegar, *char siu*, and Chinese pastries. At Fat Rice, red yeast rice is used in in both the Tchai de Bonzo (page 119) and our Char Siu recipe (page 205).

RICE COOKING WINE (*SHAOXING*) This wine is one of the most famous types of *huangjiu* and a standard ingredient in Chinese cooking. Made in Shaoxing city, in Zhejiang province on the east coast of China, Shaoxing rice cooking wine can range from clear to yellow to amber in color and adds an unmistakable flavor and fragrance to dishes, whether it is mixed into dumpling fillings, marinades, or steamed seafood. The darker varieties are simmered with soy sauce and rock sugar in red-braised preparations. For the purposes of this book, we prefer to use a clearer variety that is around 15 percent alcohol by volume, and recommend the Shaoxing Pagoda brand for dishes like Turmeric Baked Chicken (page 184).

ROSE WINE (*MEI KUEI LU CHIEW*) This is a style of sorghum-based *baijiu* that is distilled with rose petals and sugar. *Mei kuei lu chiew* literally translates to "rose essence liquor." For dishes such as Char Siu (page 205), traditional *lap cheong*, or Chinese fermented sausage, we recommend Twin Pagoda brand.

ROUSONG Also known as pork floss, this light and fluffy jerky of sorts is dried, then cooked in oil until the individual muscle fibers separate to become fuzzy and stringy. It is commonly found in congee (rice porridge) as well as Chinese-style pastries. Look for Ching Yeh or Formosa brands at Asian stores.

SAMBAL OELEK Popular throughout Southeast Asia, sambal is a condiment made with fiery red chilli peppers, vinegar, and salt. *Oelek*, which is sometimes spelled *olek* or *ulek*, refers to the mortar and pestle used to make this type of sambal. We make our own naturally fermented sambal in-house from a blend of piri piri peppers, lemon, and salt, but sambal oelek is readily available at Asian stores and the store-bought version is a perfectly fine substitute when we call for chilli sambal.

SESAME SEEDS AND TOASTED SESAME OIL The sesame plant is one of the oldest known oilseed crops and is thought to have originated in Africa, but has been cultivated in China and India for centuries. Sesame has one of the highest oil contents of any seed. Sesame oil is dark amber in color, very aromatic, and pressed from toasted white sesame seeds. It is used only as a seasoning, not for frying. Be sure to find high-quality brands that are 100 percent sesame with no other added oils. There are both black and white sesame seeds, but for the purposes of this book we always use toasted white sesame seeds.

SOY SAUCE This brewed and fermented liquid seasoning is derived from soybeans. Lower-quality products often contain wheat. There are many different types of soy sauce, but at the restaurant we use three specific types (and brands): light, dark, and sweet.

- Light soy for its savory salinity. This is our everyday soy sauce. We use San J Tamari, which is made without wheat. We prefer to use it as gluten allergies have become par for the course.

- Dark soy for its depth and caramel color. We use Dragonfly brand.

- Sweet soy, known as *kecap manis* in Indonesia, has palm sugar added, which gives the soy a thick, molasses-like consistency. We use Bango brand.

STARCHES Starches can vary widely in terms of how quickly they thicken, how much they thicken, the quality of the thickening, and, of course, their flavor after thickening.

- Cornstarch is one of the most common thickeners. Because it is almost pure starch, cornstarch is a more efficient thickener than wheat flour and is great for sauces and gravies. Cornstarch should be mixed into a slurry with cold water before use to prevent clumping.

- Potato starch is a very refined starch, contains minimal protein or fat, and has a high binding strength when cooked. It also helps make a pliable and workable dough, like with our Minchi Croquettes (page 53). Look for potato starch at your Asian grocer in small plastic bags.

- Rice flour comes in two types: sweet and regular. Regular rice flour is made from finely milled long-grain rice, whereas sweet rice flour is made from short-grain or glutinous (aka "sticky") rice. Both are gluten free. For the purposes of this book, we only call for regular rice flour—for example, in our Fat Noodles (page 94). Look for the 1-pound bags of Erawan brand at Asian stores.

- Tapioca starch is extracted from the cassava or yucca root native to Brazil. Portuguese explorers brought cassava to most of the West Indies, Africa, and Asia. Now it is cultivated worldwide, and is a staple in many world regions. The refined starch of this root thickens rather quickly, and lends a more glossy, silky mouthfeel than cornstarch. Tapioca starch must be mixed with water to form a slurry before using as a thickener. We like to use Erawan Brand.

SWEET BEAN PASTE (*TIAN MIAN JIANG*) Also called "sweet flour paste," "sweet soybean paste," "sweet flour sauce," or "sweet noodle sauce," *tian mian jiang* is a sweet bean paste made from wheat flour, sugar, salt, and fermented yellow soybeans. Commonly used in Sichuan cuisine for stir-fries and meat braises, this dark and thick sauce tastes salty, slightly sweet, and has a very savory umami flavor. *Tian mian jiang* is the base of our Umami Juice (page 285), which is the foundation of most of our stir-fries. Look for the Szechuan brand in a blue can.

SWEET POTATO NOODLES Also called "sweet potato vermicelli" or "glass noodles," these thin, translucent noodles are made from sweet potato starch and water. They are most often sold dry; either soak or boil them to hydrate. The cooked noodles have a wonderfully chewy texture and absorb tons of sauce and flavor without falling apart, as in our Tchai de Bonzo (page 119). Look for dried noodles on the shelves at your local Asian market.

TAMARIND *Tamarindus indica* is native to tropical Africa and was brought to the New World by Portuguese explorers in the sixteenth century. Now tamarind grows and is used in tropical regions across the globe. The tamarind tree produces long, curved, podlike fruit filled with small brown seeds and surrounded by a pulp that dehydrates naturally into a sticky paste. Deliciously tangy, tamarind brings an earthy acidity to dishes. Tamarind is sold in several forms, but for ease, we recommend buying a block of seedless tamarind pulp for recipes like Porco Bali-chang Tamarindo (page 193) and Fragrant Tamarind Chutney (page 49).

***TIAN JIN* PRESERVED VEGETABLE** From Tianjin China, this preserved cabbage of sorts is sun-dried, chopped, and rubbed with salt and garlic, then put into earthenware pots to ferment. Tian jin is used in small quantities for soups, stews, and stir-fries, such as our Stir-Fried Greens with Papaya, Mushroom, and Fish Pickle (page 110). Look for the Tianjin brand, sold in small brown earthenware.

TOFU PUFFS Pieces of dried bean curd (tofu) are deep-fried to create a light, slightly spongy texture. Tofu puffs are very absorbent, and as such they are a perfect addition to stews and saucy dishes. Look for tofu puffs in the refrigerated section of Asian grocers; be sure to seek out ones made with non-GMO soybeans!

TOFU SKIN Called *yuba* in Japanese, as well as "bean curd skins" or "bean curd sheets" in English, tofu skin is a by-product of the soy milk–making process; as the milk cools, a skin forms on the surface, and the skin is removed and dried into sheets. Since it's high in protein, tofu skin is often used as a meat substitute; we use it as "mock duck" in our Tchai de Bonzo (page 119). Look for vacuum-sealed packages of tofu skins in the refrigerated section at Asian markets.

WHITEBAIT Known as *yín yú* in Chinese, "whitebait" does not refer to a single species but rather a general term for small freshwater fish. Several of our recipes call for tiny dried whitebait, which add a wonderful texture as well as a baconlike flavor to our Fat Noodles (page 94) and our Bebinca de Rabano (page 122). Look for these tiny dried fish at specialty dried seafood markets in Chinatown; they are stored in glass jars and sold by the ounce.

WHOLE CANNED TOMATOES When it comes to canned tomatoes, get the best quality you can find, and always buy whole canned tomatoes. We prefer to use the San Marzano variety of plum tomatoes from Italy as they have a thick flesh with few seeds, and a strong sweet flavor.

WOOD EAR MUSHROOMS Wood ear mushrooms have a wonderful snappy texture that is great in stir-fries. They are sold dehydrated in bags and need to be rehydrated before use. We prefer buying compressed wood ear mushrooms, which come in matchbox-sized boxes and expand tenfold when rehydrated.

AROMATICS, FRESH HERBS AND UNCOMMON VEGETABLES

For maximum flavor and freshness, it is ideal to have fresh herbs growing in the garden or some potted plants in the house. However, this is not always doable, so many resort to buying herbs at local supermarkets and farmers' markets. Most herbs keep for at least 5 days if stored properly; first, any large amounts of moisture should be removed, and then should be wrapped in a damp paper towel and stored in an airtight container in the refrigerator. Many aromatics such as ginger and shallots can be stored for up to a month in a dry airy place, such as a basket on the counter, while others are best kept wrapped in the refrigerator.

BURDOCK ROOT (*ARCTIUM LAPPA*) Known as *gobo* in Japanese, and related to the artichoke, burdock is a crisp root vegetable, slender and brown-skinned with an off-white-colored flesh and a mild, earthy flavor. It is available year-round. Look for burdock that is firm in texture, as when it gets old it can be shriveled and limp. When preparing, wash and peel the skin and because burdock also discolors easily, prepare a bowl of water so that all prepped and cut portions can be kept refreshed in the bowl. Store burdock in a plastic bag in the refrigerator. It will keep for several months.

CHILLIS, DRIED (*CAPSICUM ANNUUM*) The fruit of plants from the genus Capsicum, native to South and Central America, chillies are members of the nightshade family. The substance that gives chilli peppers their fiery intensity is capsaicin, which is measured in Scoville units, ranging from 0 up to 2 million! As such a staple in regional cuisines, it is surprising to realize that it was unknown in tropical Asia until it was introduced by the Portuguese in the sixteenth and seventeenth centuries. The chilli is found in an incredible variety of colors, sizes, and flavors in different parts of the world.

We at Fat Rice are chilli maniacs. We use all kinds of chillies under the sun. We even have our farmers grow us hundreds of pounds of piri piri peppers every season to make our own chilli sambal (thanks, Pete!). For your purposes we have identified some common chillies for you to use throughout this book and divided them into categories fresh and dried.

Dried chillies are a staple flavoring for many of the dishes that we cook at Fat Rice. They add thickening power, aroma, flavor, and of course, heat, baby, heat! We use both whole flaked and powdered forms.

The drying process intensifies and gives chillies a concentrated fruity flavor. We typically remove the seeds from whole chilli peppers before use. We use common dried chillis, aka Chinese red peppers or Tianjin peppers; they are pinky sized and available at Asian grocers.

Cayenne pepper powder (extra-hot chilli pepper powder) gives a kick without a ton of flavor and coarse korean chilli flakes give color and thickening power to sambals and curries.

CHILLIS, FRESH (*CAPSICUM ANNUUM*)

When buying fresh, be sure to look for chillies that are firm, shiny, dry, and heavy for their size. Store fresh chillies wrapped in paper towels in the refrigerator for up to a week. When preparing chillies it is usually wise to wear gloves to protect any sensitive areas from the painful capsaicin within. We typically do not remove the seeds when we are working with fresh chillies in our recipes. If you prefer to have less heat, we suggest removing the seeds before using. For the purposes of this book, when referring to fresh chillies we provide two categories: "not-so-hot" and "smoking hot."

Fresh "not-so-hot" chillies (around 50,000 units on the Scoville scale) for the most part, are used raw and thinly sliced, to garnish dishes, and are very palatable. They add a nice fresh chilli heat and a vibrant color. Look for fresno, *fresh* cayenne, or Holland finger chillies.

Fresh "smoking hot" chillies (100,000+ units on the Scoville scale) offer some serious heat and are usually cooked and used for sauces and marinades. Typically, we like Thai bird, malagueta, and piri piri, which are all relatively interchangeable. For extra hotness, we use habaneros which are the kick in our Crazy Squid Rice (page 132).

CHRISTMAS BASIL (*OCIMUM BASILICUM*)

A hybrid of Thai and Genovese varieties, deep green leaves and large purple blooms; they have a slightly spicy bite and a unique fennel seed aroma. If you can't find this variety, Thai basil is a perfectly fine substitute and can be found in Southeast Asian markets.

CURRY LEAF (*MURRAYA KOENIGII SPRENG*)

The leaf of an evergreen native to India and Sri Lanka, this plant is part of the citrus family. These small, shiny, oval-pointed leaves are used in India and neighboring countries to impart distinctive flavors to curries and vegetable dishes. Curry leaves must be bloomed in hot oil until they "pop" to release their unique fragrance. Buy curry leaves fresh at Indian and Southeast Asian grocers and store them wrapped in the refrigerator for up to 2 weeks.

GALANGAL (*ALPINIA GALANGA*)

This member of the ginger family native to Indonesia has a unique pungency and bite much different than that of common ginger. Galangal is used in *rempah* (Malaysian fresh curry paste). Fresh galangal is available in Southeast Asian markets. Look for galangal that is plump, with smooth pale pink tips and tight skin, and free of mold. Fresh galangal will keep refrigerated for a couple of weeks wrapped in a paper towel. When preparing galangal, it does not need to be peeled.

GINGER (*ZINGIBER OFFINALE*)

Indigenous to South China is the underground rhizome of a reedlike plant that has fibrous roots and produces the familiar hot, fragrant spice indispensable in Asian cooking. Its intensity varies depending on how it is prepared, so we are sure to specify whether it should be peeled or unpeeled, chopped, minced sliced or julienned. Look for firm, unwrinkled roots and store in a dry airy place.

LAKSA LEAF, RAU RAM, OR VIETNAMESE CILANTRO (*PERSICARIA ODORATA*)

Native to Southeast Asia, with its minty, lemoned-up cilantro notes, laksa leaf is so called for its indispensable use in laksa (Malaysian noodle soups). Laksa leaf grows best in warm and wet environments. Look for highly aromatic leaves that are smooth and dark green and attached to a thick, juicy stem. It is found in well-stocked Southeast Asian grocers. We use laksa leaf in *rempah* and as a garnish in our Malaysian-Cristang-inspired dishes like "Portuguese" Barbecued Seafood with Big Ben's Sambal (page 139).

LEMONGRASS (*CYMBOPOGON CITRATUS*)

This long, grass-like, fibrous, and pale green herb is native to Southeast Asia and has a distinctive lemon aroma. Quintessential to much of Southeast Asian cuisine, lemongrass is found in curries, soups, and teas and is a major player in *rempah* (spice paste) of Malaysia. Trim the base and remove the tough outer layers. Usually lemongrass is sliced or finely chopped before it is blended with other herbs and spices. Look for heavy, long, relatively green stalks with chubby bulbs.

LIME LEAVES (*CITRUS HYSTRIX*) Dark green and waxy to the touch, lime leaves can be found fresh at Southeast Asian markets. They should be used immediately or frozen to preserve their aroma and flavor. They can be used whole or ground. If grinding, remove the center vein and blend in a spice grinder until it is finely chopped. Lime leaf has a distinct aroma, adding an unparalleled brightness and freshness to dishes like our Brinjal Sambal (page 64).

LOTUS ROOT (*NELUMBO NUCIFERA*) This is the edible rhizome of the lotus plant that grows in water. All parts of the plant, from the root to the young flower stalks and seeds, are edible, with the root being the most common. The lotus root has a crunchy and crisp texture when cooked. When buying lotus root, look for firm, heavy roots with smooth, clean, unblemished skins and no bruising or soft spots. Lotus root is extremely versatile when it comes to cooking: it can be sliced thin and deep-fried like a chip, stir-fried with other crisp vegetables, or even blanched and braised, like in Charlie's Peanuts (page 37).

OKRA (*ABELMOSCHUS ESCULENTUS*) Also known as *bhindi* or lady's fingers in reference to its long, elegant shape, or *quiabo* in Portuguese, this vegetable of African origin is commonly used in Brazilian, Macanese, and Indian cuisines. This narrow, five-sided, slightly fuzzy seedpod contains rows of edible white seeds that release a mucilaginous texture when cut or cooked. Due to this quality, okra is often used to thicken stews and soups. With a subtle flavor, okra benefits from being cooked with strong and/or spicy ingredients, such as in our Shrimp Curry with Okra and Tomato (page 166).

SHALLOTS (*ALLIUM CEPA*) Known in Macanese cooking as *cebolas secas*, or dry onion, shallots have a sweet strong flavor and contain minimal moisture, making them ideal for our *rempah* (spice paste) and as a fried garnish. Keep shallots in a dry airy place for up to a month.

TURMERIC (*CURCUMA LONGA*) Native to India, which produces nearly the entire world's crop, turmeric is a very important spice that dates back about four thousand years in India. Turmeric, characterized by its tuberous rhizome, has an earthy, peppery, and slightly bitter flavor with a vivid yellow color. In Macau, turmeric is often called *açafrão* (saffron in Portuguese) as it was used as an alternative to the far more expensive saffron because it imparts a similar yellow color and fragrance. Turmeric is an essential ingredient found in many of our recipes both as a fresh ingredient, and as a ground, dried spice for marinades. When buying fresh turmeric, look for firm pieces and avoid soft, dried, or shriveled ones. Store fresh turmeric in an airtight container for a week or two in the fridge, or up to several months in the freezer.

GRATITUDE AND RESPECT

We are forever indebted to all of our friends, family, colleagues, team members, guests, fans, supporters, strangers and all the amazing people who have helped us along on this adventure. Your support has guided and shaped the world of Fat Rice as we know it. We would need a whole book to thank you all properly, that have touched our lives.

To thank our families for their unconditional love, support and patience. We would have never have gotten this far without your guidance. You have helped us grow and to see our ultimate potential.

To the individuals and families in Macau, Portugal, Malaysia, and Singapore who brought us into the kitchens and willingly shared cherished family recipes and techniques with us food-obsessed kids. Your hospitality is unmatched.

To the amazing Fat Rice team. This is your book! You have helped us shape Fat Rice into what it is on a day-to-day basis with your hard work and devotion. With much testing, trial, and tribulation, we have grown together in remarkable ways.

To Alison and Charlie Lo, for taking a chance on two people who had no idea what they were getting into. For the countless recipes they tested. For growing, harvesting, and delivering vegetables. Running all over the city and shopping for hard-to-find ingredients. For dining at the restaurant on a weekly basis and giving their honest feedback. They've shown an incredible amount of love and support to all of our team members, and have always believed in us.

Craig Perman has been there with us since long before the restaurant opened. He has been a guiding force and light in the dark belly of the beast that is the entrepreneurial food business. For us, Craig has forged an amazing wine program with some of Portugal's best, small, artisanal producers. Craig scouts high quality wines that work in perfect tandem with our cuisine. As well as finding these wines, he tackles head on, the lengthy logistical nightmare of importation, label approval, and shipping. You are the man, Big Perm!

Sarah Becan is a huge part of our Fat Rice family. She has an ability to express our ideas visually, illustrating strangely-named, hard-to-describe dishes with her wildly creative imagination and cartoon comic style. We'd always dreamt of someone with her skill set, then one night, she drew a picture of (Portuguese Chicken), posted it on her blog sauceome .com, and sent us a link. It was fate—she's been part of the crew ever since. We thank her for her tireless effort towards this book and beyond, including the illustrations that have graced our windows in lieu of proper restaurant signage.

Our Chef de Cuisine, Eric Sjaaheim, for his many efforts in documenting, writing and testing the restaurant's recipes. Keeping a staff organized, and working into the early morning on the recipes in this book. He took it all in stride and embraced the adventure.

Ioan "Onu" Aldea has been Fat Rice since before day one. At the tender age of 71, he doesn't mind getting his hands dirty when others shy away. With an ear-to-ear grin, he picks hundreds of pounds of chilli pepper stems, cleans our bathrooms, waters herbs and plants, and tons of other things we don't even know about. He's the glue and makes a damn good Romanian plum brandy too! Onu! SĂ TRĂIEŞTI!

THANKS ALSO TO:

MICHAEL ALESI STEVEN ALEXANDER SAMER ALMADANI FLORITA + VITOR ALVES **APOMAC** HAJIME AMANO **JAMES AMANO** YUMIKO AMANO PEDRO ARAÚJO OF QUINTA DO AMEAL HUGO BANDEIRA **DONA VITÓRIA BAPTISA** NILES BARANOWSKI **KIKI BASSOUL RICK BAYLESS** SARAH BECAN JOHN + KAREN BROWN **LEIGH BUSH** CHRIS CHAKO **CARMEN CHAN CHEMICAL JAMES + EASY + SAL** MARY CLEMENS KATHY COLEMAN **AMY COLLINS** PAUL CONLON **TOM + PAULINE CONLON VASCO CROFT OF APHROS** DONA AIDA DE JESUS BENILDUS "BIG BEN" DE SILVA **DINO** DAVE + DENISE DYREK OF LEANING SHED FARMS **TREVOR ERB** FAT RICE REGULARS AND X-MARX SUPPORTERS FAT RICE TEAM MEMBERS PAST + PRESENT **ARMINDO + MANUELA FERREIRA** BRIAN + MARIE FITZPATRICK **COLLEEN + TIM FRANKHART BJORN FRANSSEN** SARAH FREEMAN HUGE GALDONES **GUILLERMO GALVEZ** MADALYN GARCIA **MIKE GEBERT DAN GOLDBERG** RICH GOLDSTEIN MARY GOMES **RAFAEL GONZALEZ** JOANA GRACIO **HEIDI HAGEMAN AND THE H2 TEAM BRIAN HALL** JASON HAMMEL MIGUEL HERNANDEZ **JIM HOLZTMAN** IFT **ANNABEL JACKSON DIONELE JAKUBOW** CECÍLIA JORGE LEE KATMAN **DAVID KATZ** WON KIM STEVE KINNEY **PETER KLEIN AND SEEDLING FARM + FAMILY** ABBY + MICK OF MICK KLUG FARMS ANDREW KNOWLTON **DESIREE KOH** ANDREA KUHN + FINLEY **MATTHEW KUTZ AGNUS LAM** KAT LEVITT WENDY LITTLEFIELD **ALEX LO** ALISON LO **CHARLIE LO JAMES LO** MARY LO **JULIANA LOH GALLIOT JOÃO LOPES ROSEIRA OF QUINTA DO INFANTADO** LTH FORUM **MAREK LUCKOS AUGUSTINE "GUS" LYE** LUIS MACHADO TRAVAS MACHEL **TOM MARCINIAK** RODRICK MARCUS **ANTÒNIO MARQUES DA CRUZ OF QUINTA DA SERRADINHA** JORDAN + ANGELA MARTINS JON MATHIESON VIRGINIA MATOS **GREGG MEDLEY** MGTO BEATRICE "BEA" MIGUEL **JOSEPH MIGUEL** BONNY MIGUEL-KINNEY JOHN MIHU **GRAÇA MIRANDA OF CASA DE SAIMA** JOEY NAKAYAMA **MATEUS NICOLAU DE ALMEIDA OF MUXAGAT** ONU ANA-LAURA PALIZA BROWN SONIA PALMER **PAPA JOE** RAMON PARERA OF CELLER PARDAS **IRENE + MARK PEACOCK MATTHEW PEARSON** QUENTIN PEREIRA CRAIG PERMAN **EMILY PFEIFFER** RON PIEKARZ AND FAMILY **KARA PLIKAITIS JOSH + CATHY + VICTORIA PYLE** CHANDRA RAM ADAM RAPAPORT **STEPHEN REYES** PEDRO RIBEIRO OF BOJADOR **RIQUEXO AND STAFF BETH + MON ROLDAN** CARLOS RUIVO OF LAGAR DE DAREI NICOLE RUIZ **RYAN AND THE REGGAE ON THE RIVER FAMILY** FRANCIS SADAC **LUIS SANTA MINDY SEGAL** JOE SENESE MARINA SENNA FERNANDES **FILIPE SENNA FERNANDES** MIGUEL SENNA FERNANDES **MARIO SERGIO ALVES NUNO OF QUINTA DAS BÁGEIRAS JULIE SHAPIRO** BJORN SHEN MARGARET SHERIDAN **MICHAEL SIMONEAU** LAUREL SIMS **ERIC SJAAHEIM SLAGEL FAMILY FARMS** HENRY SO HEATHER SPERLING **JUN JUN STA. ANA** MICHAEL STASHWICK **GRAHAM STEIN JC STEINBRUNNER** RONNIE SUBURBAN MIKE SULA **DIANE SWIFT** TIAGO TELES **CRISTINA TERZINA THE PIRANHAS** EMILY TIMBERLAKE SHANNON TROY **CRISTIANO VAN ZELLER OF QUINTA VALE DONA MARIA** PHIL VETTEL **VINCE STEVE VIERRA** VLADIMIR KATIE VOTA **KATIE WILSON** DAVID WONG **JOE ZANGRILLI OF ROWBOAT CREATIVE ED ZARANSKI**

ABOUT THE AUTHORS

ABRAHAM CONLON and ADRIENNE LO are the
chefs and co-owners of the Chicago restaurant
Fat Rice. They have awards and recognition from the
James Beard Foundation, *Bon Appétit*, *Food & Wine*,
Eater, and many others. HUGH AMANO is a writer
and the opening sous chef of Fat Rice.

INDEX

Copyright © 2016 by Abraham Conlon and Adrienne Lo
Photographs copyright © 2016 by Dan Goldberg
Illustrations copyright © 2016 by Sarah Becan

Published in the United States by Ten Speed Press,
an imprint of the Crown Publishing Group,
a division of Penguin Random House LLC, New York.
www.crownpublishing.com
www.tenspeed.com

Ten Speed Press and the Ten Speed Press colophon are
registered trademarks of Penguin Random House LLC.

Library of Congress Cataloging-in-Publication Data

Names: Conlon, Abraham, author. | Lo, Adrienne,
1983-author. | Amano, Hugh, author.
Title: The adventures of Fat Rice : recipes from the
Chicago restaurant inspired by Macau / Abraham Conlon,
Adrienne Lo, and Hugh Amano.
Description: Berkeley : Ten Speed Press, [2016]
Includes bibliographical references and index.
Identifiers: LCCN 2016014121 (print) | LCCN 2016019155 (ebook)
Subjects: LCSH: Cooking, Chinese–Macanese style.
Fat Rice (Restaurant) | LCGFT: Cookbooks.
Classification: LCC TX724.5.C5 C66 2016 (print)
LCC TX724.5.C5 (ebook) | DDC 641.595–dc23

LC record available at https://lccn.loc.gov/2016014121

Hardcover ISBN: 978-1-60774-895-3
eBook ISBN: 978-1-60774-896-0

Printed in China

Design by Kara Plikaitis
Prop styling by Andrea Kuhn

10 9 8 7 6 5 4 3 2 1

First Edition